Regulation

Regulation

Economic Theory and History

Edited by Jack High

Ann Arbor

THE UNIVERSITY OF MICHIGAN PRESS

Published in the United States of America by
The University of Michigan Press
Manufactured in the United States of America

1991 1991 1991 1991 4 3 2 1

Library of Congress Cataloging-in-Publication Data

Regulation : economic theory and history / edited by Jack High.
p. cm.
Includes bibliographical references and index.
ISBN 0-472-10272-9 (alk. paper)
1. Trade regulation—United States—Case studies. I. High, Jack C.
HD3616.U46R42 1991
338.973—dc20 91-28040
CIP

British Library Cataloguing in Publication Data

Regulation : economic theory and history.
I. High, Jack
363.60973

ISBN 0472102729

Acknowledgments

I owe thanks to several persons who helped in the creation of this book. The Sarah Scaife Foundation provided funding for the original conference out of which this book grew. Colleen Morretta, with her usual flair for competence, arranged the conference.

James Buchanan began the conference with an address on the constitutional aspects of regulation. The talk sparked a lively and informed discussion, which carried throughout the conference.

The Claude R. Laube Charitable Foundation provided research support for the introductory essay, and the Earhart Foundation for research support on chapter four.

Colin Day and two anonymous referees at the University of Michigan Press gave much useful advice, and their editing has made the book more readable. Rose Giacobbe and her staff at Harvard University's Graduate School of Business Administration turned the various papers into a manuscript.

Finally, I thank the authors for their scholarship, for their patience, and for their cheerful cooperation. They were, without exception, a pleasure to work with.

Contents

Introduction: A Tale of Two Disciplines

Jack High

Economic regulation is ancient. According to one authoritative account, we were kicked out of the Garden of Eden because of a regulatory dispute over food. Eve ingested a "controlled substance," as we would say in modern parlance. Unfortunately, she did so at a time when a regulator had some clout. Nevertheless, the standard historical interpretation says that the regulatory episode served the public interest, and the modern theory of regulation lends support: the bureaucracy was small; the motives of the regulator were unimpeachable; knowledge was sufficiently complete to preclude error.

The study, or at least the justification, of regulation is probably as old as the practice, but in this volume we are concerned with a relatively recent turn taken by scholars of regulation. In 1963, historian Gabriel Kolko published *The Triumph of Conservatism*. There, and in *Railroads and Regulation*, he advanced a startling thesis: "The dominant fact of American political life at the beginning of this century was that big business led the struggle for the federal regulation of the economy."[1]

How different this was from Harold Underwood Faulkner's view, that "the passage of the Interstate Commerce Act was strongly opposed by the railroad officials, who predicted dire results. . . ," or from Arthur S. Link's, that ". . . there was a progressive movement on the national level, which took form in attempts to subject railroads, industrial corporations, and banks to effective public control."[2] As James Harvey Young says, Kolko "reached down the Progressive lion's throat, grabbed its tail, and pulled the creature inside out."[3]

I thank Howard Baetjer, Clayton Coppin, Tyler Cowen, and Don Lavoie for comments.

1. Gabriel Kolko, *The Triumph of Conservatism* (New York: Macmillan Co. 1963), 57–58. See also his *Railroads and Regulation* (Princeton: Princeton University Press, 1965).

2. Harold Underwood Faulkner, *American Economic History,* 7th ed. (New York: Harper and Brothers, 1954), 490; Arthur S. Link, *American Epoch* (New York: Alfred A. Knopf, 1955), 68. Also see Faulkner's *The Decline of Laissez-Faire* (New York: Rinehart and Co., 1951), 366–82. A more recent statement that Progressive regulation served the public interest is Byrd L. Johnson's "Government Management of the Economy," in *Encyclopedia of American History*, ed. Glen Porter, (New York: Charles Scribner's Sons, 1980), 2:809–10.

3. James Harvey Young, *Pure Food* (Princeton: Princeton University Press, 1989), 280.

In 1971, economist George Stigler published "The Theory of Economic Regulation." As Kolko had before him, Stigler argued that regulation was primarily intended to benefit business. "Regulation may be actively sought by an industry, or it may be thrust upon it. A central thesis of this paper is that, as a rule, regulation is acquired by the industry and is designed and operated for its benefit."[4] Stigler's thesis differed sharply from orthodox economic opinion, which saw regulation as ". . . a means whereby public authority endeavors to curb abuses arising from imperfections in the market."[5]

According to Stigler, the ability of the state to use its coercive powers to provide subsidies, or to control entry, or to fix prices, can be used to advantage by business firms. In exchange, business firms can provide votes and money to government officials. Given the opportunity for mutually beneficial trade between government officials and firms, Stigler thought it futile to criticize regulators for providing services to businessmen. "This criticism seems to me exactly as appropriate as a criticism of the Great Atlantic and Pacific Tea Company for selling groceries, or as a criticism of a politician for currying popular support."[6] In short, both Kolko and Stigler argued that the regulation of business is by business and for business.

Kolko and Stigler were reacting to a long and well-established tradition that regulation was imposed on a recalcitrant business community for the interest of the general public. This tradition grew out of the Progressive era. Prominent intellectuals of the time argued precisely this point. Famed journalist Joseph Pulitzer, commenting on the initiation of the government's antitrust suit against Northern Securities, proclaimed, "He [Roosevelt] has subjugated Wall Street."[7] In 1903, historian and economist Elisha B. Andrews, president of Brown University, published a history of the Progressive period in which he said of Roosevelt, "In his inaugural address and in numberless speeches boldly handling the trust evil, he called for the regulation of capitalist combinations in the interest of the public."[8]

---

4. George J. Stigler, "The Theory of Economic Regulation," *Bell Journal of Economics and Management* 2 (Spring, 1971): 3.

5. Dudley F. Pegrum, *The Public Regulation of Business* (Homewood, Ill.: Richard D. Irwin, 1965), 38. Examples of this kind are common. Claire Wilcox, speaking of natural monopoly, wrote, "Government was, therefore, compelled to intervene to safeguard the public interest. Regulation was thus a substitute for competition" (*Public Policies Toward Business*, 3d ed. [Homewood, Ill.: Richard D. Irwin, 1966]).

6. Stigler, "Theory of Economic Regulation," 17.

7. Quoted in Mark Sullivan, *Our Times* (New York: Charles Scribner's Sons, 1927), 2:466. Pulitzer's rival, William Randolph Hearst, expressed more cynical sentiments on Roosevelt's trust policy. He wrote, "But the good trusts and the bad trusts of Roosevelt had no differentiation in economics, but only in politics. The good trusts were the trusts that politically supported Roosevelt and the bad trusts were the trusts that politically opposed Roosevelt." Nevertheless, Hearst believed that the prices of trusts should be regulated to prevent them from gouging the public. See William Randolph Hearst, *Truths about the Trusts* (privately printed, 1916), 4.

8. Elisha B. Andrews, *The United States in Our Own Time* (New York: Charles Scribner's Sons, 1903), 915.

James Weinstein, Martin Sklar, Douglas Anderson, and other historians have revealed the close involvement of Progressive intellectuals in regulatory reform. Nicholas Murray Butler, president of Columbia, presided over the 1907 Conference on Trusts sponsored by the National Civic Federation. He urged Congress to reform the Sherman antitrust act, allowing large firms to exist, but regulating them in the interest of the public. "There is now reason to believe," said Butler in his opening address to the conference, "that it [the Sherman act] commits the nation to a policy which is too extreme, to a policy that, in putting an end to certain admitted evils, also puts an end to certain demonstrable benefits. Many of us believe that the act unduly exalts the principle of competition and fails to lay due emphasis upon the public benefits which may follow from properly regulated and supervised combination."[9]

Prominent American economists of the period—Henry Carter Adams, John Bates Clark, Irving Fisher, Jeremiah Jenks, Edwin R. A. Seligman, Frank Taussig—participated in either the 1899 Chicago Conference or the 1907 National Conference on Trusts. Like Butler, they favored some kind of regulation, usually public exposure of corporate finances and the prohibition of offensive practices such as price discrimination.[10]

Moreover, prominent economists were closely involved in agitating for, and drafting, regulatory legislation. Jenks, who thought that "corporate regulation of the market, if not abused and if prudently regulated by government, was a progressive advance over the old competitive market," worked closely with Civic Federation leaders to organize the 1907 conference.[11] He and J. B. Clark were members of the four man subcommittee that drafted the Federation's regulation bill in 1913.[12] That bill, says Weinstein, "was almost a

9. Nicholas Murray Butler, "The Problem before the Conference," in *Proceedings of the National Conference on Trusts and Combinations* (New York: National Civic Federation, 1908), 38.

10. Generally, economists of the period favored regulation but opposed the Sherman Act because they thought that there were significant scale economies. Adams and Gunton were exceptions. Adams endorsed the Sherman Act, while Gunton opposed all regulation. Gunton's speech at the Chicago conference was so unpopular that the chairman of the session threatened to clear the galleries in order to quiet the delegates. For economists' views on the Sherman Act, see Thomas DiLorenzo and Jack High, "Antitrust and Competition, Historically Considered," *Economic Inquiry* 26 (July, 1988): 423–35. For Gunton's speech and general point of view, see *Proceedings of the Chicago Conference on Trusts*, (Chicago: Chicago Civic Federation, 1900), 276–85; and his *Trusts and the Public* (New York: D. Appleton and Co., 1899). Harvard economist Charles Bullock provides a survey of his contemporaries' views on big business in "Trust Literature: A Survey and Criticism," *Quarterly Journal of Economics* 15 (September, 1901): 167–216, reprinted in William Z. Ripley, ed., *Trusts, Pools, and Corporations* (Boston: Ginn and Co., 1905), 428–73.

11. Martin J. Sklar, *The Corporate Reconstruction of American Capitalism* (Cambridge: Cambridge University Press, 1988), 61.

12. Clark also served on Governor Charles Evans Hughes committee to propose financial regulation for the New York securities markets. See Cedric B. Cowing, *Populists, Plungers, and Progressives: A Social History of Stock and Commodity Speculation, 1890–1936* (Princeton: Princeton University Press, 1965), 38–40.

model for the final legislation." Thus, two prominent economists of the Progressive era were closely involved in the passage of the Federal Trade Commission Act.[13]

John R. Commons was appointed to the National Civic Federation's 1905 "committee on investigation" of the utility industry. Commons used this report to draft, at the urging of former Wisconsin governor Robert M. La Follette, legislation for state regulation of utilities. The Wisconsin law, which passed in 1907, "later served as a model for the laws of many other states."[14]

The prominence of the intellectuals who supported regulation because they believed it served the interests of the public would naturally give this interpretation of regulation a leading place in subsequent accounts. In intellectual affairs, however, a "leading position in" rarely means "sole possession of," and many members of the intellectual community were well aware, prior to Kolko and Stigler, that business interests influenced and benefited from regulation.

In recounting the origins of the Massachusetts railroad commission, historian Edward C. Kirkland noted:

> with the state so heavily involved, railroad corporations continually requested favors from the General Court, railroad officers and counsel haunted the state house, and the railroad lobby was so hard driven as to be a victim of occupational fatigue and carelessness.[15]

In *A Positive Program for Laissez Faire*, Chicago economist Henry Simons wrote:

> Producers are, from a political point of view, organized, articulate groups; and it is in the nature of the political process to conciliate such groups. . . . People as consumers are unorganized and inarticulate, and, representing merely the interests of the community as a whole, they always will be.

Simons condemned regulation as a "misfortune for all concerned," and recommended that the government nationalize the regulated industries.[16]

13. James Weinstein, *The Corporate Ideal in the Liberal State* (Boston: Beacon Press, 1968), 89. For contemporary praise of the Federal Trade Commission and Clayton Acts, see Allyn A. Young, "The Sherman Act and the New Antitrust Legislation," *Journal of Political Economy* 23 (1914–15): 201–20. Young was an economist at Cornell at the time he wrote the article.

14. Douglas D. Anderson, *Regulatory Politics and Electric Utilities* (Boston: Auburn House Publishing Co., 1981), 47.

15. Edward Chase Kirkland, *Men, Cities, and Transportation* (New York: Russell and Russell, 1938), 2:237–38.

16. Henry C. Simons, *A Positive Program for Laissez Faire* (Chicago: University of Chicago Press, 1934), 10–12.

Simons's opinion was virtually indistinguishable from that of Daniel Hoan, City Attorney of Milwaukee, who, in a booklet published by the Socialist Party, wrote:

> In conclusion it can safely be said that the temptation of the corporations to influence government officials has and will continue as long as private business exists. . . . This is perfectly natural. Not until the owners and the regulators of business become one and the same party will this cause of bad influence and corruption disappear. Of the three remedies suggested,—smash, regulate, or own the monopolies—the latter is the only one which will attain the object.[17]

Economist Horace Gray was also keenly aware that regulation served business interests. He said:

> Certainly many of the proponents of public utility regulation intended it to protect consumers against excessive charges and discriminations; all the early state laws bear witness to this intent. It should be remembered, however, that behind this laudable social purpose lurked the sinister forces of private privilege and monopoly. They desired immunity from prosecution under the antitrust laws, legal validation of their privileges as property rights, the protection of the state for their monopolies, and a relatively free hand to extend their economic power. All these objectives they attained under the public utility status.[18]

Among journalists, H. L. Mencken merrily debunked the opinion that regulation served the public interest. He wrote:

> The legislature, like the executive, has ceased, save indirectly, to be even the creature of the people: it is the creature, in the main, of pressure groups, and most of them, it must be manifest, are of dubious wisdom and even more dubious honesty. . . . The typical lawmaker of today is a man wholly devoid of principle—a mere counter in a grotesque and knavish game. If the right pressure could be applied to him he would be cheerfully in favor of polygamy, astrology or cannibalism.[19]

---

17. Daniel W. Hoan, *The Failure of Regulation* (Chicago: Socialist Party of the United States, 1914), 83.

18. Horace M. Gray, "The Passing of the Public Utility Concept," *Journal of Land and Public Utility Economics* 16 (February, 1940): 11. Gray's conclusions were partly based on the doctoral dissertation of his student, Burton N. Behling, *Competition and Monopoly in Public Utility Industries* (Urbana: University of Illinois Press, 1938), 72–73.

19. H. L. Mencken, "Mr. Justice Holmes," *American Mercury* (May, 1930), reprinted in Alistair Cooke, ed., *The Vintage Mencken* (New York: Random House, 1955), 192.

Until the work of Kolko and Stigler, academic research continued to document business involvement in regulation. In 1955, historian Lee Benson made it abundantly clear that commercial self-interest was the dominant force in railroad regulation. He said:

> Not surprisingly, several of the more perceptive railroad leaders came to recognize that the positive use of state power was an indispensable supplement to private, self-policing agreements.[20]

A decade later, after a detailed study of New England railroads during 1880s and 1890s, economist Paul MacAvoy concluded:

> The trunk-line railroads benefitted from regulation—the rules of the Interstate Commerce Commission against personal and locational discrimination, and against setting secret rates, had made it possible for the cartel to maintain basic long-distance grain rates of 23 to 25 cents for seven years. It had not been possible to maintain 21–22 cent rates previously, nor was it possible to maintain 17–20 cent rates in the years following the weakening of regulation.[21]

To be sure, then, both popular and academic writers knew that businessmen agitated for and benefited from regulation. But it took the stark, forceful works of Kolko and of Stigler to dislodge from the academic mind that public interest was the raison d'être of economic regulation. Despite their different approaches—one factual, the other theoretical—and despite their nearly opposite political orientations, Kolko and Stigler produced research that was strikingly compatible and, in tandem, powerfully effective. Their work undermined the predominant belief that regulation originated and functioned to serve the public.

Yet something odd happened on the way to the academic forum. Historians and economists were studying the same subject. They were reaching similar conclusions. But they were not talking to one another. They have not communicated with each other nearly as much as one might have expected fifteen or twenty years ago. In his seminal article, Stigler did not so much as refer to Kolko, let alone discuss the similarities of their work. Nor did Peltzman mention Kolko in his generalization of Stigler.[22] Historians have been

---

20. Lee Benson, *Merchants, Farmers, and Railroads* (New York: Russell and Russell, 1955), vii. Some future historian will have to explain why Benson's work did not have the same impact that Kolko's or Stigler's did.

21. Paul W. MacAvoy, *The Economic Effects of Regulation: The Trunk-line Railroad Cartels and the Interstate Commerce Commission Before 1900* (Cambridge, Mass.: MIT Press, 1965), 201.

22. Sam Peltzman, "Toward a More General Theory of Regulation," *Journal of Law and Economics* 19 (August, 1976): 211–40. Among economists, George W. Hilton and Alfred Kahn

better. McCraw devoted a section of his superb survey article to economists' views. Horwitz recently provided an excellent summary of economists' contributions to regulation theory.[23] Some notable historians of regulation are cognizant of Stigler, Peltzman, and a few other economists.[24] Yet there are fundamental advances in economics of which historians seem unaware. Just as most economists have ignored the history of regulation, so most historians have neglected the economics of regulation.

It seems almost self-evident that economists and historians of regulation should stay in close touch with the others' research, not simply as a professional courtesy, but to improve our understanding of the subject.

Where two disciplines reach similar conclusions, our confidence is strengthened, provided that we know about both sets of conclusions. But even where the conclusions begin to diverge, we need to stay in contact, because we need to know why. We need to get our theory and our stories straight.

Not only can the two disciplines cross-check their conclusions, they can also cross-fertilize their hypotheses. Theoretical results can motivate factual investigation, and factual discoveries can inspire theoretical development. Tacking between abstract principle and concrete event has long been a tenet of good literary style, and philosophers of science now tell us that it is a tenet of good science as well. Economics and history are natural complements. By paying attention to the work of the other, each can do more effective work than can either discipline working in isolation. As Don Lavoie puts it, theory and history are "two inescapable aspects of what is ultimately one integrated intellectual endeavor."[25] Two parallel developments in the history and economics of regulation illustrate the complementarity between these two lines of research.

On the history side, there was no denying Kolko's basic point—businessmen favored regulation and wielded considerable influence over it. Nevertheless, historians pointed out that businessmen did not always favor regulation, nor did they always act in unison, nor were they the only ones

---

are exceptions. In his "Consistency of the Interstate Commerce Act," *Journal of Law and Economics* 9 (October, 1966): 110, Hilton writes, "Professor Kolko's recent demonstration of the origins of the Act in railroad pressure, and of the cartelizing behavior of the Commission in its first thirty years was a major piece of historical revision." See also Alfred Kahn, *The Economics of Regulation* (Cambridge, Mass.: MIT Press, 1988), 2:27; Richard Posner mentions Kolko's *Railroads*, but not *Triumph* in "Theories of Economic Regulation," *Bell Journal of Economics and Management Science* 5 (Autumn, 1974): 335–58.

23. Thomas K. McCraw, "Regulation in America," *Business History Review* 49 (Summer, 1975): 159–83; Robert Britt Horwitz, *The Irony of Regulatory Reform* (Oxford: Oxford University Press, 1989), chap. 2.

24. Richard H. K. Vietor's chapter in this volume is one example. See also Donna Wood, *The Strategic Uses of Public Policy* (Boston: Pitman Publishing, 1986).

25. Don Lavoie, "Euclideanism versus Hermeneutics: A Reinterpretation of Misesian Apriorism," in *Subjectivism, Intelligibility, and Economic Understanding*, ed. Israel M. Kirzner (New York: New York University Press, 1986), 194.

involved in the regulatory process. Vietor, for example, points out that "Twenty-one of the nation's fifty-two major rail systems were represented by witnesses before the Senate Interstate Commerce Committee [of 1905]. All but one company, the Chicago Great Western Railroad, completely and forthrightly opposed expanding ICC rate regulatory powers."[26] Nevertheless, the Hepburn Act, which granted the ICC rate-making power, passed the following year. It is misleadingly simple to say that the regulatory bodies are captured by the regulated industry.

It is equally misleading to portray railroad regulation simply as the tool of businesses that were customers of the railroads. As Vietor documents, the coal industry opposed passage of the Hepburn Act, the agricultural industry favored it, and the lumber industry was split.[27]

Historical research has found such a pattern common. The regulated industry influences regulation, but does not control it. As a rule, neither the regulated industry nor its antagonists have been able to capture regulatory reform. In banking, in electricity, in coal, in natural gas, in food, in sports, in retail sales—in just about every regulatory episode that historians have studied—individual interests have been too diverse for a single group to control.

Writing in 1970, Ralph Hidy underscored this point. "Among historians centering their efforts on specific periods such as the Progressive era," he wrote, "the greatest need is to recognize the divisions of opinions, postures, and actions within firms, industries, and other groupings. . . . Public policy is never made by one pressure group or any one group in government; that might be a tentative working hypothesis."

Morton Keller described this diversity as "The Pluralist State," the title of an article in which he wrote, "American regulation today, as over the past century, is determined by the peculiar characteristics of the society: a roiling diversity of interests and authorities; the pressure of economic, technological, and demographic change; the deep national ambivalence towards the private power of corporations and the public power of the state."[28]

A similar development took place in economics. The economic theory of regulation started off as capture theory. Peltzman has said of Stigler's seminal work, "The specific conclusions Stigler reached bear the imprint of the then accumulating evidence in favor of some form of the C[apture] T[heory].

---

26. Richard H. K. Vietor, "Businessmen and the Political Economy: The Railroad Rate Controversy of 1905," *Journal of American History* 64 (June, 1977): 50. See also K. Austin Kerr, *American Railroad Politics, 1914–1920* (Pittsburgh: University of Pittsburgh Press, 1968) and, for a vigorous denial of Kolko's thesis, Albro Martin, *Enterprise Denied* (New York: Columbia University Press, 1971).

27. Vietor, "Businessmen and the Political Economy," 50–55.

28. Ralph W. Hidy, "Business History: Present Status and Future Needs," *Business History Review* 44 (Winter, 1970): 496. Morton Keller, "The Pluralist State," in *Regulation in Perspective*, ed. Thomas K. McCraw (Cambridge, Mass.: Harvard University Press, 1981), 94.

Indeed his article comes across as an effort to rationalize those results."[29] But economists were quick to point out that the regulated industry was not the only economic group to benefit from or to influence regulation.

In several regulated industries studied by economists—including railroads, telephone, utility, taxicabs, and airlines—some consumers received special benefits from regulation. These consumers would receive subsidies in the form of below-cost prices. Hilton wrote "The incentives upon the commissioners are to generate monopoly gain in one activity, either through administering a cartel or maintaining a monopoly, and then to dissipate it in uneconomic activity."[30] Sharing the gains from regulation with consumers would not be necessary if consumers did not wield some power over regulators.

Hilton provided an economic rationale for regulatory behavior that created cartels and dissipated part of the gains. This behavior follows from the situation in which regulators find themselves. Commissioners normally have short tenure, and one of the most promising lines of future employment for a commissioner is with the regulated industry. Moreover, since the regulatory body is charged by the legislature with protecting the public interest, commissioners have an incentive to subsidize particular groups. So regulators restrict entry into an industry, enabling producers to raise prices and earn some monopoly rents. The regulators then require the industry to dissipate some of these rents by subsidizing particular groups of consumers.

Constructing a more general theoretical model, in which regulatory profits were shared among various groups, was the primary achievement of Peltzman. In his survey of economists' work on regulation, Tollison calls Peltzman's model "the single most important theoretical development in the post-Stigler literature on regulation."[31] Peltzman derived from comparative statics exercises what historians and economists had been arguing for some years, that "no single economic interest captures a regulatory body."[32]

Another parallel development in both the history and the economics of regulation deserves some notice, because it represents a significant advance over what may be called the "cartel approach" to regulation. Historical research has documented that firms within the same industry will often take

29. Sam Peltzman, "The Economic Theory of Regulation after a Decade of Deregulation," in *Brookings Papers on Economic Activity*, ed. Martin Neil Baily and Clifford Winston (Washington, D.C.: Brookings Institution, 1989). Thomas K. McCraw, "Regulation in America," 174, writes, "In some respects, Stigler's was the Kolko model updated."

30. George W. Hilton, "The Basic Behavior of Regulatory Commissions," *American Economic Review* 62 (May, 1972): 50. See also Richard A. Posner, "Taxation by Regulation," *Bell Journal of Economics and Management Science* 2 (Spring, 1971): 22–50.

31. Robert Tollison, "Regulation and Interest Groups," in this volume.

32. Sam Peltzman, "Economic Theory of Regulation," 9. This is also a main theme in Gary Becker, "A Theory of Competition Among Pressure Groups for Political Influence," *Quarterly Journal of Economics* 98 (August, 1983): 371–400.

diametrically opposite positions over regulation. During the fight for pure food legislation, firms in the whiskey industry opposed one another, at times fiercely. So did firms in the catsup and baking powder industries. During the passage of the Hepburn Act, lumber companies on the west coast opposed the bill, while lumber manufacturers in the south favored it. Eastern coal companies favored environmental legislation that required utility companies to install coal scrubbers; western coal companies opposed it. Conflict between firms in the same industry is sufficiently common that sociologist Donna J. Wood has called it "the strategic use of public policy."[33]

These historical episodes require a reformulation, or at least an extension, of regulation theory. If the regulator functions as the agency for a cartel, then firms within the same industry should not take opposing sides on regulation.

As Tollison points out in his contribution to this volume, the theoretical treatment of intraindustry conflict was first analyzed by Buchanan and Tullock. When firms in the same industry have different costs of production, it "opens the door to possible regulations that impose relatively greater costs on higher cost, marginal firms, causing some of them to leave the industry." The reduced supply leads to higher prices for firms remaining in business. Thus, economists have extended the theory of regulation to encompass intraindustry conflict, and have used the theory "extensively in the areas of social and environmental regulation."[34] Again, we see economics and history studying similar problems and reaching similar conclusions.

The chapters in this volume are intended to encourage closer communication between historians and economists of regulation. Besides bringing together between two covers research from both disciplines, the volume reveals some further similarities and complementarities that strengthen our understanding of regulatory activity.

Perhaps the most pressing need in the theory of regulation at the present time is to come to terms with deregulation. In his contribution to this volume, Tollison points out that "interest group theory must be able to cope with both regulation and deregulation in an explanatory sense. Interest groups can drive the economy in either direction."[35] Tollison himself has studied the economic forces that liberalized the corporate charter laws in the United States and repealed the Corn Laws in Great Britain. However, other episodes of deregulation do not seem to fit economic theory so well. Airlines and telecom-

33. See Donna J. Wood, *Strategic Uses of Public Policy*; Jack High and Clayton Coppin, "Wiley and the Whiskey Industry," *Business History Review* 62 (Summer, 1988): 286–309; Richard H. K. Vietor, *Environmental Politics and the Coal Coalition* (College Station: Texas A&M University Press, 1980), 125–27; Vietor "Businessmen and the Political Economy;" Robert Crandall, *Controlling Industrial Pollution* (Washington, D.C.: Brookings Institution, 1983), 120–23.

34. Tollison, "Regulation and Interest Groups."

35. Tollison, "Regulation and Interest Groups."

munications, two of the industries studied in this volume, are examples. These episodes of deregulation carry additional weight because so much of the history of regulation in these industries does correspond to economic theory.[36]

Vietor makes it abundantly clear that the early regulation of airlines created a "government-induced cartel." For awhile this cartel was run by the postmaster general. Vietor writes, "Hoover's Postmaster General, Walter F. Brown, proposed legislation to give himself wide-ranging authority over routes, mail rates, and discretionary contract awards." Although this regime ended in scandal in the 1930s, the Black-McKellar Act "restructured the airline industry, creating the horizontal oligopoly until 1970s."[37]

For forty years, the Civil Aeronautics Board regulated prices and entry into the airline business. Then, beginning in 1975, "airline regulation came unravelled with amazing speed. The political process, especially in view of its active support by regulators, confounded the conventional wisdom of the policy literature."[38]

Crandall points out that telecommunications is an "unnatural monopoly," that is, a monopoly put in place by government decree. Through the 1970s, regulation operated much as economic theory would predict—"Incumbent carriers [were] often protected from competition from new carriers or new services," and cross-subsidies ran from urban to rural, from long-distance to local, and from business to residential customers. But then the government filed an antitrust violation against AT&T, and issued a divestiture order in 1982. Again, as it had in the airline industry, the iron triangle of legislators, regulators, and the regulated industry had been broken.[39]

In neither of these episodes of deregulation do Congress or regulators succumb to powerful pressures from industry. In the Kennedy hearings, all the airlines initially opposed deregulation. And although MCI brought its own antitrust suit against AT&T, and no doubt encouraged the Justice Department to do the same, MCI was neither large enough nor powerful enough to exert strong pressure. Obviously, politicians and regulators are more independent of commercial interests than the traditional theory of regulation would have us believe. This independence must be incorporated into the theory, and it must be done in such a way that it will account for regulation as well as deregulation.

The independent force exerted by regulators is yet another parallel development, although still inchoate, of history and economics. Thomas McCraw's

36. See Martha Derthick and Paul J. Quirk, *The Politics of Deregulation* (Washington, D.C., Brookings Institution, 1985), 13–26. Derthick and Quirk argue that ideas and public opinion triumphed over economic interests in the deregulation of airlines, trucking, and telecommunications.

37. Richard Vietor, "The Hubris of Regulated Competition," in this volume.

38. Vietor, "The Hubris of Regulated Competition."

39. Crandall, "Halfway Home," in this volume.

portrait of Charles Francis Adams is a vivid illustration of the influence that regulators exert upon regulation. Adams consciously chose railroad regulation as a means of advancing his career. McCraw writes of Adams, "Now, in 1867, married, past thirty, and still frustrated by his law practice, he deliberately set about to build a career on the foundation of his writing ability; he would educate himself in all aspects of the railroad question, publish his analyses and thereby publicize his growing expertise, and use the resulting reputation to gain an official public post."[40] The result of Adams's pursuit of a career was a deep and long-lasting influence on the regulation of railroads.

Adams's case is not unusual. The other prophets of regulation—Brandeis, Landis, and Kahn—advanced their careers through their distinctive influences on regulation, which, in Kahn's case, also meant deregulation. Were it not for his able efforts as President Carter's chairman of the Civil Aeronautics Board, the airline industry might not have been deregulated. It probably would have ended, as did telecommunications, in the halfway house between competition and deregulation.[41]

Clayton Coppin and I argue that the independent influence of regulators can be integrated into the theory of regulation through the notion of bureaucratic entrepreneurship. The analogy with entrepreneurship in markets is pertinent here. In order to succeed, business entrepreneurs must convince other firms, and ultimately the consumer, of the superior value of their innovation. Although the entrepreneur depends on others, he or she is nevertheless an independent force in the market, in the sense that he or she exercises judgment and leadership that shape the market process. The same is true of regulators. The success or failure of their initiatives depends on the legislator, and ultimately on the voter, but regulators nevertheless exercise their own independent influence on the regulatory process. Moreover, this influence can sometimes increase, sometimes decrease, and sometimes merely change the form of regulation.[42]

Deregulation is itself part of a broader issue in the history and economics of regulation: Why do some industries fall under the regulatory umbrella

40. Thomas K. McCraw, *Prophets of Regulation* (Cambridge, Mass.: Harvard University Press, 1984), 6.

41. Vietor says, "The deregulation process received a great boost in 1977, when President Jimmy Carter appointed Alfred Kahn to chair the CAB. This quintessential policy entrepreneur took charge at the perfect time." See "The Hubris of Regulated Competition." For a detailed account of Kahn's influence on regulation at both the state and national levels, see McCraw, *Prophets of Regulation*, chap. 7.

42. For an illuminating account of bureaucratic entrepreneurship by an insider, see Stephen Breyer, *Regulation and Its Reform* (Cambridge, Mass.: Harvard University Press, 1982), 317–40. Breyer's strategy was brilliant, and had the hearings been in hands less competent than those of Breyer and Kennedy, airline deregulation may never have gotten off the ground. The airlines, labor unions, and some regulators initially offered intense opposition to deregulation. See Vietor, "The Hubris of Regulated Competition."

while others do not? Although regulation has become so widespread in recent years that the term *regulated industries* is something of a pleonasm, it is nevertheless true that some industries are subject to industry-specific regulation (utilities, for example, are subject to rate regulation) while other industries are not.

The economic theory of regulation explains this differential as the outcome of political self-interest. Tollison writes, "Thus, there is a vote-maximizing rationale for why one observes the extensive regulation of natural monopolies (utilities) and purely competitive industries (agriculture) and little or no regulation of the automobile and steel industries."[43]

A detailed historical investigation might well support this broad theoretical conclusion. Nevertheless, there are some regulated industries that do not fit. The sports industry is one of these. No matter how we classify football, basketball, and baseball—as monopolistic, as oligopolistic, or as competitive industries—a simple industry structure argument is not going to explain regulation. Football and basketball are subject to antitrust regulation; baseball is not. This is often referred to as the "baseball anomaly," which has not, at least until now, received a satisfactory explanation.

To explain the regulatory pattern of sports, Ellig goes beyond looking at simple industry structure. He looks at the internal organization of the industry. He finds that the vertical integration of the baseball leagues binds together the interests of major and minor league teams. If the major league teams resist a bill to subject baseball to antitrust law, so do their minor league affiliates. These affiliates exist in over a hundred cities across the country. They are often a source of pride in the community and are supported by scores of local civic leaders and local executives. Collectively, when these people speak, Congress listens.

In contrast, football and basketball do not have minor leagues. Colleges and universities control the apprentices, and their interests do not closely coincide with the interests of the professional leagues. The National Collegiate Athletic Association wants professional football and basketball leagues subjected to antitrust law.

This difference in the organizations of professional sports is how Ellig explains the baseball anomaly. Using a straight-line political interest argument and relying on traditional historical sources, Ellig concludes that "Baseball's lower organizational costs, combined with the sheer size of its minor league system, give it a comparative advantage in lobbying relative to other major sports."[44]

If Ellig is right, we can well understand Congressman Celler's complaint, uttered after the 1950 hearings on baseball's antitrust exemption, that

43. Tollison, "Interest Groups and Regulation."

44. Jerome Ellig, "The Baseball Anomaly and Congressional Intent," in this volume.

"They came upon Washington like locusts. They were in every nook and cranny—baseball players, the owners, and their cohorts."[45]

Both deregulation and the baseball anomaly indicate that economists' traditional classification of industry structure, while it may have relevance, is not sufficient to explain the historical record of regulation. This insufficiency is further illustrated by the place of technology in regulation. Traditionally, technology has been incorporated into regulatory studies mainly because it provides a public interest rationale for the regulation of natural monopolies.

The term *natural monopoly* is a theoretical one, derived from the shape of a firm's average cost curve relative to the size of the market. High fixed costs combined with low marginal costs will result in a declining average cost over some range. If this range covers the whole of the market, that is, if the average costs decline for the entire quantity demanded, then the industry is categorized as a natural monopoly, meaning that the good can be supplied most economically if one firm produces for the whole market. High fixed and low marginal costs are the result of technological conditions facing producers.[46]

There is no doubt that technological considerations affect the organization of individual firms and also of industries. There are important economic differences, based in technology, between "center" and "peripheral" firms. Center firms are characterized by capital intensity, by economies of scale or scope or speed, and by genuine economic advantages of large size. Peripheral firms are characterized by labor intensity, few economies of scale or scope, and few economic advantages of large size.

Theoretical concepts such as capital intensity and economies of scale have been studied in detail by business historians. In fact, historians have contributed more to our understanding of technology's effects on business organization than economists have.[47] These theoretical ideas have a firm basis in historical fact. Surprisingly, recent research suggests that we cannot say the same thing for natural monopoly.

We usually take it for granted that industries like telecommunications and electric utilities are natural monopolies. But this is based more on impression than on empirical evidence. Speaking of telecommunications, Crandall says, "There are no dispositive studies of the economies of scope in telecom-

---

45. Ellig, "The Baseball Anomaly."

46. See the discussions by Hirsh, in this volume, and Greg A. Jarrell, "The Demand for State Regulation of the Electric Utility Industry," *Journal of Law and Economics* 21 (October, 1978): 272–76.

47. See Alfred Chandler, *Strategy and Structure* (Cambridge, Mass.: MIT Press, 1964) and *The Visible Hand* (Cambridge, Mass.: Harvard University Press, 1977); Glenn E. Porter, *The Rise of Big Business* (New York: Thomas Y. Crowell Co., 1973). For the implications of this historiography for antitrust regulation, see Thomas K. McCraw, "Rethinking the Trust Question," in *Regulation in Perspective*. I have taken the terms *center firms* and *peripheral firms* from McCraw.

munications, and even the studies of scale economies are rather flawed because they cannot accurately capture the effects of technical progress."[48]

Walter Primeaux has recently studied scale economies in the electric utility industry. He concludes that ". . . it is not true that electric utility companies operate at higher costs in a duopoly than in a monopoly market structure." Nor does it appear that consumers receive lower prices from regulated monopolists than from competitive electric utilities. Primeaux says, "All in all, adverse pricing effects were not found to exist where direct competition existed; indeed, the opposite was true. Consumers derived substantial price benefits from the direct competition."[49]

We can adduce further historical evidence on this point. Although consolidations occurred in both telecommunications and electric utilities, neither industry evolved monopolies without the help of regulation. Kolko documents the efforts of AT&T to secure regulation at both the federal and state levels. By 1913, says Kolko, "AT&T realized that its long-term objectives of political stability and economic rationality could be attained only by federal regulation, and its commitment to the cause was intensified." He quotes Theodore Vail, president of AT&T, as saying, "We believe in and were the first to advocate state or govenrment control and regulation of public utilities."[50]

In the electric utility industry, Hirsh says that ". . . regulation emerged as a managerial innovation coming largely from the industry itself." Samuel Insull, who became president of Chicago Edison in 1892, was one of the leaders. According to Hirsh, ". . . as early as 1898, Insull advocated that private companies see public regulation as a means to achieve legal and unequivocal monopoly status. . . . Like executives in other industries, Insull advocated regulation by proclaiming it would be 'in the public interest.'"[51]

So, while the technology of telecommunications and electric utilities very likely classify them as center industries, it is doubtful that either were, or

48. Crandall, "Halfway Home." Blankart and Knieps have recently said, "The correct specification of technological change in econometric models seems to be a difficult task, particularly if dynamic sectors are under consideration and no clear solution is currently available. . . . In spite of the extensive empirical work done in recent years, the actual degree of (dis-)economies of scale in telecommunications system[s] remains uncertain" (Charles B. Blankart and Guenter Knieps, "What Can We Learn From Comparative Institutional Analysis? The Case of Telecommunications," *Kyklos* 42 [1989]: 582).

49. Walter Primeaux, *Direct Electric Utility Competition* (New York: Praeger, 1986), 9 and 282. William Emmons reached a similar conclusion after studying utility rates in 1930 and 1942. He writes, "prior to the New Deal, electricity prices were significantly lower in markets served by two competing electric utilities than in comparable markets served by a single firm." Emmons also found that public ownership resulted in lower rates than regulated monopolies. See William Emmons, "Measuring the Effects of Market Structure, Ownership, and Regulation: Evidence from the U.S. Electric Utility Industry, 1882–1942," working paper, Harvard University Business School.

50. Kolko, *The Triumph of Conservatism*, 180.

51. Richard F. Hirsh, "Regulation and Technology in the Electric Utility Industry: An Historical Analaysis of Interdependence and Change," in this volume.

are, natural monopolies. As plausible as the natural monopoly reasoning might be theoretically and as appealing as the regulation of natural monopoly might sound in the abstract, both ideas are rendered doubtful by historical research. Had economists made a more careful study of the events surrounding and conditions facing these industries, they might have been less ready to accept the public interest arguments so eagerly put forward by business executives.[52]

The subject of technological change in regulation, like most subjects in economic dynamics, almost seems to require the combined efforts of history and economics. Effective regulation will always alter the environment of the firm. It will alter the opportunities for profit. As a consequence of altered profit opportunities, technology may develop differently in the regulated environment than in the competitive environment. The precise ways in which the development of technology will differ, and the extent to which it will differ, are matters for empirical study.

Vietor's description of the rapid changeover, after deregulation, in the airline fleet of American Airlines suggests that existing aircraft, especially the widebodies, were not the most efficient way of providing service. Sunit Khanna, in his survey of the effects of regulation on technological change, says, "There is, however, reason to believe that regulatory policies of the CAB, resulting in nonprice competition, might have enhanced the tendencies of the trunk carriers to procure relatively large size aircraft."[53]

Hirsh's study of the electric utility industry reveals both the incentives to change the direction of technology and the course of the change when the competitive environment changes. Once electrical utilities had established their monopolies on the basis of large-scale technology, the industry had every incentive to exploit that particular technology. This strategy for technological change worked well for both firms and regulators, and eventually displaced nearly all smaller technology. Not until large steam turbines reached their limits of scale, and Congress passed the Public Utility Regulatory Policies Act of 1978, were smaller technologies able to compete. In particular, the generation of electric power in conjunction with, or as a by-product of, other industrial processes, is making a comeback. Known as cogeneration, this process produced 29.0 percent of electrical power in 1922, but only 3.5 percent in

---

52. Even if natural monopolies exist, regulation is certainly not the only, and perhaps not even the best, way to serve the consumer. For a discussion of the theoretical issues, see Harold Demsetz, "Why Regulate Utilities?" *Journal of Law and Economics* 12 (April, 1969): 1–22; Oliver Williamson, "Franchise Bidding for Natural Monopolies," *Bell Journal of Economics and Management Science* 7 (Spring, 1976): 73–104; Victor Goldberg, "Regulation and Administered Contracts," *Bell Journal of Economics and Management Science* 7 (Autumn, 1976): 426–48.

53. Sunit K. Khanna, "Economic Regulation and Technological Change: A Review of the Literature," *Public Utilities Fortnightly* (January 21, 1982): 41. On American Airlines's changes in its fleet, see Vietor, "The Hubris of Regulated Competition."

1978. Over the next ten years, thanks to the 1978 act, over 27.0 percent of new electric power will likely come from small-scale producers.[54]

Regulated firms will also resist the introduction of new technology if the innovation threatens their profitability. In the telecommuncations industry, Khanna notes that ". . . every regulatory response to an offer of new technologies in this industry resulted in efforts by the American Telephone and Telegraph Company either to foreclose entry by offering excessive rate reductions, or to impose severe technical requirements which made it difficult for the new entrants to interconnect with the Bell system.[55]

Similarly, the recent innovations in small-scale technology for electric utility generation is motivated by the profit seeking of small, unregulated, entrepreneurial firms. "As can be imagined," Hirsh tells us, "many utility managers are displeased by these developments."[56] Once again, the historical record of regulation harmonizes with the economic principle that firms will follow the star of profitability, wherever it might lead.

The connections considered here, between the economics and history of regulation, show that the subject can be profitably pursued in tandem. Regulation lends itself almost naturally to the joint considerations of abstract theory and concrete particular. It may be no exaggeration to say that a satisfactory understanding of regulation cannot be attained by either discipline working in isolation.

54. Hirsh, "Regulation and Technology in the Electric Utility Industry."

55. Khanna,"Economic Regulation and Technical Change," 40. See also Crandall, "Halfway Home."

56. Hirsh, "Regulation and Technology." On the generation of new technology, Hirsh writes, "The new driving force for development of generation technologies may therefore come from the unregulated, small-power generation industry. . . . One already sees much innovation occurring."

CHAPTER 1

The Hubris of Regulated Competition: Airlines, 1925–88

Richard H. K. Vietor

Airline regulation and deregulation, taken together, have served as a uniquely interesting laboratory for testing basic concepts of political economy and business management.

During the forty years of federal regulation (from 1938 to 1978), economists studied airlines to understand how federal intervention affected key aspects of market structure—especially entry, price, and supply and demand.[1] Political scientists cited this experience to illustrate diverse theories of regulatory origin, capture, and process.[2] Students of business administration focused on the regulated airlines' marketing, logistics, and competitive strategies.[3]

More recently, economists have been fascinated by the unanticipated consequences of deregulation, while political scientists are still trying to explain why and how it happened. The business conduct and market performance of deregulated airlines have challenged even the most sophisticated

---

1. Among the best studies by economists are Richard E. Caves, *Air Transport and its Regulators: An Industry Study* (Cambridge, Mass.: Harvard University Press, 1962); Samuel B. Richmond, *Regulation and Competition in Air Transportation* (New York: Columbia University Press, 1961); and William A. Jordan, *Airline Regulation in America: Effects and Imperfections* (Baltimore: John Hopkins University Press, 1970); Alfred E. Kahn, *The Economics of Regulation* (New York: Wiley and Sons, 1971), 2:209–20.

2. Samuel P. Huntington, "Clientalism: A Study in Administrative Politics," Ph.D. diss., Harvard University, 1951; Marver H. Bernstein, *Regulating Business by Independent Commission* (Princeton: Princeton University Press, 1955); Emmette S. Redford, *The Regulatory Process: With Illustrations from Commercial Aviation* (Austin: University of Texas Press, 1969); Robert C. Fraser, Alan D. Donheiser, and Thomas G. Miller, Jr., *Civil Aviation Development: A Policy and Operations Analysis* (New York: Praeger, 1972).

3. Paul W. Cherington, *Airline Price Policy: A Study of Domestic Airline Passenger Fares* (Boston: Harvard Business School Division of Research, 1958); Stanley C. Hollander, *Passenger Transportation: Readings Selected from a Marketing Viewpoint* (East Lansing: Michigan State University Press, 1968); William Fruhan, *The Fight for Competitive Advantage* (Boston: Harvard Business School Division of Research, 1972).

ideas about contestability, information and transaction costs, economies of scale, and the public and private interest theories of government.[4] For business administration, the speed and starkness of deregulation have shed new light on the process of strategic and organizational adjustment to competitive change.[5]

Despite the richness of this scholarly output, economic and political explanations remain relatively unintegrated; the economic studies tend to be cross-sectional, seldom focusing on the dynamic process of an evolving market structure; the policy explanations strive unsuccessfully for monocausality; and, with some exceptions (e.g., Meyer, *Airline Deregulation*, and Levine, "Airline Competition"), neither the economic nor policy explanations take into account the strategic conduct of the firm or its surprising effects on market structure. By examining the history of regulation and deregulation, this chapter seeks to provide a middle-level theory of regulation: a dynamic view of the market-structuring effects of regulatory policy, the multiple interactive causes of deregulation, and the strategic response of a major carrier—American Airlines.

The chapter is organized in five sections: (1) an explanation of the origins of airline regulation, 1925–38; (2) its effects on market structure, 1938–69; (3) a discussion of the causes of deregulation, 1969–78; (4) a description of American Airlines' strategic adjustment to deregulation and an overview of

---

4. Among the economic studies of deregulation are John Meyer, Merton J. Peck, John Stenason, and Charles Zwick, *Airline Deregulation: The Early Experience* (Boston: Auburn House Publishing, 1981); John Meyer and Clinton Oster, *Deregulation and the New Airline Entrepreneurs* (Cambridge, Mass.: MIT Press, 1984), and *Deregulation and the Future of Intercity Passenger Travel* (Cambridge, Mass.: MIT Press, 1987); Elizabeth E. Bailey, David R. Graham, and Daniel P. Kaplan, *Deregulating the Airlines* (Cambridge, Mass.: MIT Press, 1985); Elizabeth E. Bailey and Jeffrey R. Williams, "Sources of Rent in the Deregulated Airline Industry," *Journal of Law and Economics* 31 (April, 1988), 173–202; Steve Morrison and Clifford Winston, *The Economic Effects of Airline Deregulation* (Washington, D.C.: Brookings Institution, 1986); Robert J. Andriuliatis, David L. Frank, Tae H. Oum, and Michael W. Tretheway, *Deregulation and Airline Employment: Myth Versus Fact* (Vancouver: University of British Columbia Centre for Transportation Studies, 1987); and Michael E. Levine, "Airline Competition in Deregulated Markets: Theory, Firm Strategy, and Public Policy," *Yale Journal of Regulation* 4, no. 2 (Spring, 1987), 393–494. On the politics of deregulation, see Bradley Behrman, "Civil Aeronautics Board," in *The Politics of Regulation*, ed. James Q. Wilson (New York: Basic Books, 1980), 75–120; Stephen Breyer, *Regulation and its Reform* (Cambridge, Mass.: Harvard University Press, 1982); Thomas K. McCraw, *Prophets of Regulation* (Cambridge, Mass.: Harvard University Press, 1984); Martha Derthick and Paul J. Quirk, *The Politics of Deregulation* (Washington, D.C.: Brookings Institution, 1985); Anthony E. Brown, *The Politics of Airline Deregulation* (Knoxville: University of Tennessee Press, 1987).

5. See Debra Whitestone and Leonard Schlesinger, *People Express (A)* (Boston: HBS Case Services, no. 483–103, 1983); Martha Weinberg, *Continental Airlines (A)* (Boston: HBS Case Services, no. 385–006, 1984), *Frontier Airlines (A)* (Boston: HBS Case Services, no. 184–041, 1983); and Richard Vietor, *American Airlines (A)* (Boston: HBS Case Services, no. 385–182, 1985).

market structure and performance, 1978–87; and (5) some middle-level theoretical conclusions.

"Market Failure" and Origins of Regulation, 1925–38

The airline business in the United States started out as a dangerous, heavily subsidized, mail delivery service. Government literally created the market. During World War I, Congress had funded the development and large-scale production of military aircraft. As the war ended, the Post Office inaugurated scheduled airmail service, with operations provided by Army pilots. For several years, the industry limped along with a short supply of skilled pilots, few control systems, rudimentary airports, and an uncoordinated route structure. Recognizing these weaknesses, the industry itself sought government help—regulation of airways and subsidies for commercial airmail.[6] Congress tried to meet these needs with the Kelly Airmail Act of 1925, providing for competitive bidding and subsidies for contract airmail service, and the Air Commerce Act of 1926, authorizing the Department of Commerce to regulate air navigation and safety.[7]

The subsidies, amounting to $7 million per year by 1930, stimulated demand for airmail service and intense competition among suppliers. Route mileage increased tenfold, with more than a dozen carriers organized to provide regular service. But nothing in the 1925 act facilitated a rational route structure, modification of initial bids, or development of passenger service. Frustrated by the industry's slow development, Hoover's Postmaster General, Walter F. Brown, proposed legislation to give himself wide-ranging authority over routes, mail rates, and discretionary contract awards. Congress granted Brown his request, save for the waiver of competitive bidding, in the McNary-Watres Act of 1930.[8]

Brown wasted no time cashing this "blank check." He called a meeting of the principal airmail carriers, none of whom were breaking even on passenger service, and asked them to "agree among themselves as to the territory in which they shall have the paramount interest."[9] The "pioneer" carriers readily acceded to this cooperative approach, and with some arm-twisting

6. David D. Lee, "Herbert Hoover and the Development of Commercial Aviation, 1921–26," *Business History Review* 58, no. 1 (Spring, 1984), 78–84.

7. Paul T. David, *The Economics of Air Mail Transportation* (Washington, D.C.: Brookings Institution, 1934); Francis A. Spencer, *Air Mail Payment and the Government* (Washington, D.C.: Brookings Institution, 1941), 29–39; Charles C. Rohlfing, *National Regulation of Aeronautics* (Philadelphia: University of Pennsylvania Press, 1931).

8. J. Howard Hamstra, "Two Decades—Federal Regulation in Perspective," *The Journal of Air Law and Commerce* 12, no. 2 (April, 1941), 108–14.

9. Irving Glover, Second Assistant Postmaster, "Memorandum to the Postmaster General," May 20, 1930, reprinted in House Committee on Post Office and Post Roads, *Air Mail Hearings*, 73d Cong., 2d sess., (February-March, 1934), 227.

from Brown, three transcontinental routes were designated and awarded: a southern route to American Airways, a central route to TWA, and a northern route to United Airways. Six other carriers received the remaining contracts. "There was no sense," as Brown later explained, "in taking the government's money and dishing it out to every little fellow that was flying around. . . ." Administrative integration and consolidation was the only way he could think of "to make the industry self-sustaining."[10]

With this government-induced cartel in place, the airline business made some rapid advances. Improvements in aircraft technology, together with noncompetitive mail contracts, stimulated the growth of passenger service. The principal carriers grew by acquisition as well as extension, in a depression-induced build-up of holding company pyramids. TWA was acquired by General Motors (along with Eastern, Western, and Douglas Aviation); United formed a holding company with National Air Transport, Pratt & Whitney, Boeing, and Sikorsky; and American was acquired by Aviation Corporation (along with Texas Air, Continental Air, Robertson Aircraft ["the Lindbergh Line"], and several others).[11]

On February 9, 1934, the pyramids and the cartel came crashing down. President Franklin Roosevelt, responding to allegations of conspiracy, cancelled all existing airmail contracts and ordered the Army to deliver the airmail. Brown's infamous "spoils conference" with airline industry leaders in 1930 had come to light as a full-blown political scandal.[12]

Congress hastily revised the airmail act (the Black-McKellar Act of 1934), curtailing the Postmaster General's authority, reimposing strict competitive bidding, and giving the Interstate Commerce Commission control of entry, through certification. The act's most distinctive feature was punitive; in the best tradition of the Big Stick, it prohibited existing carriers from bidding on contracts, banned interlocking directorates, and restricted airlines with mail contracts from "engag[ing] in any other phase of the aviation industry." With this, the aviation trusts were destroyed.[13]

The 1934 act restructured the airline industry, creating the horizontal oligopoly that would last until 1970s. With new executive officers, new names, and new incorporation papers, eleven carriers emerged from the conglomerates. The "Big Four"—American Airlines, United Airlines, Trans World Airlines, and Eastern Airlines—held about 80 percent of market share

10. Quoted in Robert J. Serling, *Eagle: The Story of American Airlines* (New York: St. Martins/Marek, 1985), 65.

11. Senate Committee on Post Office and Post Roads, *Revisions of Air Mail Laws,* 73d Cong., 2d sess. (March, 1934), 76–86.

12. Franklin D. Roosevelt, Executive Order no. 6591, February 9, 1934; see also Senate Special Committee, *Investigation of Air Mail and Ocean Mail Contracts*, 73d Cong., 2d sess., parts 1–9, 1934.

13. *Public Law 308*, 48 Stat. 933, 39 U.S.C. 463 (1934); Charles Rhyne, *The Civil Aeronautics Act Annotated* (Washington, D.C.: National Law Book Co., 1939), 29–31.

(in revenue passenger miles). Seven others—Northwest, Pennsylvania Central, Braniff, Western Air Express, Chicago & Western, Mid-Continent, and National—shared the remaining 20 percent. The act also imposed a competitive bidding system that, as the only feasible means of entry, resulted in absurdly low bids. Aggravated by stagnation, industry profitability turned negative for the next few years, giving the impression that "excess competition" was a sort of market failure.

While perhaps excessive, competition was by no means rejected out of hand. An ad hoc Aviation Commission, appointed by Congress to reconsider long-term aviation policy, firmly rejected nationalization (the "European model"), and concluded that air transport was "not a natural monopoly." Although it recommended that Congress create an independent commission to regulate entry and set minimum standards of service, it wished to preserve a constructive "spirit of emulation" among carriers:

> There must be enough competition to serve as a spur to the eager search for progress, but there must not be so much as to raise costs materially through the duplication of facilities. There must be no arbitrary denial of the right of entry of newcomers. . . . [14]

The Commission was recommending regulated competition, in the belief that regulators could decouple services from prices and optimize for both.

The airline industry now lobbied hard for unified economic regulation by an independent commission. Half the total investment in aviation had allegedly been lost, and without legislation, complained Edgar Gorrell, president of the Air Transport Association, "there is nothing to prevent the entire air carrier system from crashing to earth under the impact of cutthroat and destructive practices."[15]

When the Roosevelt administration endorsed legislation in 1938, Congress passed the Civil Aeronautics Act.[16] The act created a Civil Aeronautics Authority (later Board) with broad authority to control entry and exit by certification, to approve or amend tariffs, to set mail rates, to control mergers, to authorize interfirm agreements, and to control methods of competition.[17]

14. Federal Aviation Commission, "Report of the Federal Aviation Commission," Senate Document 15, 74th Cong., 1st sess. (January, 1935), 52–53.

15. House Committee on Interstate and Foreign Commerce, *To Create a Civil Aeronautics Authority*, 75th Cong., 3d sess. (March, 1938), 38; Edgar S. Gorrell, "Rationalization of Air Transport," *Journal of Air Law* 9 (1938): 43.

16. The Roosevelt administration preferred that all regulatory responsibilities for transportation be consolidated in a single agency—either the ICC or a new cabinet department. See Franklin D. Roosevelt, "Message of Transmittal," January 31, 1935, in Federal Aviation Commission, *Report*, iii-iv; Senate Subcommittee on S. 3659, Committee on Interstate Commerce, *Civil Aviation and Air Transport*, 75th Cong., 3d sess. (April, 1938), 1–2.

17. The original (1938) act actually combined regulatory and developmental (air traffic control and safety) functions under the same administrative roof. But after just two years,

These extraordinary powers were based on two criteria: "the promotion of adequate, economical, and efficient service . . . at reasonable charges," and "competition to the extent necessary to assure the sound development of an air-transportation system. . . ."[18]

The regulatory principle expressed here was clearly different from the public utility concept that had evolved from *Munn v. Illinois*.[19] Nor was it a simple "capture" of policy by industry.[20] Rather, and from the start, it was a muddled attempt to structure markets and guide competition toward a socially optimal mix of service, innovation, and economic growth.

Regulation-Defined Airline Markets, 1938–69

During its first thirty years, the Civil Aeronautics Board (CAB) took several tacks, depending on its makeup (particularly its chairman) and on airline market conditions. Prior to 1955, the board fostered rapid growth through route extensions, tight control over mergers and new entrants, and "route strengthening" for the smaller trunk carriers. Since the act had grandfathered the routes of the major carriers, the Big Four started out from a dominant position. As the CAB added 56,000 miles of new routes in the late 1940s (doubling the prewar network), it implemented a policy of "route strengthening" to favor the growth of the smaller trunk carriers (e.g., Northeastern, Northwestern, Braniff, Continental, Delta, National, Western, Mid-Continent, and Southern).[21] The board also promoted growth by certifying and nurturing noncompeting "feeder lines," which had grown into thirteen relatively stable, local carriers with 22,000 miles of routes and $54 million in revenues by 1954 (see tables 1 and 2).

Control of entry was a difficult issue for the Civil Aeronautics Board. Because airmail subsidies artificially stimulated entry, and because low natural entry barriers encouraged cream skimming, entry restrictions appeared warranted, even necessary. But with the postwar glut of aircraft and pilots, hundreds of "irregulars" commenced service, exempt from certification. For a time, these irregulars showed extraordinary imagination and flexibility in skirting each new CAB rule. At its peak in 1951, the market share of the irregular carriers reached 7.5 percent of revenue-passenger miles and 21.0

Congress amended the act, restoring air traffic control and safety to the Commerce Department (and changing the name of the Civil Aeronautics Authority to the Civil Aeronautics Board); see *Reorganization Act of 1940*, 54 Stat. 735; also, House of Representatives, House Report 2505, 76th Cong., 3d sess. (1940).

18. *Civil Aeronautics Act of 1938*, 52 Stat. 973; see also Rhyne, *Civil Aeronautics Act Annotated*.

19. The Board itself drew this distinction in Civil Aeronautics Board, "Acquisition of Marquette by TWA—Supplemental Opinion," 2 CAB 409 (1940): 411–13.

20. See, for example, George Stigler, "Theories of Economic Regulation," *Bell Journal of Economics and Management Science* 2 (1971): 3–21.

21. Civil Aeronautics Board, *Annual Report*, (Washington, D.C., GPO 1946–49).

TABLE 1. Market Share of Certified Carriers, 1939–54 (percentage of revenue-passenger miles)

	1939	1949	1954
Big Four	82	70	71
Other Trunks	18	28	25
Local Carriers	—	2	4

Source: Civil Aeronautics Board, *Handbook of Airline Statistics, 1973* (Washington, D.C., 1973), 23.

percent of cargo. It took nearly a decade for the Board to plug every loophole, alienating quite a few congressmen in the process.[22] On the major trunk routes, the board had no real decision rule for settling requests for competitive entry and service rivalry. Case-by-case decision making reflected a balancing act, slightly tilted toward a "presumption in favor of competition on any route which offered sufficient traffic to support competing services without unreasonable increase of total operating costs."[23] Too much service rivalry, without pricing flexibility, clearly threatened to raise costs, add excess capacity, and dilute traffic.[24]

The Board's ad hoc decision making contrasted sharply with a running debate in policy circles over the structure of the "national aviation system." Central planning, it seemed, still had a credible following among legislators and bureaucrats during the 1940s. But the board's authority, much less vision, was limited with regard to route structure. While it generally recognized that the linearity of inherited mail routes was less than optimal, there was no consensus for a plan.[25] By default, point-to-point, nonstop service became the standard for aviation policy.

22. *Investigation of Nonscheduled Air Service*, 6 CAB (1946), 1049; *Large Irregular Carriers, Exemption*, 11 CAB (1950), 609; U.S. Congress Select Committee on Small Business, *Future of Irregular Airlines in United States Air Transportation Industry*, 83d Cong., 1st sess. (1953), and House Judiciary Committee, *Report Pursuant to H. Res. 107 on Airlines*, 85th Cong., 1st sess. (April 5, 1957).

23. *Transcontinental and Western Air North-South California* 4 CAB 373 (1943); *Colonial Air et al., Atlantic Seaboard Op.*, 4 CAB 552, 555 (1943).

24. In a 1947 case, for example, this ambivalence toward city-pair competition (among trunk carriers) was clear, as the examiner sought to distinguish "between the cutthroat, disruptive type of competition where the existing carrier is fighting for financial survival and the constructive kind of competitive service imposed to stimulate traffic, reduce costs, encourage better service, and otherwise promote the development of the industry." See Civil Aeronautics Board, *Docket no. 679, Detroit Washington Service Case*, "Report of Examiner" (March 17, 1947), 84.

25. See, for example, The President's Air Policy Commission, *Survival in the Air Age* (Washington: GPO, 1948); Congressional Aviation Policy Board, *National Aviation Policy*, 80th Cong., 2d sess.; James M. Landis, "Air Routes Under the Civil Aeronautics Act," *Journal of Air Law and Commerce* 15 (Summer, 1948): 299–303.

TABLE 2. Certified Local Carriers in 1954

Allegheny	Ozark
Bonanza	Piedmont
Central	Southern
Frontier	Southwest
Lake Central	Trans-Texas
Mohawk	West Coast
North Central	

While the CAB fumbled to regulate competition, technological change and the business cycle periodically rocked airline markets. In 1947, the industry plunged into a second reequipment cycle (the first had been the prewar shift to DC-3s), converting to larger, faster, four-engine aircraft capable of seating forty to sixty people. As the carriers incurred new debt to expand capacity, recession struck in 1948, load factors plummeted, and operating margins turned sharply negative.[26]

The CAB responded to this crisis by urging all major carriers to raise rates by 10 percent and to offer promotional fares to fill empty seats.[27] Accused by the incumbent airlines of encouraging "competition for competition's sake," the board substantially curtailed its encouragement of city-pair rivalry and shut the door to new entry.[28] Eventually, it approved most of the mergers precipitated by recession; by 1954, the sixteen trunk carriers were reduced to thirteen, and twenty-three locals to thirteen.

Shortly after the Korean War, this policy of structural stability was completely reversed. In April, 1955, President Eisenhower appointed Ross Rizley, previously a congressman from Oklahoma, to chair the Civil Aeronautics Board. With prosperity helping to fill capacity and sustain record high airline earnings, Rizley concluded that more competition would best serve the public interest.[29] In a series of fourteen decisions over the next eighteen months, the CAB reduced the number of noncompetitive city pairs in the top 100 markets from forty to sixteen. In all, competition was introduced or strengthened in 559 city-pair markets.[30]

At this very moment of intensified rivalry, the jet age commenced. First turboprops, developed in England, and then real jets were introduced into

26. The load factor dropped from 79 percent to 60 percent in two years; see Civil Aeronautics Board, *Annual Report* (1948), 3.

27. Cherington, *Airline Price Policy*, 186–289.

28. Civil Aeronautics Board, *Docket no. 1102, Southern Service to the West*, "Report of the Hearing Examiner" (June 21, 1959), 99, and 12 CAB 518 (1951), 534.

29. Ross Rizley, "Some Personal Reflections After Eight Months as Chairman of the Civil Aeronautics Board," *Journal of Air Law and Commerce* 22 (Autumn, 1955): 445–52.

30. Samuel Richmond, *Regulation and Competition*, 112–90.

commercial aviation. In a daring effort to tie up production lines at both major aircraft manufacturers, Pan American ordered 25 Boeing 707s and 25 DC-8s in October, 1955. United followed suit, then American, and, within a few months, the industry had committed to $1.4 billion worth of new equipment—about $200 million more than its total net investment.[31]

Once again, this reequipment cycle added capacity and debt and undermined return on investment. An investigation of passenger fares, opened in 1956, evolved into a collective rate case that yielded rate hikes of 10 percent in 1958 and 5 percent in 1960. The board justified these increases by an array of utilitylike rate-making standards, with a rate of return pegged at 10.25 percent.[32]

The crux of this rule making was the board's adoption of a target load factor—set at 63 percent. The CAB's Bureau of Air Operations argued that airline passengers should not be burdened with the cost of excess capacity: "Airline management is both responsible and capable of exercising control of load factors over reasonably extended periods by tailoring capacity to the requirements of traffic."[33] Of course, estimation of unit operating costs, and thus the revenue requirement, were linked to this crucial target.

Nowhere is the hubris of regulated competition more evident. The board's view that capacity utilization was a managerial prerogative, independent of price and entry regulation, was myopic. It somehow decoupled the economic linkages between the firm and the market—between price, capacity investment, market share, and earnings. Excess capacity was the perverse result of a hybrid regulation that prevented price competition but not service rivalry. Soon enough, however, this would become painfully obvious (see fig. 1).

Regulatory Failure and Regulatory Reform, 1969–78

Basic Conditions and Regulatory Failure

Even before 1969, the foundations were in place for serious problems with airline regulation: the point-to-point route structure, excess service rivalry and capacity, bundled pricing, and collective, utility-type rate making. Nonetheless, healthy economic growth and dramatic productivity gains from technological innovation had more than made up for regulatory inefficiencies.

But the macroeconomy began to change. Slower economic growth, ris-

31. Richard Caves, *Air Transport*, 307–13. Net investment, as of 1955, was reported as $1,239,305,000 (in U.S. Congress House Judiciary Committee *Report on Airlines*, 18).

32. William Jordan, *Airline Regulation in America Effects and Imperfections* (Baltimore: John Hopkins University Press, 1970), 62–65.

33. Emmette S. Redford, *The General Passenger Fare Investigation*, Interuniversity Case Program no. 56 (University, Ala.: University of Alabama Press, 1960), 43–44.

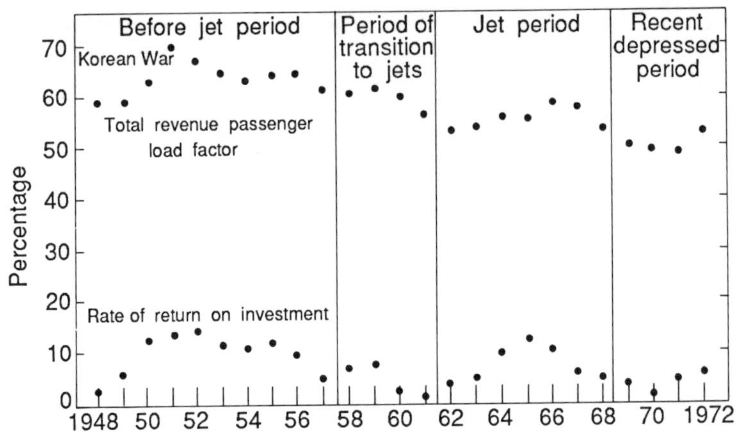

Fig. 1. Load factors and rates of return, 1948–72, domestic trunklines. (From Civil Aeronautics Board, *Regulatory Reform: Report of the C.A.B. Special Staff* [Washington, D.C.: CAC, 1975], 130.)

ing inflation, and higher interest rates staggered airline markets. Demand, which had been growing at an annual rate of 18 percent from 1965 through 1969, slowed to 4 percent between 1969 and 1975. Supply shocks in the early 1970s, combined with the ratcheting upward of wage costs, sparked a virtual explosion of airline operating costs. Between 1969 and 1978, the price of jet fuel increased 222 percent, amounting to nearly one-fifth of operating costs; labor costs, which accounted for 45 percent of airline expenses, increased 135 percent (to $22,422 per employee).[34]

Once again, new technology and a fourth reequipment cycle coincided with a downturn in the business cycle. Pan American, as before, was first to buy 25 wide-bodied Boeing 747s (with 350 to 450 seats). Domestic carriers followed suit, ordering McDonnell-Douglas DC-10s and Lockeed L-1011s, as well as 747s. By 1975, trunk carriers were operating 282 wide-bodied aircraft. At $22 to $25 million per aircraft, this capacity cost more than $6 billion—nearly four times cumulative operating profits.[35]

Taken together, these dramatic changes in demand (for service) and supply (of available seats) amounted to a reversal in the airline industry's economic structure. Since the conversion to jet aircraft began in the late 1950s, the industry had enjoyed declining unit costs of capacity (with productivity growth outstripping inflation).[36] But in 1969, nominal unit costs turned around, rising 77 percent by 1978. Real capacity costs stopped declining, stuck at their 1970 level for the next seven years (fig. 2). Realized costs per

34. Civil Aeronautics Board, *Handbook of Airline Statistics* (1972), 464 and (1978), 136.
35. Civil Aeronautics Board, *Handbook of Airline Statistics* (1974), 134–35.
36. William Fruhan, *Fight for Competitive Advantage*, 24.

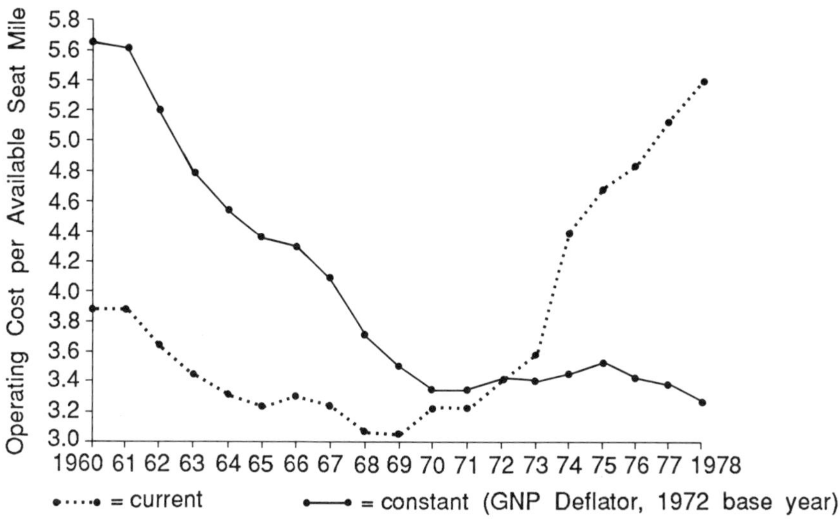

Fig. 2. Unit cost of airline capacity for domestic trunk carriers by available seat miles, in cents. (Data from CAB, *Handbook of Airline Statistics,* 1972, 1974, 1976, 1978.)

unit of output changed even more dramatically, due to the decline in capacity utilization. In nominal terms, costs per revenue passenger mile (RPM) exploded (fig. 3). Dramatic price increases now became necessary, forcing the CAB to open an industrywide rate case that attracted political attention to its own regulatory failings.

Excess capacity, a persistent feature of regulated competition (and of airmail subsidies), was the crux of the problem. In the absence of price and entry freedom, capacity was the principal means of competition, and choice of aircraft was the most important managerial prerogative. Modernity, speed, and comfort were critical aspects of service rivalry. No major carrier could afford to fall behind in new aircraft acquisition; thus, the repetition of frantic reequipment cycles, even to the point where domestic carriers ordered inappropriate and unnecessary 747s.[37]

37. To the extent that equipment rivalry encouraged technological innovation, it was an acknowledged benefit of CAB regulation. Development of the DC-3, for example, and later the DC-10, were the direct results of American Airlines' efforts to be more competitive. Similarly, Pan American played a major role in Boeing's development of the 747. In part, these results were the consequences of perverse service rivalry and reflected the economic security and service obligations induced by regulation. Moreover, this rapid turnover of aircraft may not have been an unmixed benefit. Richard Caves pointed long ago to the fact that excessive equipment competition may have precluded some desirable utilization of older aircraft for lower fare service; see Caves, *Air Transport and its Regulators*, 241; Kahn, *Economics of Regulation*, 2:213–14. On the reequipment cycle, see Louis J. Hector, "Problems in Economic Regulation of Civil Aviation in the United States," *Journal of Air Law and Commerce* 25 (1958): 101–7.

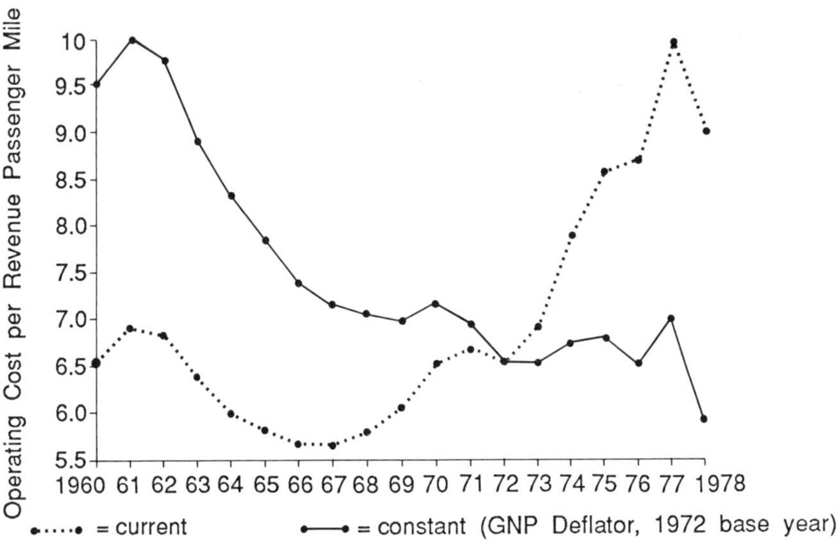

Fig. 3. Unit cost of airline service for domestic trunk carriers by revenue passenger miles, in cents. (data from CAB, *Handbook of Airline Statistics,* 1972, 1974, 1976, 1978.)

Even more dramatic was the quantitative side of capacity competition. Customers, especially business travelers, desired convenience and choice in frequency of departure and nonstop service. In the absence of pricing flexibility, the addition of capacity by one competitor in a city-pair market was likely to take market share from the others. In fact, market share appeared historically to vary disproportionately to capacity share—an empirical relationship called the *S-Curve*. For rivals serving the same city-pair, this phenomenon posed a kind of Prisoner's Dilemma.[38]

Load factors, falling since 1965, hit a record low in 1971 of 48 percent. But meanwhile, the rapid growth in the number of flights had already caused severe air traffic congestion, especially in the largest urban markets—Chicago, Los Angeles, New York, and Washington. On those routes, where price-insensitive business customers sought maximum convenience, excess capacity was rampant. Load factors on domestic 747 flights actually fell to 33 percent in 1971–72.

After a series of private talks, American, United, and TWA petitioned the CAB to approve capacity restrictions. Between 1971 and 1974, several

38. A city-pair rival with a minority share of capacity was likely to have a lower load factor than competitors. Since overall load factors were often near the break-even point, it was difficult for a minority-share competitor to make a profit. This condition created a perverse incentive to increase capacity, even though the load factor would fall if one's rival(s) followed suit; see William Fruhan, *Fight for Competitive Advantage*, 126–39.

agreements were implemented, reducing the number of weekly round-trip flights from 10 percent (Washington-Los Angeles) to 38 percent (New York-San Francisco). In these markets, load factors improved considerably, to the point where travelers actually complained of difficulties getting tickets.[39] Secor Browne, the CAB chairman from 1969 to 1973, complemented these capacity cartels with a virtual moratorium on new route authorizations. In the five years beginning in July, 1969, only two applications were granted. The rest were denied or left pending indefinitely.[40]

With capacity and route expansion foreclosed as outlets for product differentiation, the trunk carriers devised new means of service competition. "Capacity wars" gave way to "lounge wars." On wide-bodied aircraft, lounges were introduced in first class, then in coach. When American installed piano bars, TWA countered with electronic draw-poker machines. Live entertainment proliferated, with musicians, magicians, winetasters, and Playboy Bunnies.[41] This heightened service rivalry, meanwhile, spilled over into other city-pair markets, where some of the grounded aircraft were put to use. When smaller carriers complained, the industry's consensus on behalf of regulation began to waiver.

The *Domestic Passenger Fare Investigation* was the CAB's principal response to this crisis in capacity utilization. This proceeding, begun in January, 1970, and concluded five years later, yielded fare increases totaling 38 percent. Although the investigation produced several regulatory innovations, its impact on economic efficiency was subject to intense criticism.[42] The mileage-based pricing prevented fare flexibility and marginal-cost pricing, while the industry averaging of costs protected the least efficient carrier. By 1975, the CAB's efforts had done little to improve airline performance; gross overcapacity, high prices, and weak earnings prevailed.

---

39. William A. Jordan, "Airline Capacity Agreements Correcting a Regulatory Imperfection," *Journal of Air Law and Commerce* 39 (1973): 184–86; Senate Judiciary Committee, Subcommittee on Administrative Practices and Procedure, *Civil Aeronautics Board Practices and Procedures—A Report*, 94th Cong., 1st sess., Committee Print (Washington: GPO, 1975), 145–46. These capacity agreements were ruled unlawful in Civil Aeronautics Board, *Docket no. 22908*, *Capacity Reduction Agreements Case*, "Report of the Examiner" (November 18, 1974).

40. Commissioner G. Joseph Minetti, quoted in Senate Judiciary Committee, *CAB Practices and Procedure*, 84–86.

41. William Jordan, "Airline Capacity Agreements," 203.

42. The CAB's procedure and methodology had been subject to criticism since the late 1950s, when Commissioner Louis Hector resigned and sent an open letter to President Eisenhower, criticizing the board's lack of rational criteria, policy flip-flopping through case-by-case, oral decisions, justified after the fact by written opinions; see Louis J. Hector, "Problems of the CAB and the Independent Regulatory Agencies," A Memorandum to the President, (September 10, 1959). In the DPFI, the Board adopted an elaborate new set of standards, including (1) determination of an industrywide, average cost, (2) a target load factor of 55 percent, (3) a 12 percent rate of return, (4) a rate structure based on mileage, (5) an assumed price elasticity of demand of -0.7 percent, and (6) an automatic quarterly process for reporting costs and calculating fare adjustments. See Senate Judiciary Committee, *CAB Practices and Procedure*, 109–113.

New Ideas and Policy Entrepreneurship

From this point on, airline regulation came unraveled with amazing speed. The political process, especially in view of its active support by regulators, confounded the conventional wisdom of the policy literature. What could have broken the symmetry of the "iron triangle"—the regulated industry, congressional interests, and regulators—to which theory had attributed such immutable power? How, indeed, could a "captured" agency cross its captors to advocate its own demise?[43] No single explanation can suffice. Changes in basic economic factors, technological innovation, and regulatory failure were necessary, but not sufficient, preconditions. New ideas about government regulation and "policy entrepreneurship" also contributed.

Intellectuals, especially economists, played an unusual role in the process of airline deregulation. The work of John Meyer, Richard Caves, and Michael Levine (a lawyer) had earlier established a scholarly thread of criticism. But now, as the industry's performance worsened, other critical voices joined in.[44]

Not all of these critics were conventional academics. Many of them were Washington commuters, visiting at the Brookings Institution and the American Enterprise Institute, and taking appointments in the government. By 1974, their critique of regulation had been widely disseminated through the economic-policy literature familiar to Washington insiders.[45]

The institutional dissemination of their regulatory critique seemed part of a broader loss of faith in government management. The underlying political ideology, which accepted a liberal, active role for the federal government, was seriously eroded during the early 1970s by various microeconomic problems, macroeconomic problems, and two key noneconomic issues—the Vietnam War and Watergate. In the second half of 1974, with the presidency weakened, with the world economic order destabilized after the first oil shock and the demise of fixed exchange rates, and with the domestic economy sliding into a high-inflation recession, the time for reform, and for political entrepreneurship, was ripe.

---

43. For a detailed analysis of the theoretical literature that pertains to airline deregulation, see Jonathan L. Katz, "The Politics of Deregulation: The Case of the Civil Aeronautics Board," Ph.D. diss.: Columbia University, 1985, chaps. 2 and 3.

44. See John R. Meyer, Merton J. Peck, John Stenason, and Charles Zwick, *The Economics of Competition in the Transportation Industries* (Cambridge, Mass.: Harvard University Press, 1959); Michael E. Levin, "Is Regulation Necessary? California Air Transporation and National Regulatory Policy," *Yale Law Journal* 74 (1965):1416–47; Theodore E. Keeler, "Airline Regulation and Market Performance," *Bell Journal of Economics and Management Science* 3 (Autumn, 1972):399; George W. Douglas and James C. Miller III, *Economic Regulation of Domestic Air Transport: Theory and Policy* (Washington, D.C.: Brookings Institution, 1974); Paul MacAvoy and John W. Snow, *Regulation of Passenger Fares and Competition among the Airlines* (Washington, D.C.: American Enterprise Institute, 1977).

45. Derthick and Quirk, *The Politics of Deregulation*, 29–39.

TABLE 3. Comparison between Interstate and Intrastate Service, June, 1973, to June, 1974

City Pair	Fare	Miles	Passengers
Los Angeles–San Francisco[a]	$18.75	338	7,483,419
Chicago-Minneapolis	38.39	339	1,424,621
San Francisco–San Diego[a]	26.21	456	399,639
Dallas/Ft. Worth–New Orleans	44.44	442	522,223
Dallas/Ft. Worth–Houston[a]	23.15/13.89	239	1,620,000
Las Vegas–Los Angeles	28.70	236	1,181,466
Houston–San Antonio[a]	23.15/13.89	191	490,000
Boston–New York	24.07	191	2,493,882

Source: Senate Judiciary Committee, Subcommittee on Administrative Practices and Procedure, *Civil Aeronautics Board Practices and Procedures,* 94th Cong., 1st sess., Committee Print (1975), 41.

[a]Intrastate markets.

Stephen Breyer and Senator Edward Kennedy were the first to seize this political opportunity. Kennedy hired Breyer, from the Harvard law faculty, to revitalize the agenda of his Subcommittee on Administrative Practice and Procedure. Together, they chose regulatory reform as a strategic issue.[46] Breyer shrewdly suggested that they start with airlines, for several reasons: (1) the industry's visibility and glamour, (2) the weak theoretical reed (excess competition) by which regulation was justified, (3) the industry's failing performance, (4) the relatively simple political-interest structure (only firms and unions, neither of which had much political clout), and (5) the existence of nonregulated, intrastate airlines whose performance compared favorably with that of CAB-regulated trunk carriers.

Senator Kennedy's subcommittee held hearings on airline regulation in the spring of 1975. Orchestrated by Breyer to present a "story" and maximize attention in the press, these hearings were immensely successful. The central theme was that CAB regulation had caused airline fares to be higher than necessary. Witnesses from the airlines and from the CAB found it impossible to rebut the critical logic of Senator Kennedy and his well-prepared staff.[47] The numbers, especially from California and Texas, spoke for themselves (table 3).

What had been an academic debate now became a political issue into which a wider array of interest groups were drawn. The Ford administration proposed legislation to reform airline regulation in 1975, and a coalition of consumer activists, together with a number of airport authorities and munici-

46. K. Harrigan and D. Kasper, *Senator Kennedy and the CAB*, Case no. 9–378–055 (Boston: Harvard Business School, 1977).

47. Stephen Breyer, *Regulation and its Reform*, 321–22.

palities, lent support to the administration's initiative.[48] CAB Chairman Richard O'Melia appointed a special staff to review the board's performance, and, in July, 1975, the special staff issued a lengthy critique that astonishingly recommended deregulation.[49] During the next two years, the congressional committees with jurisdictional responsibility for airline regulation held hearings on various proposals for liberalization of entry and fares. Organized labor was uniformly and adamantly opposed to deregulation. Pilots, machinists, clerks, flight attendants, engineers, teamsters, and transport workers were quick to realize the implications of more competition for wages, benefits, work rules, and job security. Air safety, stability, and "the growth of aviation" were their principal arguments against regulatory reform.[50]

The airlines themselves started out in unanimous opposition to any significant reform, let alone general deregulation. But in the course of the political debate, a few defected as they realized that a unique opportunity lay at hand. Air Wisconsin, Frontier, and Hughes Air West hoped to grow; Pan Am sought entry to domestic markets, and eventually mighty United realized that its market dominance might be a competitive advantage.

Still, most carriers remained vehemently opposed. Although a self-styled "great believer in market forces," Frank Lorenzo, the chairman of Texas International, anticipated some structural problems from all out competition.

> [If] the Aviation Act of 1975 goes into effect, we will, over a period of years, end up with a couple of very large airlines. There will be many small airlines that will start up here and there, but they will never amount to a very significant amount of the transportation market. . . . The operating and financial advantages will go to the large carriers with substantial resources, and to very small carriers that temporarily have lower labor costs, primarily because they are nonunionized.

When asked by Senator Howard Cannon if regulatory liberalization "would be an attack on the labor movement," Lorenzo answered, flatly, "yes."[51]

Executives at American Airlines opposed deregulation as adamantly as anyone. Al Casey, American's chairman, was so intransigent that Senator Cannon (once he had come around to the idea) facetiously nominated him for

48. *Economic Report of the President, February, 1975* (Washington: GPO, 1975), chap. 3.

49. CAB, *Regulatory Reform: Report of the CAB Special Staff* (Washington: CAB, 1975); also, 284–91.

50. See Senate Commerce Committee, Subcommittee on Aviation, *Regulatory Reform in Air Transport*, 94th Cong., 2d sess. (April-June, 1976), 827; Senate Committee on Commerce, Science, and Transport, Subcommittee on Aviation, *Regulatory Reform in Air Transportation*, 95th Cong., 1st sess. (March-April, 1977).

51. *Regulatory Reform in Air Transporation*, 95th Cong., 1st sess. (March-April, 1977): 510.

"dinosaur-of-the-month." Likewise, Robert Crandall, who eventually became president of American, warned that deregulation needlessly risked degradation of service, safety, and the integrated air transport network.[52]

While Congress deliberated, new leadership at the CAB experimented with regulatory liberalization. Chairman John Robson, appointed by President Ford in 1975, played the peculiar role of "a Hamlet deregulator . . . beset by doubts and unsure of what to do, but . . . inclined to deregulation."[53] While not challenging the CAB's procedural framework, he liberalized charters, expanded competitive route authority, and experimented with fare competition—the off-peak "peanuts fare" by Texas International, and American's broad rejoinder, the "Super Saver."

The deregulation process received a great boost in 1977 when President Jimmy Carter appointed Alfred Kahn to chair the CAB. This quintessential policy entrepreneur took charge at the perfect time. With a powerful intellect, a dedication to microeconomic efficiency, and a quick and infectious humor, Kahn set about reorganizing the CAB. Under Kahn, the board decided several landmark cases that tested open entry and unrestricted price competition.[54]

The policy options, now, were narrowing. Early in 1978, both houses of Congress passed bills to liberalize regulation. Airline executives, such as American's Crandall, faced with the prospect of a policy "that would leave the airlines half free and half fettered," now shifted gears and called for the total elimination of economic regulation.[55]

In October, 1978, Congress passed the Airline Deregulation Act. President Carter signed it ten days later. The act would now place "maximum reliance on competitive market forces." The Civil Aeronautics Board would automatically certify entry, unless doing so damaged the public interest. Fares would be flexible within a wide zone of reasonableness, and mergers would be readily approved. If all went well, the Civil Aeronautics Board would cease to exist by 1985.[56]

---

52. Rush Loving Jr., "The Pros and Cons of Airline Deregulation," *Fortune* (August, 1977): 212; Robert Crandall, "Speech in Detroit," May 28, 1975 (Robert Crandall Papers at American Airlines, Dallas, Texas).

53. Anonymous interview, quoted in Jonathan Katz, "The Politics of Airline Deregulation," 141.

54. See especially, Civil Aeronautics Board, *Docket no. 30277, Chicago-Midway Low Fare Route Proceeding* (July 12, 1978); *CAB Order no. 38–7-40*, 74.

55. Robert Crandall, "Airline Regulation: Sense and Nonsense," speech for the Rotary Club of Tulsa, July 12, 1978; see also Alfred Kahn, "A Funny Thing Happened on the Way to Cincinnati," speech for the American Association of Airport Executives, Cincinnati, Ohio, May 22, 1978.

56. Certain regulatory functions involving customer services (baggage complaints, bumping, and smoking), interline ticketing, and joint fares, would devolve upon the Department of Transportation. See House Committee on Public Works, *Legislative History of the Airline Deregulation Act of 1978*, 96th Cong., 1st sess. (1978).

TABLE 4. Trunk Airlines: Operating Profits/(Losses) First Half, 1980 (in millions)

	Revenues	Expenses	Profit/(Loss)	Percentage Margin
American	1,746	1,867	(120)	(7.0)
Braniff	741	801	(60)	(8.1)
Coninental	497	522	(25)	(6.6)
Delta	1,582	1,508	74	4.6
Eastern	1,704	1,700	4	0.3
Northwest	740	791	(51)	(6.9)
Pan Am	1,672	1,781	(109)	(6.3)
TWA	1,581	1,633	(52)	(4.0)
United	2,108	2,222	(113)	(5.4)
Western	470	513	(42)	(9.2)
All Trunks	$12,845	$13,340	$(495)	(4.0)

Source: Merrill Lynch, *Airline Industry Annual Financial Statistics* (1982).

Deregulation, 1978–88

Destabilization, 1978–80

The first year of airline deregulation "was one of the most difficult and tumultuous years of our history," commented Bob Crandall. "As an industry, we seemed bent on giving away the store."[57] And 1980 proved worse still. All but two of the major carriers lost money, with American Airlines' first half losses the worst in the industry (table 4). Passenger traffic slumped because of the recession, and the price of jet fuel had doubled again.[58] Intense competition for key routes, with wild fares discounting, caught the industry and its regulators by surprise.

The major carriers were not at all prepared for the suddenness of competition. Although the deregulation act had proposed an orderly phase-out of regulation, reallocation of routes and fare competition swept past the board's half-hearted attempts at stabilization. A sort of reverse tar baby–effect set in. By the spring of 1980, carriers were virtually free to determine the routes they served and the prices they charged.[59]

57. Robert L. Crandall, quoted in Richard Vietor, *American Airlines (A)*, 1.

58. Again, difficult macroeconomic conditions coincided with important changes within the industry. The second oil shock drove jet fuel prices from 40 to 90 cents a gallon—or about 25 percent of operating costs. With inflation at 10.1 percent, wages per employee reached $26,691. As GNP growth turned negative 0.7 percent, airline traffic fell 4.0 percent. (American's traffic dropped 15.0 percent from a 1979 level inflated by United's strike.)

59. Office of Economic Analysis, Civil Aeronautics Board, *Competition and the Airlines: An Evaluation of Deregulation* (Washington: CAB, 1982), 22.

New entry by low-cost, no-frills, point-to-point carriers contributed to the shock. Former intrastates, charters, commuters, and start-ups sensed tremendous opportunities to make money on low-density, ill-served routes as well as high-density, over-priced ones. With low overhead, nonunion labor, depreciated aircraft, leased facilities, and few extraneous services, these companies—PSA, Air Cal, Southwest, Capitol, and World, and eventually Midway, New York Air, and People Express—put intense competitive pressure on the established carriers.[60]

In May, 1979, World Airways, a former charter, offered a one-way fare of $108 between New York and Los Angeles and New York and San Francisco. This touched off the "transcon wars" among the major carriers, undercutting revenues of more than $750 million, just for those two routes. TWA expanded the war to the "semi-transcon" market, matched by all of the other majors. Pricing "madness" went from bad to worse when Eastern tried to enter, with an unrestricted transcontinental fare of $99. World went to $88, the others matched, and the price war spread to "peripheral transcon" markets of Boston, Washington, and Philadelphia.[61]

Hastily, now, the majors began dropping unprofitable routes and entering the potentially profitable markets of their competitors. Braniff challenged American in the Southwest, while Delta attacked American's hub at Dallas from the East. Eastern expanded out of LaGuardia toward the west, and United contested more of the major city-pair markets connected to its hub in Chicago. Such unrestricted competition forced a dilution of yields (effective revenue per passenger mile), pushing break-even load factors higher (table 5).[62]

Accelerated "hubbing" was the clearest short-term strategic response by the major carriers. This practice, of concentrating connecting flights at a particular airport, had been used to a limited extent since the 1960s. Both Delta and Eastern had developed a significant hub at Atlanta; United at Chicago; American at Dallas, and Allegheny (now US Air) at Pittsburgh. But hitherto, regulation had severely constrained the use of the hub-and-spoke route structure as an operating strategy.[63] Only after receiving route flexibility could the majors contemplate the potential economies of scale and scope that the hub-and-spoke system had to offer.[64]

But fleet composition, at least in the short-run, was a major constraint to route restructuring. As Crandall explained in 1980,

60. Ibid., 108.

61. Thomas Plaskett (vice president of marketing, American Airlines), "Address to American Airlines Marketing Meeting" (Spring, 1981), 31.

62. Salomon Brothers, *Industry Analysis* (May 31, 1983), 6.

63. Steven Morrison and Clifford Winston, *The Economic Effects of Airline Deregulation*, 7; Michael Levine, "Airline Competition in Deregulated Markets," 413.

64. CAB Office of Economic Analysis, *Competition and the Airlines*, 49.

TABLE 5. Load Factor of Trunk Airlines (Twelve Months ending June 30, 1980)

	Actual	Break-even	Spread
American	62.5%	66.8%	(4.3)
Braniff	55.0	61.4	(6.4)
Continental	56.6	61.5	(4.9)
Delta	60.6	58.6	2.0
Eastern	65.3	65.2	0.1
Pan American	60.8	64.2	(3.4)
Northwest	53.1	56.4	(3.3)
TWA	60.8	64.7	(4.2)
United	61.8	65.9	(4.1)
Western	56.6	61.3	(2.9)
All Trunks	60.4%	63.3%	(2.9)

Source: Merrill Lynch, *Airline Industry Annual Financial Statistics* (1982).

> the established carriers bought their airplanes years ago expecting to operate them over a stable and franchised route system developed within the structure of Civil Aeronautics Board regulations. Critical decisions about which airplanes to buy, and in what numbers, were based on marketing assumptions that seemed reasonable at the time. They could not—and did not—anticipate the free-for-all we have today.[65]

Thus, the four-engine Boeing 707s, designed for transcontinental service in the mid-1950s when oil was cheap and load factors high, had become uneconomical by 1980. On most domestic routes, so had the 747s and the older-model 727s. Although a new generation of aircraft (Boeing 757 and 767) was nearing the start of production, few of the major carriers could afford the price, at nearly $25 million each.

This was the real market-structuring impact of regulation. Four decades of CAB control had not only shaped entry, price, supply, and demand, but had penetrated to the operational core of the regulated firms. Route structure and fleet composition, the essential plant and operating method of the airline business, were artifacts of public policy. Yet most other aspects of the business—work rules and crew assignments, terminal and gate investments, organization of maintenance, and all critical marketing activities—were shaped to fit the routes and fleet. Managers that recognized this clearly, and could implement effective changes quickly, had an immense competitive advantage.

65. Robert L. Crandall, "Remarks Before the 33rd Annual Conference of Airport Operators Council International," Mexico City (September 30, 1980), 8.

Strategic Adjustment at American Airlines

In terms of strategy, organizational structure, and performance, American Airlines' adjustment to deregulation, starting as the second-largest, but least efficient of incumbent domestic carriers, was the most thoroughgoing and successful. As such, it provides the sharpest contrasts for examining the effects of regulatory change on business practice. Conversely, its size and revealed market power show how effective strategy, like regulation, can shape market structure to create sustainable rents.

American Airlines was not prepared for deregulation. Its break-even load factor was the industry's highest. Its labor costs were higher than the industry average and its productivity growth lower. Its fleet was the least fuel efficient, and its route structure the industry's most fragmented.[66] During the period in which regulation broke down (1968–74), American's management had made several serious errors: overexpansion into hotel properties, acquisition of too many wide-bodied aircraft, cutbacks in the development of computerized reservation systems, a failed merger attempt, and, finally, a managerial crisis. In September, 1973, George Spater, American's chairman, admitted to making an illegal contribution to the Nixon campaign. He resigned, leaving American with operating losses, major organizational problems, and ruined morale.[67]

C. R. Smith, American's colorful chief executive from 1934 to 1968, came out of retirement just long enough to choose a new chairman—an outsider named Albert Casey, president of the Times Mirror Company. Casey, a rough-and-tumble Boston Irishman with a self-deprecating sense of humor, specialized in finance, liked a lot of people, but knew nothing about airlines. His immediate challenge was to restore confidence and, eventually, to prepare the organization for the demands of deregulation.

Casey found a top-heavy organization with inadequate management systems. Cost controls, planning, marketing, and the piece-parts of operations were thoroughly fragmented. The budgetary system, according to Casey, "was a disaster." Cost control became Casey's first priority. "Very early on," he recalled, "I found that Bob [Crandall] knew more about the company than anybody else," even though he had only been there one year. Robert Crandall, with an MBA degree from Wharton, had held finance positions at Eastman Kodak and Hallmark Cards before coming to American, and was experienced in managing information systems. Together, Casey and Crandall "got down and ripped the airline apart," creating cost controls and a centralized budget-

66. American Airlines, "Market Activity Report, 1980"; Merrill Lynch, *Airline Industry Annual Financial Statistics* (December, 1982).

67. Robert J. Serling, *Eagle: The Story of American Airlines* (New York: St. Martins/Marek, 1985), 414–17.

ing system. This project significantly deepened Crandall's understanding of American and prepared him to lead the company's structural adjustments after deregulation.[68]

Casey, meanwhile, encouraged the modernization and expansion of SABRE—American's computerized reservation system. This huge, real-time computer network had become a vital component of modern airline operations. Although American had been the pioneer, it had allowed United and TWA to surpass its system by the early 1970s. Beginning in 1975, American caught up, developing new features and test marketing SABRE in travel agencies, which were just becoming important distribution channels for the airlines (responsible for about one-third of airline ticket sales). In 1976, when United prematurely announced plans to market its own reservation system (APOLLO), American was ready, and scooped the market. Recognizing SABRE as a strategic (rather than operational) component of competitive advantage, Crandall invested heavily.[69]

Between 1975 and 1979, Casey got rid of some managerial deadwood, sold off the Americana Hotel chain, centralized maintenance, training, and computer operations, and moved American's corporate headquarters out of New York City to the Dallas-Fort Worth Airport. In June, 1980, he appointed Crandall president and chief operating officer, with a new group of young but experienced executives.

Crandall moved quickly to staunch American's losses. Over the next three months, his management team developed a five-part plan to restructure American Airlines, creating a smaller but more efficient company with a long-term goal of remaining a viable, full-service, national airline.[70] The plan was implemented immediately.

First, they grounded the fifty-three 707s. These aircraft—about one-fifth of American's capacity—were losing money every time they took off. This decision—to shrink the airline—was a drastic step that threatened, due to the S-Curve, an irretrievable loss of market share. But Crandall felt that competition would not ease any time soon and the red ink could not be sustained. Another difficult decision was to cancel its order for 757s, which American could not afford. The 747s, meanwhile, were sold or converted to freighters.

With fewer aircraft, American would obviously need to reduce its number of direct, point-to-point, nonstop flights—but not necessarily the number of city-pairs served. Route flexibility, in the face of the cutthroat competition during 1980, provided a unique opportunity for American to restructure routes

68. Albert Casey, retired CEO, American Airlines, interview with the author, April 1, 1987.

69. Duncan Copeland, "Evolution of Airline Reservation Systems: 1945–1985," Harvard Business School Working Paper (1988).

70. American Airlines, "Profit Improvement Plan" (1980).

toward optimizing aircraft utilization, cost reduction, and market retention. Now, Wes Kaldahl, American's chief planner, took a look at available cities, airport gates, and weather conditions, at traffic patterns and demographic trends, at competitor's systems, and, above all, at the economies of scale and scope in route design.

Since 1977, American had concentrated 142 daily departures (29 percent of its system total) at the huge Dallas/Ft. Worth Airport. These flights were grouped in a series of connecting "complexes" (a near simultaneous arrival and departure of multiple aircraft), the largest of which used 19 gates. A similar, but smaller, hub operation had developed at Chicago's O'Hare Airport. The scale advantages in these arrangements derived from the concentration of labor resources and costly ground equipment (e.g., aircraft pushers, baggage haulers, service vehicles, and maintenance equipment) at a single point, increasing their utilization and spreading those costs across more arrivals and departures (and passengers). Economies of scope were even greater. By serving two groups of city markets on either side of a hub, through the hub, an airline could serve many more city-pairs, at higher frequencies, with fewer aircraft and flight crews. Thus, a hub connecting twenty cities to the east and twenty more to the west provided one-stop service to 440 city-pairs. At that level, an increment of one flight added 43 more markets.[71]

On the revenue side, effective "complexing" was a critical part of this operating strategy. Large complexes, with one-hour stopovers would make it possible to gather traffic from diffuse sources, substitute one-stop service for nonstop service, retain customers end-to-end, and increase load factors on previously thin routes. Delta, with its regional hub at Atlanta, provided a model.

Once these economics were clear, the other issues easily fell into place. Kaldahl recommended a major restructuring, focusing 50 percent of American's traffic at the Dallas/Ft. Worth (DFW) "Superplex." The number of transcontinental, nonstop flights were reduced; two dozen miscellaneous routes, nine Mexican routes, and several Northeast business routes were discontinued. But through Dallas/Ft. Worth, 22 new destinations would be served within a year, increasing city-pair combinations from 655 to 1,519, and daily departures to 213.[72] By 1984, this number would reach 300, in eleven daily connecting complexes, of which the largest used 35 gates (see figs. 4 and 5). This level of concentration was nearly matched at O'Hare, with 224 daily departures serving 65 cities.[73]

With a smaller fleet and a more efficient route structure, American could do with fewer employees. Crandall announced layoffs combined with an carly

71. Wesley G. Kaldahl, "Address to a Lenders Meeting" (May 4, 1982).
72. American Airlines, "The Dallas/Ft. Worth Connecting Complex" (January 20, 1982).
73. W. G. Kaldahl, "Presentation to Airline Analysts" (July 2, 1985), 7.

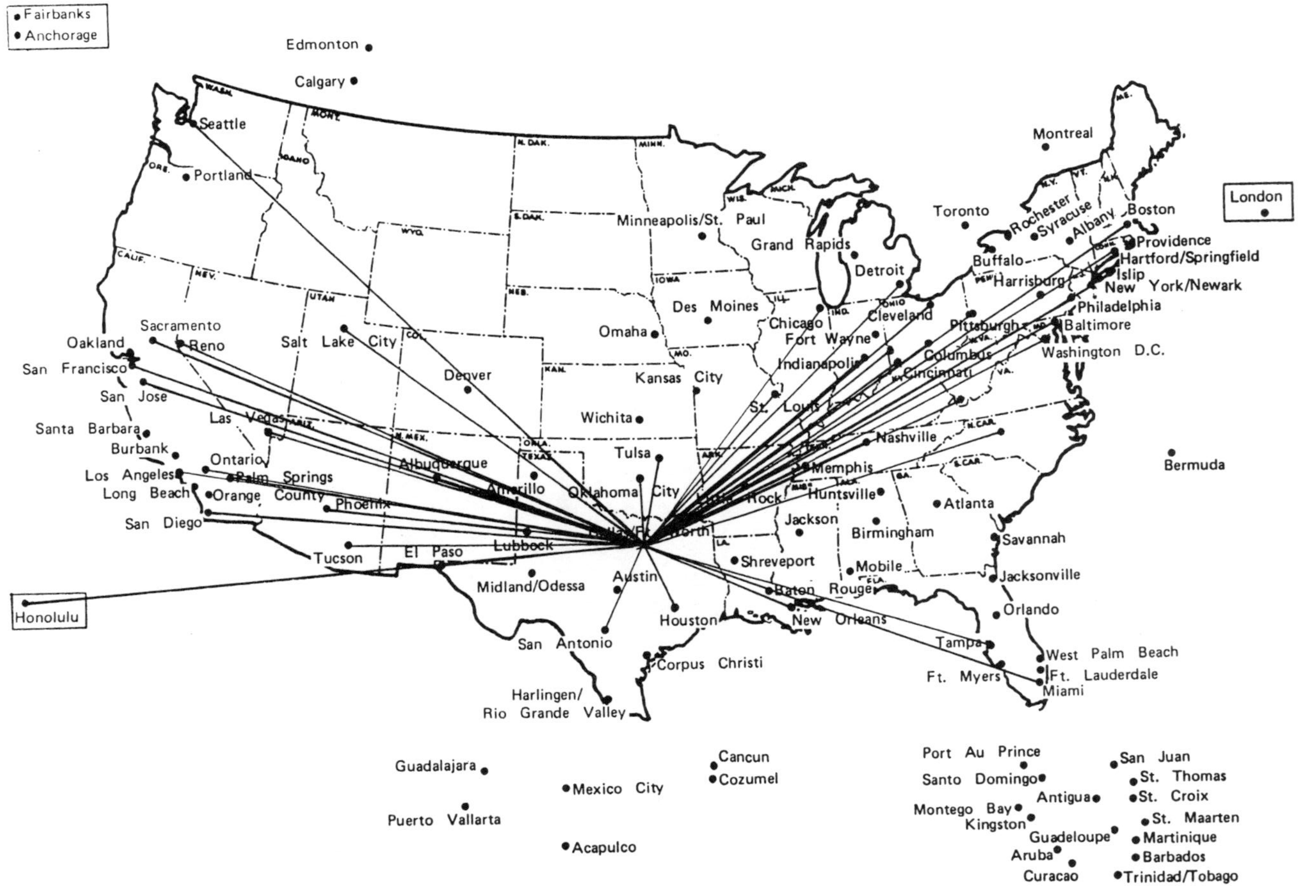

Fig. 4. Cities served by American Airlines through the DFW Hub, 1980. (Complied from American Airlines, Market Activity, 1980.)

Fig. 5. Cities served by American Airlines through the DFW Hub, 1984. (Compiled from American Airlines, Market Activity, 1984.)

retirement program, reducing personnel from 41,000 to 35,500 by the end of 1981. Labor productivity, in every job classification, was reviewed and improved, to the extent allowed by labor contracts.

Miscellaneous costs, especially fuel, were attacked on every front. Long-term fuel contracts were renegotiated, more efficient fuel-loading and flying procedures were adopted, and aircraft were modified and repainted to reduce drag. Seating density was increased everywhere, at the same time reducing weight with new, slimline seats.

Despite all these efforts, American could not hope to compete on cost alone. Differentiation, with a full range of services targeted toward business travelers, was American's only prior competitive advantage. Thus, the last part of the plan was a marketing strategy that applied American's traditional strengths to its emerging hub-and-spoke network. Service, traffic control, and distribution were its critical components.[74]

Service, to every extent possible, would be maintained at existing levels, unaffected by cost cutting. This included reservations, ticketing, baggage handling, in-flight services, and, above all, on-time departures. To hold business travelers on the system, the hub connections had to work, with little more than an hour between flights.

Pricing to maximize revenue yield and fill seats would be implemented through SABRE. Peak-load and promotional pricing would need sufficient restrictions to prevent dilution (crossover by business travelers from premium fares to discount categories) but enough flexibility to avoid selling too many discount seats and thus preempting premium customers. Before long, American's reservation system could manage this more complex fare structure, allocating seats on each flight to five different classes of fares or restrictions, and shifting allocations on a daily basis.

SABRE also gave American an advantage in distribution channels. The incredible complexity of route and pricing options made travel agencies an appealing channel for perplexed travelers; it also made computerized reservation systems a virtual necessity for travel agents. With $85 million in additional investment since 1976, American's SABRE now became the industry's biggest and most profitable distribution system, not to mention an awesome source of market and strategic data. Crandall saw this, and pushed SABRE's expansion as fast as possible, to capture 27 percent of the travel agency market by 1983.

To cap the marketing plan, American devised a scheme to create brand loyalty and bond its frequent flyers to the hub. With SABRE delivering the necessary automated record keeping, American rolled out its AAdvantage program in the spring of 1981. AAdvantage gave mileage credits for flying

74. Thomas G. Plaskett, vice president, marketing, American Airlines, interview with the author, August 1984; Thomas Plaskett, "American Airlines Marketing Meeting" (Spring, 1981), 24.

American. These could accumulate to award levels for free seats. By inventing the frequent flyer program, American seized a first-mover advantage, capturing 6.3 million subscribers whose loyalty, given the cumulative nature of awards, strengthened over time.

With this short-run plan underway and showing results by the end of 1981, Crandall's management team turned to the longer-term issues of competing in an unregulated environment: labor productivity and costs, fleet modernization, and expansion.

Crandall's approach to American's labor derived from two premises; unit labor costs had to be reduced for American to survive, but a "sledgehammer" approach would undermine the morale necessary for a service-oriented strategy. Crandall led a massive program, beginning with a series of "president's conferences" and bimonthly videotapes, to communicate to employees the realities of competition. No details were spared as to what competitors were doing and what that would mean for American's costs and service in every aspect of its business. This initiative continued for two years, using virtually every conceivable channel to communicate with employees.[75]

In 1982, as the nation plunged into recession, Crandall's message took a sharper edge, comparing the potential benefits of work rule changes to the unattractive alternatives. As contract renegotiations began, Crandall asked the unions, beginning with the Transport Workers Union (TWU), for utilization across job categories and part-time work. Pilots and flight attendants were asked to give more hours of productive (flying) time. In return, he offered guaranteed job security and profit sharing.[76] As negotiations dragged on into 1983, Crandall scheduled closings in unprofitable cities, prepared paycuts, and sold off a few more aircraft. When negotiations broke down in February, Crandall announced plans to eliminate work rules, unilaterally. The TWU signed a new contract in March, accepting the work rule changes and a drastically lower, "B" wage scale for newly hired employees.[77] Pilots, engineers, and flight attendants followed suit.[78]

---

75. R. L. Crandall, interview with the author, August, 1984; interview with Judith Leff, September, 1987; see also, C. A. Pasciuto, vice president of Employee Relations, American Airlines, "Remarks Before Western Railroad Association" (April 28, 1983).

76. American Airlines, "The Plan for Achieving Union Productivity Improvements" (1982); "A Blueprint for the Future . . . ," American Airlines' Proposal to the Transport Workers Union (1982).

77. "An Even Better Blueprint for the Future," American Airlines' Proposal to the Transport Workers Union (1983). This revised offer included a wage increase, more vacation days, and improvements in medical benefits.

78. The "two tier pay scale," as American takes pains to explain, is not a phrase coined by the company. Indeed, management did not initially see the "B" rate as a separate wage system. Rather, it was a front-end adjustment to lower costs of new employees. The same applied to flight attendants; it was a temporary measure, scheduled to reconverge with the "A" scale after several years, and disappear altogether after nine years. With the pilots, American committed to recall more than 500 already on furlough, but at wages 15 percent less than they were making before,

TABLE 6. American Airlines Selected Consolidated Financial Data (in thousands, except per-share amounts)

	1980	1983	1985	1987
Total operating revenues	$3,820,978	$4,763,307	$6,131,028	$7,197,974
Total operating expenses	3,907,233	4,481,825	5,594,395	6,736,910
Operating income (loss)	(86,255)	281,482	536,633	461,064
Earnings (loss) per common share	(5.70)	4.79	5.94	3.28
Total assets	3,277,883	4,728,165	6,421,101	8,423,349
Dividends paid per common share	.10	—	—	—

Source: American Airlines, *Annual Reports.*

With this "two-tier" wage system in place, American was ready to expand. In the spring of 1984, American ordered 67 MD Super 80s, with a price-protected option on 100 more. This stretch version of an older McDonnell Douglas design, with two fuel efficient engines and a two-pilot cockpit, could deliver 32 percent lower operating costs. With 142 seats (compared to 115 seats in a 727–100), it was the right size for most of American's hub-and-spoke routes.[79] Better yet, McDonnell Douglas agreed to a favorable short-term lease rate and an option to return the aircraft after five years, without penalty.

With the aircraft it needed, with the expansion of its DFW and Chicago hubs completed, with the dominant reservation system, and with declining average labor costs, American moved to complete its expansion. In July, 1985, Crandall announced American's reentry into the East with two new hubs—at Nashville and Raleigh/Durham. Both cities were growing rapidly, with high-tech and research-oriented industries, and would provide American a north-south route structure that straddled the hubs of two major competitors—Delta and Piedmont.[80] American, now, had largely completed its strategic adjustment to deregulation (see table 6).

Market Structure and Industry Performance

Four strategic patterns, or competitive types, were evident in the deregulated environment. Few, however, were as successful as American's.

for five years. American's management hoped that these temporary differentials would make American more competitive until its operating costs came down and its low-cost competitors accrued their own seniority and overhead costs. From the union's perspective, this temporary concession was the least unattractive means of protecting old-timers from the cutbacks and benefit losses that deregulation made inevitable.

79. American Airlines, "Fleet and Route Planning Issues" (1984).

80. American Airlines, "American's Planned North/South Hubs," Presentation to the Board of Directors (July 17, 1985).

Building on their prior advantages, four other carriers besides American—United, Delta, Northwest, and TWA—eventually developed full-service, price-differentiated, hub-and-spoke trunk systems. United unsuccessfully tried integration into travel-related businesses before refocusing on airline operations to take advantage of its dominant size. Both Delta and TWA decided to acquire regionals (Western and Ozark) to gain the scale and hub strengthening deemed necessary to compete with American and United.

A second pattern, full-price, hub-and-spoke regionals, proved transitory. Four carriers—Western at Salt Lake City, Republic at Detroit and Minneapolis, US Air at Pittsburgh, and Piedmont at Charlotte—strengthened their hubs to attain regional dominance and preempt competitive entry (despite relatively high costs).[81] Evidently, this was not a durable approach, once the national carriers expanded. All four regionals merged into nationals (US Air combining with Piedmont and acquiring Pacific Southwest Airlines), to obtain minimum scale and scope.[82]

A low-cost, limited service, low-fare strategy was pursued by several new entrants, by two failing trunks, and by one previously intrastate carrier. New York Air and People Express were the most important, but eventually unsuccessful, new entrants with this strategy. Continental and Braniff were major carriers that, after bankruptcy, rebuilt their operations as low-cost, discount carriers. Continental, a subsidiary of Texas Air, pursued a distinctive strategy of voiding labor contracts and benefit obligations through bankruptcy. By the end of 1987, Texas Air had acquired People Express, Frontier, and Eastern, was attempting to rationalize operations, and was struggling to service debt of about $6.5 billion.[83] Only Southwest, with long experience at no-frills, low-cost service, had remained profitable, and even grown, with this strategic choice.

A fourth competitive strategy was adopted by commuter airlines struggling to survive in smaller, low-density markets. Initially, this was a viable business, with appropriate aircraft, sensible schedules, and low-cost labor. But the majors, with their hub operations, needed to control traffic fed from smaller communities. The commuters, meanwhile, needed gate space and services where they connected at the major airports. Joint marketing tie-ins, between majors and commuters, seemed to serve both interests. Eventually, however, these evolved into "code-sharing" (colisting flights on computerized reservation systems), shared aircraft colors, capital infusions, and new names. By 1988, tie-ins had given the eight largest carriers effective control over

81. Bailey and Williams, "Sources of Rent in the Deregulated Airline Industry," 173–202.

82. Six other small regional carriers have remained independent. They are Air Wisconsin, Alaska Air, Aloha, American West, Jet America, and Midway.

83. Weinberg, *Continental Airlines (A)*; "House of Mirrors," *Wall Street Journal*, April 7, 1988.

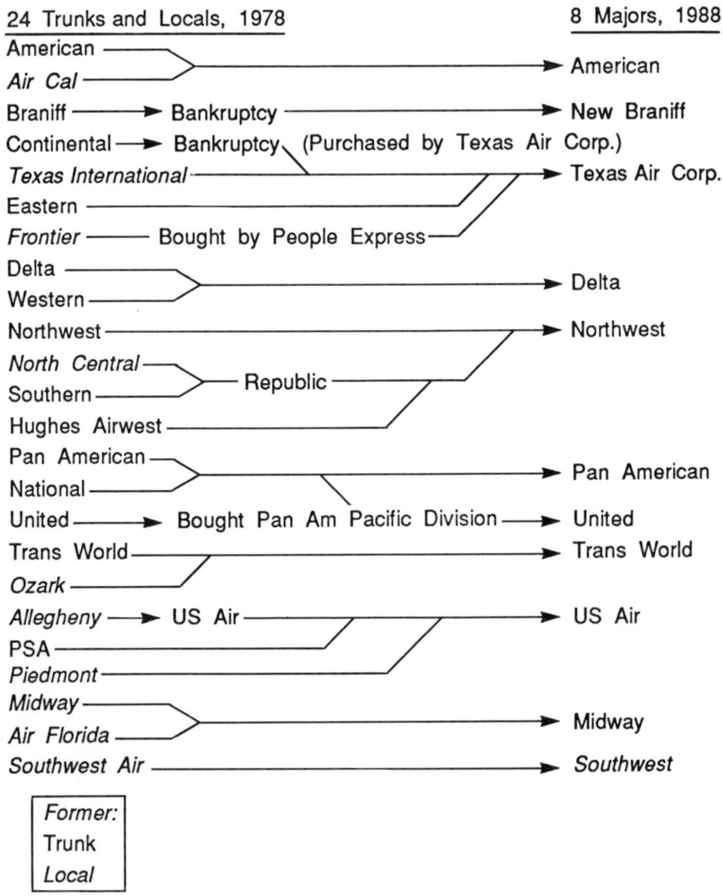

Fig. 6. Consolidation of pre-deregulation trunk and local airlines. (From *Air Transport World,* June, 1987, 64–65.)

forty-eight of the fifty largest commuters.[84] Foreclosure of entry was one of the consequences.

All of these strategic responses to deregulation, and the structural adjustments that accompanied them, had an obvious impact on overall industry structure. Figure 6 shows the wave of mergers that occurred between 1981

84. Clinton V. Oster Jr. and Don H. Pickrell, "Marketing Alliances and Competitive Strategy in the Airline Industry," *Logistics and Transportation Review* 22 (1986): 371–87; "Major U.S. Airlines Rapidly Gain Control Over Regional Lines," *Wall Street Journal*, February 17, 1988.

TABLE 7. Market Shares of the Largest U.S. Airlines at Selected Airports

Airport	Airline	1978	1985
Chicago (O'Hare)	United	33.1	41.8
	American	18.6	30.3
Atlanta (Hartsfield)	Delta	50.1	52.3
	Eastern	38.6	41.5
Dallas-Fort Worth	Braniff	33.7	—
	American	29.8	61.1
	Delta	16.6	23.8
Los Angeles International	United	27.8	16.2
	Western[a]	16.9	14.1
	American	16.4	12.6
Denver	United	32.0	35.8
	Frontier[b]	19.9	25.4
	Continental	19.3	22.5
St. Louis	TWA	39.4	57.1
	Ozark[c]	20.6	27.2
Pittsburgh	Allegheny	46.7	79.8
Minneapolis	Northwest	31.7	42.5
	North Central[d]	21.4	36.7
Houston	Continental	19.0	57.6

Source: Federal Aviation Administration.

Note: Market shares are based on each carrier's proportion of revenue passenger enplanements at each airport.

[a]Delta has acquired Western.

[b]Frontier has sold a significant portion of its assets to United; Continental purchased the remaining assets.

[c]TWA has merged with Ozark.

[d]Republic, which was formed by the combination of North Central and Southern, has merged with Northwest.

and 1988. Most of the action involved acquisitions of regionals by trunks. The eight largest surviving carriers were still those certified by the CAB in 1938. Rationalization of industry structure did raise Big Four concentration to 61 percent—higher than in 1978, but less than in 1934.[85] Even more salient was the concentration that developed at the hubs (see table 7). For travelers who wished to originate or terminate at a hub city, carrier choice was now more limited, and there was some evidence of uncompetitive pricing. However, for travelers flying between nonhub cities, concentration was less important since airlines competed through different hubs.

The effects of deregulation on market structure and performance were just as dramatic as on industry structure, but not quite so clear. Several

85. "Texas Air's Hard Bargainer," *New York Times*, September 16, 1986.

TABLE 8. New Entrant Airlines, 1979–88

Entrant	Entry	Exit[a]
Midway Airlines	1979	
New York Air	1980	1986
People Express	1981	1986
Jet America	1981	1986
Muse Air	1981	1985
Pacific Express	1982	1984
Northeastern International	1982	1984
Hawaii Express	1982	1984
Best Airlines	1982	1984
Sunworld	1983	1988
America West	1983	
Air One	1983	1984
Regent Air	1983	1983
Frontier Horizon	1984	1986
Air Atlanta	1984	1987
Florida Express	1984	1987
Presidential Air	1985	1987
Transtar	1985	1987

Source: DOT, *Air Carrier Monthly Traffic Statistics* (1986 and 1987); *Air Transport World* (June, 1987): 64–65.

[a]Most of these companies have gone bankrupt. A few, including New York Air, People Express, and Muse Air, have been acquired and/or consolidated on the verge of bankruptcy.

exogenous events, including the second oil shock, the air traffic controllers (PATCO) strike in 1981, and the 1982–83 recession, also shaped the patterns of adjustment. With this qualification in mind, we can observe significant changes in the following market characteristics: (1) entry and exit conditions, (2) price level and pricing mechanisms, (3) segmentation, (4) distribution channels, (5) cost structure, (6) operations, (7) demand, (8) service levels (and safety), and (9) industry profitability.

Entry into the industry and into individual city-pair markets clearly opened up as soon as the CAB lowered its barriers. As table 8 indicates, several start-ups entered the business during the first few years of deregulation. Relatively low minimum-efficient scale and capital costs made this possible. But, as the table also shows, few of these entrants survived to 1988. Despite the hopes of economists, particularly those associated with contestability theory, the airline industry did not turn out to be frictionless.[86] By building economies of scale and scope, by segmenting markets with strategic

86. Elizabeth E. Bailey and John C. Panzar, "The Contestability of Airline Markets during the Transition to Deregulation," *Law and Contemporary Problems* (Winter, 1981): 809–22; William J. Baumol, John C. Panzar, and Robert D. Willig, *Contestable Markets and the Theory of Industry Structure* (New York: Harcourt Brace Jovanovich, 1982).

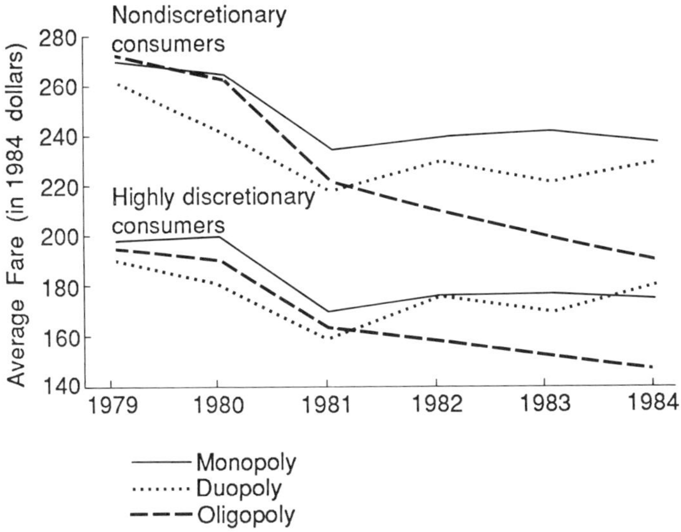

Fig. 7. Fare changes by type of market and type of consumer, 1979–84. (From John R. Meyer and Clintin V. Oyster, Jr., *Deregulation and the Future of Intercity Passenger Travel* [Cambridge, Mass.: MIT Press, 1987], 110.)

pricing, and by developing control of distribution channels, the incumbent firms responded strategically to create competitive advantages and eventually foreclose entry. As the data came in, economists revised their views of the industry's contestability.[87] At best, it appeared to be a transitional condition.

Deregulation prompted an immediate reduction of prices and a continuing fragmentation of pricing structure. Here too, the early pricing responses seemed to support the logic of contestability. As figure 7 indicates, even monopolists lowered their fares. Eventually though, prices stabilized in the least competitive markets and then increased. Price structure, meanwhile, fragmented into a wide range of special packages, discounts, and incentive deals. By 1987, the proportion of passengers using some sort of discount fare had risen from 37 percent (1977) to 91 percent.[88] Yield management became the sine qua non of airline marketing. Sophisticated customer and competitor analyses, drawing on computerized data bases, was performed daily to optimize revenue by adjusting schedules, fares, and seat allocations among discount categories. This development should not have been surprising, in view of airline economics (lumpy bundles of seats with diverse marginal costs) and a history of similar, albeit constrained, pricing practices.[89]

87. Bailey, Graham, and Kaplan, *Deregulating the Airlines*; for a good review of the revisionist literature, see Dipendra Sinha, "The Theory of Contestable Markets and U.S. Airline Deregulation: A Survey," *Logistics and Transportation Review* 22 (1987): 405–19.

88. "Assessing the Effects of Airline Deregulation," *New York Times*, March 20, 1988.

89. Cherington, *Airline Price Policy*, 210–89.

Commoditylike price wars at the outset of deregulation were partly the result of the market's desegmentation. Carriers only gradually implemented strategies to resegment the market by price, service, brand image, and loyalty (frequent flyer programs).

Among the most striking features of airline deregulation was the development and newfound strategic importance of distribution channels (methods of selling tickets). Under regulation, distribution channels were unimportant and unsophisticated. But with the transition to competition, customer access and control suddenly became critical for sellers, while the fluidity of adjusting markets caused extreme informational problems for buyers. Computerized reservation systems, with a relatively small incremental cost of adding a travel agency and huge economies of scale (and scope), quickly became a competitive bottleneck that first movers took a tremendous advantage of. By 1988, American (SABRE) and United (APOLLO) controlled 70 percent of the travel agency channel, leaving competing systems (TWA, Delta, and Eastern) with too small a base and other carriers in abject dependency.[90] Accordingly, Frontier and ten other carriers brought a civil antitrust suit, seeking damages and divestiture of SABRE and APOLLO. The case was based on the "essential facility" doctrine—the same concept that the government had used successfully to attack the Bell System. Although civil charges were dismissed late in 1988, the Department of Transportation continued to review proposals for divesting the airlines of their reservation systems.

Cost reduction was a predictable result of deregulation. The most dramatic and politicized aspect of this process was the decosting of labor. Elimination of work rules, increases in "hard" hours for flight crews, and wage givebacks all contributed to lower costs.[91] Continental, by reducing labor costs to 1.33 cents per available seat mile, set a competitive baseline for the others. Delta, even with its traditionally nonunion work force, remained at the high end with costs of 3.54 cents per average seat mile.[92]

Like American, every major carrier eventually moved to reduce costs

---

90. By 1985, travel agents accounted for 57 percent of all airline tickets sold; see *United Airlines v. Aeronautics Board*, 766 F.2d 1107, 1109 (7th Cir., 1985); Civil Aeronautics Board, *Investigation into the Competitive Marketing of Air Transportation*, *Order 82–12–85* (Washington, D.C.: GPO,1984); Senate Committee on Commerce, Subcommittee on Aviation, *Computer Reservation Systems*, 99th Cong., 1st sess. (March 19, 1985).

91. James Blumestock and Evelyn Thomchick, "Deregulation and Airline Labor Relations," *Logistics and Transportation Review* 22 (1986): 389–403; John Meyer and Clinton Oster, *Deregulation and the Future of Intercity Passenger Travel*, 83–107. However, a study by Canadian economists indicates that "since deregulation, the growth rate of compensation in the U.S. airline industry exceeds that of the transport/utility sector of the economy and nearly matches that of the U.S. business sector." See R. J. Andriuliatis, David L. Frank, Tae H. Oum, and Michael W. Thretheway, "Deregulation and Airline Employment: Myth versus Fact," Center for Transportation Studies, University of British Columbia (1986), 27, 31–32.

92. AMR Corporation, *1986 Annual Report*, 12.

across the entire range of operations: fuel, overhead, fleet and route structure, as well as labor. In all, the cost per passenger-mile traveled declined by about 30 percent (from 4.5 to 3.3 cents in real term) between 1981 and 1987.[93]

Perhaps the most important change in market structure was the fundamental redesign of operations. The hub-and-spoke route structure, combined with "complexing," was a major innovation over the predominantly point-to-point, nonstop operations encouraged by regulation. Besides the economies of scale and scope previously discussed, the full development of hub operations, combined with feeder tie-ins, created powerful barriers to point-to-point or selective entry by potential competitors.[94] Complexing, moreover, aggravated air traffic congestion and placed a greater-than-ever premium on gates and landing "slots." These scarce commodities, according to economists, had become bottleneck facilities that generated rents and hampered competition. Proposed solutions, such as the sale or auction of slots, were second-best, since dominant firms had the deepest pockets. Not surprisingly, American's Bob Crandall was a vocal advocate of a market for peak-hour slots.[95]

Aggregate demand for air transportation appeared to be stimulated by deregulation. At least the number of passengers had doubled since the start of deregulation, and the annual growth rate of revenue-passenger miles had increased.[96] These very gains make it difficult to assess the impact of deregulation on service quality. Higher traffic levels, with no concomitant improvement in air traffic control systems or airport capacity, caused all sorts of operating problems. By 1987, the number of departures handled per controller had risen by 52 percent.[97] Traffic-related problems, especially the now-frequent delays, could arguably be attributed to deregulation's success.

On the other hand, some service degradation was clearly a product of the deregulated carriers' freedom of strategic choice. One major change was the sharp reduction of nonstop, point-to-point service. Frequency of flights, on

93. *New York Times*, March 20, 1988.

94. Bailey and Williams, "Sources of Rent"; David K. Massey, "Hub Strategies," *Airline Executive* (June, 1987): 37–41. In commenting on this point, however, Meyer suggested that the prospect of point-to-point hub overflights with appropriate new aircraft, like 757s, 767s, and 737–300s, may partially undermine hub dominance.

95. Lawrence T. Phillips, "Structural Change in the Airline Industry: Carrier Concentration at Large Hub Airports and its Implications for Competitive Behavior," *Transportation Journal* 25 (Winter, 1985): 18–28; Robert Crandall, interview with author, March, 1987.

96. Revenue-passenger miles grew 7.6 percent annually between 1968 and 1978, and 8.7 percent from 1978 to 1987 (Merrill Lynch, *Airline Industry* [November, 1985]; Department of Transportation, *Air Carrier Monthly Traffic Statistics* [June, 1987]).

97. In 1986, the number of federal controllers was down to 22,000, from 27,000 before the PATCO strike in 1981. While the incidence of near-collisions had increased, most other safety measures had improved due to continuing advances in avionics; see Federal Trade Commission, Bureau of Economics, *The Deregulated Airline Industry: A Review of the Evidence* (January, 1988), 76–77.

TABLE 9. Air Travel Monthly Consumer Complaints for Major U.S. Airlines

U.S. Airlines (Majors/Nationals)	Rank	Complaints per 100,000 Passengers October, 1987	Complaints per 100,000 Passengers October, 1986
Northwest Airlines	1	17.78	4.62
Continental Airlines	2	15.11	3.04
Eastern Air Lines	3	13.25	2.04
Pan American World Airways	4	12.82	4.25
Trans World Airlines	5	9.59	3.11
United Airlines	6	5.49	2.55
America West Airlines	7	3.85	.15
USAir	8	3.61	1.10
Piedmont Airlines	9	3.28	.38
American Airlines	10	2.98	1.14
Delta Air Lines	11	2.17	.70
Alaska Airlines	12	2.13	.26
Pacific Southwest Airlines	13	2.04	.74
Southwest Airlines	14	1.52	.64

Source: U.S. Department of Transportation, *Air Travel Consumer Report* (November, 1987).

Note: The number of passengers flown is from RSPA form 41 reports filed by the airlines and reflects the most recent enplanement data available at the time of the complaint report. Thus, the number of passengers in the complaint report is from a period two months earlier than the period for the complaints themselves. For example, a June complaint report is based on June complaints and April enplanement figures.

the other hand, improved 14 percent overall (between 1977 and 1984), and 20–30 percent in major cities.[98] Consumer complaints about lost baggage, crowding in reservation and ticketing services, overbooking and bumping, and in flight services increased dramatically for all airlines, but with a sizeable differential across companies. As deregulation forced cost reductions and allowed service segmentation, some carriers obviously chose to focus greater resources on service than others (table 9).

Industry performance is a final, important aspect of deregulation's effects. On the one hand, the load factor, a basic measure of capacity utilization and the industry's perennial problem under regulation, had improved considerably from the early 1970s (fig. 8). Labor productivity, in terms of average seat miles, had also improved by 23 percent since 1978.

On the other hand, financial results were dismal. Several major carriers had suffered persistent losses, while four (Continental, Braniff, Frontier, and Peoples) failed altogether. Of course, a few firms were reasonably profitable—most notably American and US Air—but the average was very low. Total net income for the major carriers over the nine years since deregula-

98. FTC, *Deregulated Airline Industry*, 61–83; Morrison and Winston, *Economics of Airline Deregulation*, 25–47.

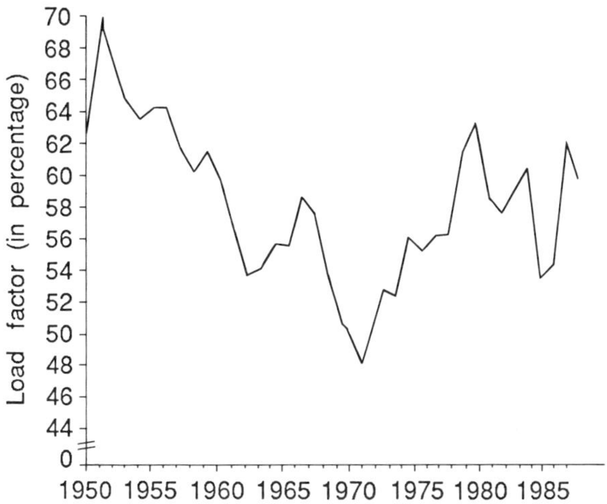

Fig. 8. Domestic trunk load factors, 1950–87. (Data from E. E. Bailey, D. R. Graham, and D. P. Kaplan, *Deregulating the Airlines* (Cambridge, Mass.: MIT Press, 1985), 204–5; Department of Transportation, *Air Carrier Monthly Traffic Statistics* [1986 and 1987].)

tion was $750 million, on sales of $313 billion. Return on equity, which had averaged 1.3 percent (1970–77), fell to a pitiful 0.1 percent.[99]

Regulation, Markets, and Firms

This brief history of the domestic airline industry can tell us something about the economic and political dynamics of regulatory policy. Perhaps we can draw some preliminary conclusions that apply generally to such industries as trucking and rail transport, telecommunications, natural gas, and commercial banking.

First, economic regulation can best and most usefully be understood as a market-structuring process. It shapes virtually all of the market's important characteristics. In this sense, the market, after years of regulation, becomes an artifact of policy that bears little resemblance to any natural economic or technological factors. This process, moreover, does not stop at the boundary of the firm. That is, regulation shapes the organizational resources of the firm, right down to its operational core. This is clear in the case of American Airlines, and would be much the same for firms in other industries undergoing deregulation: AT&T or CSX or El Paso Natural Gas or Bank America.

Second, by examining airline regulation from start to finish (more or

99. Alfred Kahn, "Airline Deregulation—A Mixed Bag, But a Clear Success Nevertheless," *Transportation Law Journal* 16, no. 2 (1988): 248–49 and n. 58.

less), we have an unusual opportunity to generalize on a dynamic theory of political process. This history makes clear that no monocausal explanation—either economic or political—is sufficient. The microeconomic and political circumstances that gave rise to regulation were entirely different from those that forced deregulation.

To explain the onset of airline regulation, its workings, and eventual reform, we need to relate several factors. Dramatic changes in basic conditions—especially macroeconomic and ideological circumstances—were key. Economic regulation, in general, was a policy response to the extraordinary failure of markets in the 1930s. Technological developments, which repeatedly undermined the microeconomic characteristics on which regulation was superimposed, were also important. So were new ideas about regulation's failings and alternative approaches. Entrepreneurship in the business and the policy arena helped force the change in policy. And finally, regulation itself contributed by failing to deal effectively with all of these other changes.

Third, the sudden impact of deregulation on the incumbent airlines combined with the inherent competitiveness of the industry provide a sharper than usual perspective on the links between regulation, markets, and firms. In the American Airlines case, we see rapid and thoroughgoing adjustment of the firm's business strategy and organizational resources. As an artifact of regulation, American Airlines was ill suited to unrestricted competition. Crandall saw this; he understood the industry's underlying economics, recognized key elements of its emerging value-chain, and hastened to adapt before anyone else.

The consequences of this sort of adjustment for market structure were completely unanticipated by economists.[100] Perhaps the profession's tendency to treat firms as data points, operating autonomously within abstract markets, accounts for this. At any rate, the airline story should help us appreciate the extent to which business conduct—especially strategy—is designed to create and capture rents and, thus, to reshape market structure itself.

Finally, we can see in the airline story that regulated competition, in contrast to regulated monopoly, is a flawed concept, at least in the U.S. political and legal context. The idea that certain market characteristics could be shaped by the government, without affecting management's other prerogatives, reflects a kind of hubris. The boundaries between markets and firms and the economic linkages among market characteristics form a complicated and seamless web. When regulators, no matter how well intentioned, intervene to manage markets, they affect important aspects of the business, directly or indirectly.

Regulated competition entails more detailed regulation, more careful and complicated cost allocations, more antitrust policing by regulators, and con-

100. This point is acknowledged, and thoughtfully discussed, in Michael Levine, "Airline Competition," 393–417.

stant efforts at fine tuning. Unintended consequences abound. Today, in telecommunications, natural gas, and financial services, public policy is rapidly evolving (or drifting) into just such a species. In telecommunications, equal access, open network architecture, and even price caps are complicated new regulatory mechanisms designed to manage competition. In natural gas, the open-access regime of Order 436 is the same. And in financial services, Congress is coping with the consequences of competitive, but regulated, Savings and Loans, and debating a mixed mode for commercial banking as well. Ironically, the appropriate model for these new systems is not airline deregulation but, rather, the failed experience of airline regulation.

CHAPTER 2

Regulation and Interest Groups

Robert D. Tollison

It has been twenty years since Stigler (1971) published his reformulation of the capture theory of economic regulation and seventeen years since Posner (1974) reviewed the state of this literature and assessed the empirical evidence with respect to its scientific viability.[1] This seems like an appropriate time and occasion to assess the development and application of the theory of economic regulation over the interim.

Several important things have happened in the post-Stigler era. First, Stigler's basic theory has been generalized in a powerful and useful manner by Peltzman (1976). Second, following Stigler's lead, additional research has been done on the origins of government regulation. Third, the idea of heterogeneous firms in the same industry competing against one another for regulatory rents has been formally developed and tested. Fourth, the modifier *economic* has been dropped from the title "The Theory of Economic Regulation." There is an economic theory of regulation, and whether this regulation be economic or social, it can be explained by the forces that drive the demand and supply of regulatory outcomes (Becker 1976). Fifth, some analysts have carried this analysis even further by dropping "economic regulation" from the title and substituting "government." These authors have written about and tested what has come to be called the interest-group theory of government. Their goal is to explain all legislation and governmental activities by interest-group principles. Sixth, the study of the process of economic regulation has been greatly amplified and strengthened by the application of agency theory to regulatory bureau behavior. Seventh, Stigler's theory has been applied in the context of regulatory federalism, where the price effects of regulation can be exported across governmental boundaries. Eighth, powerful new statistical techniques, originally developed in the efficient markets/rational expectations literature in the theory of finance, have been brought to bear on the study of the effects of regulation on firms and industries. Finally, empirical support for

---

I thank Donald Boudreaux, Jack High, William F. Shughart II, and George J. Stigler for helpful comments.

1. For precursors of Stigler in political science, see Bentley 1908 and Truman 1951.

all of these branches of the tree planted by Stigler has developed rapidly since Posner's (1974) review of the evidence, which was somewhat scanty at the time he wrote.

This chapter will center on these several aspects of the development of the economic theory of regulation since 1971. The topics covered include Peltzman's more general theory, the origin of regulation, heterogeneous firms and regulation, social versus economic regulation, the interest-group theory of government, the agent-principal problem in a regulatory context, the exportation of the price effects of regulation, event analysis, and modern deregulation.

One final proviso is in order. Both Stigler (1971) and Posner (1974) spent time discussing the alternative, public-interest theory of government and regulation. This chapter has nothing new to add to this topic. Interested readers can consult their original discussions.

Peltzman's Generalization

In his basic paper, Stigler made the following observation: "These various political boons are not obtained by the industry in a pure profit-maximizing form" (1971, 6). This comment contained the seed that later led to Peltzman's (1976) generalization of Stigler's theory. Figure 1 illustrates.

Profits are measured along the vertical axis, and price along the horizontal axis. A vote-maximizing regulator/politician seeks to trade off wealth between consumers represented by the price variable and producers represented by the profit variable. Higher indifference curves for the regulator are read in a northwestern direction in figure 1. Point *A* on the horizontal axis corresponds to a competitive industry making zero economic profits. Point *B* corresponds to profit-maximization by a pure monopolist. Note that the shape of the regulator's indifference curves show the nature of Stigler's conjecture. Point *B* is not a political equilibrium unless consumer interests are ignored totally by the regulator. (This would imply a *V* curve parallel to the profit axis tangent to point *B*.) A normal political equilibrium is given by point *E*, where the regulator equates his or her marginal rate of political substitution (of consumer for producer votes) to the slope of the transfer locus as defined by the profit hill.

Peltzman's model contains many useful implications. For example, why are certain types of industries regulated and others not? In figure 1, it is easy to see that the improvement in regulator utility (votes) is greater when industries that are either purely competitive or pure monopolies are regulated. Movements from points such as *A* (pure competition) or *B* (pure monopoly) to point *E* create more political wealth for the regulator than movements from intermediate positions such as *C* (oligopoly?). Thus, there is a vote-maximizing rationale for why one observes the extensive regulation of natural monopolies (utilities) and purely competitive industries (agriculture) and little or no regulation of the steel and automobile industries.

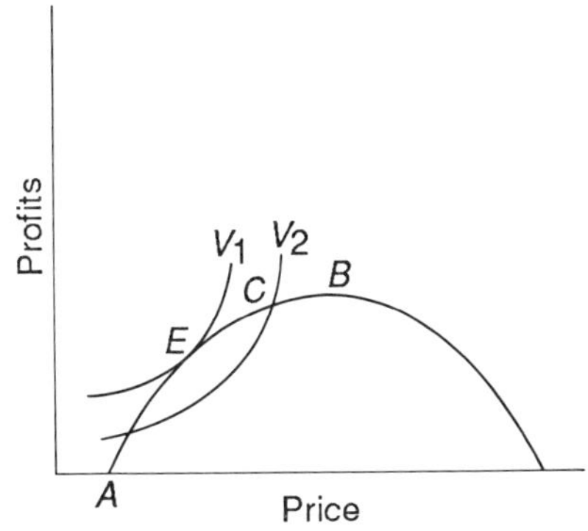

Fig. 1. A regulatory equilibrium

In a private setting, it is well known that fixed costs have no influence on short-run price and output. However, fixed costs matter to the political equilibrium level of price and profit in figure 1. Imagine that the profit hill (which is a function of price and costs) shrank by a constant amount throughout its range, reflecting an increase in fixed costs in the industry. Obviously, the optimal political price would change. In general, the vote-maximizing regulator will make trade-offs in such a fashion that increases in industry profit are shared with consumers through a regulatory price reduction and decreases in industry profit are buffered by regulatory price increases. Hirshleifer (1976, 243) called this the principle of "share the gain and share the pain." There are numerous other interesting applications of Peltzman's model, which is without doubt the single most important theoretical development in the post-Stigler literature on regulation. Moreover, the model frames many of the subsequent developments in the literature which will be reviewed in this chapter. First, there is the issue of the origin and timing of regulatory intervention, posed by the movement from points *A* or *B* to *E* in figure 1. Second, there is the more complex case where heterogeneous competitors compete for regulatory rents and the relevant trade-off is between consumers who lose from higher prices, losing firms that exit the industry, and winning firms that capture a regulatory windfall. Third, how does Peltzman's theory handle so-called social regulation? Fourth, is Peltzman's theory a theory of regulation or a theory of government? Fifth, there is the black box of the vote-maximizing regulator in Peltzman's model. From where do the *V* curves come? Who monitors the political equilibrium process? What can be said about the process of economic regulation? And so on. Sixth, what happens if there are competing governments in the Peltzman theory? Seventh, how can the researcher detect the wealth effects of regulation discussed in the Peltzman model? These and several other issues are addressed in the remainder of this chapter.

The Origins of Regulation

Economists have typically taken a cross-sectional approach to the study of regulation. Given that regulation exists in some jurisdictions and not in others, differences in such variables as price and output can be compared in the two cases. Much less attention has been devoted to the question of why regulation comes into existence in the first place. In other words, what explains the timing of major regulatory events such as the passage of a new law mandating a regulatory program?

One way to address this issue is through a case study. In this approach, the revealed beneficiaries of a regulation are identified ex post, once the regulatory scheme is in place. These beneficiaries presumably played a big role in the original passage of the regulation; hence, the case study retraces the history of the regulation in such terms. There is nothing wrong with this approach, and it has been usefully applied in a variety of contexts to show why certain regulatory programs came into existence. One simple way, for example, to apply this method is to look at the legislative hearings that preceded the passage of a law. Who showed up to testify, and what did they say?[2]

The case study, however, offers little help in the predictive problem of explaining the *timing* of major regulatory events. Why did the revealed beneficiaries of a regulation succeed in capturing the regulatory process in, say, 1914 and not before or after? What constellation of political forces led to the observed timing of regulatory intervention in the economy? This is a positive, predictive problem for the theory of economic regulation.

Stigler (1971) laid out a method for addressing this issue in his original paper on the subject. He attempted, with mixed results, to explain the onset (the date) of occupational regulation across U.S. states. In other words, the initial year of regulation was the dependent variable, and variables that reflected the estimated costs and benefits of the regulation to the relevant interest groups (barbers, for example) made up the right-hand side of the model. For example, do more concentrated economic interests lead to earlier occupational licensure?

The subsequent literature has not risen very much to Stigler's challenge on this issue, but there are some developments worth reporting. Stigler and Friedland (1962) reported cross-sectional regression results for electricity prices across U.S. states for 1922. Their results suggested that state regulation of electricity prices had no detectable effect on the level of these prices; prices

2. An obvious problem with this approach is free-riding behavior by interest groups and unrelated individuals who stand to benefit from the regulation. Still, it is a practical way to find out which groups found it worthwhile to lobby. Another problem is to disentangle the private-interest motivation of the testifying groups from their transparent public-interest rhetoric about the virtues of the regulation.

in regulated states were statistically the same as prices in unregulated states. Needless to say, this was an obviously shocking result to economists. Jarrell (1978) unraveled this conundrum by examining the timing of municipal and state regulation of electric utilities over the period prior to 1922. He found that both municipal and state regulation occurred first where the demand for regulation was the greatest, that is, where electric utility markets were the most competitive. The predicted effects of economic regulation are borne out in Jarrell's results as prices and profits rose substantially in the states that were regulated early. Thus, the 1922 cross-section used by Stigler and Friedland obscured the earlier run-up of prices in the high-demand, regulated states vis-à-vis the low-demand, unregulated states. Jarrell thus showed that electricity price regulation did make a difference in price and output, as one would normally expect.

Shughart and Tollison (1981) applied the timing method to explain the evolution of more liberal corporate chartering laws across U.S. states from 1837 to 1913. The older system of corporate chartering was excessively bureaucratic and cumbersome, requiring legislative enactment of a firm's charter in some cases. The new system was a great deal less costly in that obtaining a charter required going to the appropriate state office, filing the appropriate forms, and paying a fee.[3] Shughart and Tollison sought to explain the year in which states adopted more liberal chartering laws with a model that incorporated proximate measures of the costs and benefits of such laws to local (state) manufacturing interests. Greater costs suggest later passage; greater benefits suggest earlier passage. Such a theory leads to a robust explanation of the timing of this significant episode of legal change and deregulation in U.S. history. This latter point is important in that the interest-group theory must be able to cope with both regulation and deregulation in an explanatory sense. Interest groups can drive the economy in either direction.[4]

Finally, there has been some work seeking to use the economic theory of regulation to explain the passage of the Sherman Act in 1890. Stigler (1985) tested some basic theses such as that agricultural interests were concerned about transportation costs, but he essentially found no coherent empirical explanation for the passage of the first U.S. antitrust law. Thus, while the

3. Why did the state let go of such an obviously lucrative monopoly? The answer appears to be that firms in both England and the United States had recourse to the joint-stock form of organization without state approval (the so-called unincorporated joint-stock companies). Hence, the demand for state charters fell, and the state fell back to its next best alternative, which was liberal chartering for a fee. Liberal chartering also enabled states to keep track of a firm's activities, in case future regulatory possibilities presented themselves. See Anderson and Tollison 1983.

4. Anderson and Tollison (1985) discuss the repeal of the Corn Laws in England in 1846 as the result of an interest-group process led by the Anti–Corn Law League, the prototype of the modern lobbying organization. This episode, in any event, is another case where interest groups led a deregulation movement.

interest-group theory works well in explaining the origin of some regulations, it does not seem to work so well in the case of others. A possible explanation has been proposed by McChesney (1987). The legislature will sometimes pass a vaguely defined statute to be enforced in an unpredictable manner in order to ferret out relevant interest groups in the economy and to increase the demand of these groups for relief from cost-increasing government regulation. McChesney called this process rent extraction. Simplistically, then, the passage of the Sherman Act led to groups (labor, maritime interests, and so on) at a later date seeking exemptions from the antitrust laws. In such a way, the demand for the services of present and past legislators was increased, and reactive interest groups that could be tapped for political support were identified. The Federal Trade Commission Act of 1914 is an even better example of such a law than the Sherman Act. A useful way to think of this sort of governmental behavior is by analogy to fishing—the government is simply trolling for business.[5]

Explaining the timing of specific government regulations provides a challenge to economists and other students of government regulation. The progress made thus far is not really impressive, and there are many regulatory histories waiting to be written (or, one should say, rewritten).[6]

Heterogeneous Firms

In the simple version of the capture theory, a unified industry captures a regulatory process at the expense of consumers. Indeed, even in Peltzman's general theory of regulation, consumer and producer interests are stylistically traded off against one another. However, much economic regulation is driven by a different set of combatants. Much regulation is fueled by competitor versus competitor interests. The most obvious example of this type of regulation is where the producers of butter obtain a regulation raising the price of margarine. But this is not what is meant here; what is meant is competitor versus competitor in the same industry, that is, some butter producers against others.

Buchanan and Tullock (1975) were the first to articulate such a theory of regulation in the context of pollution controls. Since their paper, other applications of the basic concept have appeared (see, for example, Maloney and McCormick 1982). The basic idea is straightforward. Firms in an industry are heterogeneous with respect to costs; the industry supply curve is upward sloping. This opens the door to possible regulations that impose relatively

5. The treatment of the antitrust laws in an interest-group context may seem far-fetched to some. Nonetheless, if the shoe fits, wear it. Modern, private antitrust litigation is little more than competitors using the courtroom to subvert competition. Indeed, the Federal Trade Commission has been a major rule-making agency; see Mackay, Miller, and Yandle 1987.

6. The parallel to the work of Kolko (1965) here is apparent. Regulatory history can be an enticing field of work when approached from the perspective of the interplay of interest groups.

greater costs on higher-cost, marginal firms, causing some of them to leave the industry. All firms face higher costs as a result of direct regulation, but the exit of higher-cost firms raises market price in the industry. Depending upon relevant elasticities, the increase in price can outweigh the increase in costs for the lower-cost producers. If so, the regulation increases their wealth at the expense of both consumers and the higher-cost firms that had to leave the industry.

This approach to the explanation of regulation has been used extensively in the areas of social and environmental regulation. Fundamentally, it offers a better understanding of why direct administrative controls over production are preferred to less intrusive regulation such as environmental user fees or property rights. Requiring all producers to adopt the same expensive technology for pollution control can make lower-cost producers better off in terms of the heterogeneous firm theory. Although there is some debate about the matter, safety regulations such as the cotton dust standard have also been analyzed in terms of this general approach.[7] Indeed, a recent paper by Bartel and Thomas (1987) suggested that the regional economic impacts of environmental and occupational and health safety legislation are best explained by the heterogeneous firm approach (higher-cost, rust belt firms benefit at the expense of lower-cost, sun belt firms).

In a more innovative spirit, Marvel (1979) used this theory to explain the origin of the British factory acts in the 1830s. Contrary to the conventional wisdom that such laws were in the public interest because they limited the working hours of women and children, Marvel argues that the regulation of hours favored steam mill over water mill owners. The latter could only operate when the water flow was sufficient, and hence ran long hours when stream conditions were good. The hours restrictions curtailed the ability of the water-driven mills to make up for lost output when streams were low. According to Marvel's estimates, the resulting rise in textile prices transferred a significant amount of wealth to steam mill owners, who could operate on a regular basis. This is only part of the interest-group story of the factory acts, but Marvel laid out an innovative and plausible private-interest explanation of this legislation based on the idea of heterogeneous firms.[8]

Moreover, the theory of regulation based on heterogeneous firms is still evolving. High (1990) has recently produced a model in which the relevant winning coalition along the industry supply curve is composed of the higher-cost firms in the industry. And, in fact, this result seems more in keeping with the relevant empirical evidence about the impact of environmental and safety

---

7. See Maloney and McCormick 1982; Hughes, Magat, and Ricks 1986. Also see Pashigian 1984.

8. Anderson and Tollison (1984) offered a complementary theory to Marvel's by pointing out the role played by senior factory operatives in securing passage of hours legislation. The operatives viewed women and children as competitors in the labor market. Anderson and Tollison primarily analyzed the background of those who testified on the proposed legislation.

regulation, which, as noted above, has been shown to benefit primarily higher-cost, rust belt firms at the expense of lower-cost, sun belt firms (Bartel and Thomas 1987). High and Coppin (1988) also found evidence of high-cost firms winning the regulatory battle during passage of the Pure Food and Drug Act. In any event, the evolution of the heterogeneous firm model has been an important development in the theory of economic regulation since 1971.[9]

Social versus Economic Regulation

Stigler (1971) called his article "The Theory of Economic Regulation." This has come to be a somewhat misleading title. As the previous discussion indicates, much, if not all, of the regulation that goes under the heading of social and safety regulation has been successfully analyzed with the tools that Stigler initially deployed. In short, the best way to understand any regulatory scheme is to answer the twin questions, who wins and who loses. As Becker (1976) emphasized, it is best to think in terms of an economic theory of regulation rather than a theory of economic regulation.

Indeed, even the most innocuous sounding regulatory programs have been analyzed with the interest-group model. These include environmental, health, and safety programs (Bartel and Thomas 1987), the British factory acts (Anderson and Tollison 1984), various antitrust policies and practices (Mackay, Miller, and Yandle 1987), the banning of the importation of slaves into the United States (Anderson, Rowley, and Tollison 1988), immigration restrictions (Shughart, Tollison, and Kimenyi 1986), apostolic decrees by the Roman Catholic Church (Ault, Ekelund, and Tollison 1987), Luddism (Anderson and Tollison 1986), population growth (Kimenyi, Shughart, and Tollison (1988), farmer opposition to futures markets (Pashigian 1988), and still others. The point is not to review this literature in detail but to stress the generality of the economic approach to regulation. There simply is no viable distinction in the literature among "types" or "kinds" of regulation. There is not one theory for one type of regulation and another for another type. There is one unified economic approach to regulation and other governmental wealth-transfer programs.

The Interest-Group Theory of Government

An even more general point has been made. The idea that the economic theory of regulation applies only to off-budget governmental operations such as price and entry regulation has also gone by the board in the literature. It is now argued quite systematically that all governmental activities, off- and on-

9. This literature is often discussed under the rubric of the strategic uses of regulation. See McCormick 1984 for a review article. What is meant is the same—competitor competing against competitor for regulatory rents.

budget, can be modeled as a response to interest-group pressures. This point of view is normally expressed as the interest-group theory of legislation (Tollison 1988).

This approach can be sketched as follows (see McCormick and Tollison 1981). Demanders of legislation are those who can afford to organize to lobby for $1 by spending less than $1. Suppliers of legislation are those who find it efficient to let demanders have $1 without spending more than $1 to resist having their wealth taken away.[10] Politicians and bureaucrats are brokers in this process, pairing demanders with suppliers and clearing the market for governmental wealth transfers. Efficient brokers seek concentrated demanders and diffuse suppliers; inefficient brokers are replaced in the next election.

There have been many contributions to this literature, representing the emergence of an empirically testable theory of the state. Landes and Posner (1975) provided a theory of the demand for interest-group legislation in which the legislature and the independent judiciary play key roles. In a nutshell, they stress legislative and judicial behavior that serves to enhance the durability or present value of interest-group legislation. For example, if legal disputes are always resolved in terms of what the propounding legislature intended, laws become worth more to interest groups because they are more durable. In effect, the legislature can promulgate a type of long-term contract with interest groups. This insightful paper has other useful implications about the interest-group theory of government, and it has had a major impact on the theory of the demand for legislation.[11] There have also been several successful empirical tests of the Landes-Posner model (Crain and Tollison 1979a and 1979b; Anderson, Shughart, and Tollison 1989; Crain, Shughart, and Tollison 1988).

McCormick and Tollison (1980 and 1981) provided cross-sectional evidence about the role of legislative institutions and pressure groups in supplying wealth transfers and regulation across U.S. states. Important explanatory variables in their approach were legislative size, house/senate ratio, number of trade associations, population, and income. They provided a reduced-form model of the supply of legislation and transfers. They also analyzed the pay and occupational characteristics of the political brokers who stand at the center of the interest-group process. They addressed such issues as how legislators are compensated and why lawyers are such successful politicians (and the answer is not that they have a comparative advantage in writing legislation).

---

10. Note that the concept of supply is qualified here. Supply is not voluntary in the usual use of the term; it is coercive by virtue of the government's monopoly of force.

11. A theory of the demand for interest-group legislation presumes that interest groups already exist, having overcome free riding and costs of organizing to form a group to lobby. This prior problem of group formation is still largely a mystery to economists. Perhaps it is groups that have organized for some other basic purpose that have the lowest marginal costs of lobbying.

And Becker (1983), of course, has provided a general equilibrium rationale for the impact of interest groups on the overall cost of governmental policies. He argued that competition among pressure groups causes the social costs of political intervention to be minimized. This important theoretical result is still finding its way into the literature on interest-group theory.

In addition to this work, there have been numerous other specific applications of interest-group theory to explain various government processes. These include constitutional change (Crain and Tollison 1979a), executive vetoes (Crain and Tollison 1979b), corporate chartering laws (Shughart and Tollison 1981), legislative organization (Crain, Leavens, and Tollison 1986), political business cycles (Shughart and Tollison 1986), the redrawing of legislative districts (Crain, Davis, and Tollison 1990), and many others. The basic point, however, is simple. The theory of economic regulation began as an explanation of a subset of off-budget governmental activities. It has grown to encompass all government off-budget activity (economic and social regulation) and to raise a serious challenge to other theories of the state in the form of the interest-group theory of government. The latter theory asserts the working hypothesis that all governmental activities can be usefully formulated in interest-group terms.[12]

There have also been interest-group theories of government growth and change formulated on a grander scale. Olson (1982) models the rise and decline of nations as being fundamentally affected by the formation and activities of interest groups.[13] In short, the longer interest groups have been around, the more they are able to foul up the economy (thus causing a lower growth rate). Olson's hypothesis has achieved widespread attention and some empirical support in tests using data on growth rates of U.S. states. Ekelund and Tollison (1981) modeled the mercantile economies (ca. 1500–1700) of England and France in interest-group terms. They argued and reported evidence in favor of the hypothesis that a competition among interest groups explains the rise of free enterprise in England (the alternative theory is that Adam Smith routed the mercantilists). As stressed earlier, economic history offers many opportunities to study the effects of interest groups on economic life.[14]

The idea that interest groups matter in an economy has thus become quite widespread. Moreover, the evidence is growing that their effects are profound and telling on such variables as economic growth rates. But keep Becker's (1983) point in mind: government is not free. Interest groups are clearly a cost of the governmental process, but they may be an expression of a social cost–minimizing coalition in the transfer society.

12. Indeed, interest-group theory has been applied to quasi-governmental settings such as the National Collegiate Athletic Association (Fleisher and Tollison 1988) and the medieval church (Ekelund, Hebert, and Tollison 1989). There have also been analogies to interest groups inside a corporation (Faith, Higgins, and Tollison 1984).

13. Also see Mueller 1983.

14. See Anderson and Hill 1980 for an excellent study in this genre.

The Agent-Principal Relation

The agent-principal problem is an economic problem. The principal is a residual claimant who holds an ownership right in the activities that his or her agent conducts. The problem of the principal is to devise contractual and monitoring arrangements so that his or her interest is reflected in the labors of the agent. This stylized economic setting has generated a great deal of economic research and interest among economists because it obviously applies to many activities in an economy, such as the corporation, the labor union, the not-for-profit firm, and so on.

The agency problem has also had an impact on the economic theory of regulation and legislation. The issue can be put as follows. A bureau head, say a regulatory bureau head, is the agent. Members of Congress serving on an oversight committee are the principals. The members of Congress evaluate and set political trade-offs, as in the Peltzman model, by reading their election returns. The issue is how effective are the politicians in seeing to it that the bureaus under their jurisdiction make the appropriate political trade-offs and transfers?

The answer, in an emerging literature pioneered by Weingast (Weingast and Moran 1983), appears to be that bureaus are quite attuned to the preferences of their overseers. Weingast has studied the FTC and the SEC, and, in both cases, he found strong support for such an hypothesis. Contrary to the common impression, then, government agencies do not appear to have a lot of discretion or to be out of the control of the voters through their elected representatives. They appear to heed the trade-offs of their overseers carefully. The agency relation, thus, has much to teach us about politics and regulation. And issues abound for future research. Does it matter whether the agent is appointed or elected? Does it matter whether there is a single agent or multiple agents (as in a regulatory commission)? What is the postregulatory employment relation for staff and commissioners? And so on.[15]

What is at stake here for students of regulation and government is to pierce the black box of bureaucracy and to understand its inner workings better. How does one explain the process of economic regulation and, more generally, bureaucratic performance? The agent-principal framework offers a sensible route by which to develop a better understanding of such issues.

Regulatory Federalism

The Peltzman theory was written as if the regulator were embedded in a single, unified government. If, instead, the regulator is placed in the context of competing governments, at the same or different levels, interesting issues and applications of interest-group theory arise.

15. See Faith and Tollison 1983; Crain and McCormick 1984; Shughart, Tollison, and Goff 1986; Lindsay and Maloney 1988.

Maloney, McCormick, and Tollison (1984) addressed the behavior of the Peltzman regulator in the setting of competitive governments at the same level. Their theory was based upon the presence of comparative advantage and Ricardian rents across governments. Suppose a state has a comparative advantage in production of a good or service and, at the same time, most of the consumers of the good live in other states. What one has here is obviously a very low-cost margin for political wealth transfer. The benefits accrue in-state to voters; the costs fall out-of-state on nonvoters. This theory predicts significant interstate exportation of economic regulation where the underlying conditions hold. Maloney, McCormick, and Tollison test this theory on interstate electricity prices and find it supported in the data. The more a state's electricity production is exported, the higher its price. There are obviously numerous other testable implications of this theory.[16]

The issue of the locus of regulation across different levels of government has received a great deal of attention from a normative perspective—who should regulate what according to welfare principles—but not very much attention from a positive economics perspective. As noted earlier, Jarrell (1978) has discussed the evolution of electric utility regulation from the municipal to the state level. Stylistically, of course, costs and benefits to interest groups are the key to understanding this issue. Is it more effective, for example, to lobby and monitor regulators in fifty separate states or in Washington, D.C.? Are there economies of scale to be gained from unified federal regulation that cannot be achieved under myraid state standards? And so on. The point is that this is an important issue that has been largely untouched in the post-Stigler literature.

Event Analysis

The major methodological development in the literature on regulation is event analysis (Schwert 1981). This analysis derives from the efficient markets/rational expectations hypothesis in the theory of finance. This hypothesis maintains that security prices reflect all the available information about the forces impacting on firm wealth. Hence, unanticipated changes in regulation will be reflected in a firm's share prices, and the effect of regulation on firm wealth can be measured directly by event analysis. It is not necessary to go into the technical details of this procedure here. Essentially, an event window is constructed over which the unanticipated change in regulation took place or was announced (for example, in the *Wall Street Journal*). Other factors affecting firm share prices are held constant (the movement of the market in general), and the wealth effects of the regulation are estimated. Obviously, these effects can be positive (capture) or negative (consumer protection).

16. See Easterbrook 1983 for a dissenting view about the empirical importance of such interstate effects.

Because Schwert (1981) surveys much of the relevant literature, there is no need to do so here. Event analysis, however, offers an extremely useful device for studying the effects of regulation and other related economic activities. In the announcement of a merger, for example, how do the share prices of the remaining competitors behave? Expectations of a price increase will lead to increased wealth for competitor firms who expect to live under this price umbrella; the likelihood of a more efficient competitor will lead to an expectation of a lower price and to decreased wealth for competitor firms. This and many other interesting issues have been addressed in the literature using event analysis. The advantages of the approach are powerful, and much useful work can be done along these lines to evaluate the effects of past and present regulation.

Modern Deregulation

I have discussed the origin of regulation and some preliminary thoughts on the companion issue of deregulation and its sources. Deregulation is obviously an important issue for the theory of economic regulation. Not only must the theory be able to explain the onset of regulation, but it must also be able to explain the exit of regulation from the political marketplace.

Peltzman (1989) has recently addressed this challenge to the theory, specifically focusing on the deregulation of selected U.S. industries in the late 1970s and early 1980s. This deregulation episode was quantitatively important, and Peltzman wanted to see if the theory of economic regulation could explain it.

He framed the issue in a general way by emphasizing that the theory of economic regulation, as presently constituted, is mostly an architecture for describing positions of political equilibrium, and it has not been expanded sufficiently to account for the process of entry into and exit from the political market for regulation. With the issue thus framed, Peltzman argued that the Chicago theory can explain episodes of deregulation, primarily as a function of regulatory-induced cost increases that reduce the gains to producers from sustaining regulation and increase the potential gains to the benefactors (consumers) of deregulation. In essence, he proposed a cyclical theory of regulation. Regulation (or entry) occurs and a rent-transfer process is begun; over time, the rents are eroded because the regulator cannot enforce a perfect cartel; and, finally, deregulation (or exit) becomes politically profitable. It is the present value of the regulatory transfer at the onset of regulation that drives behavior in Peltzman's dynamic model of economic regulation.

This is certainly an intriguing idea. Although it is not clear why cost increases and rent dissipation cannot be controlled by the regulator, the answer is probably traceable to Stigler's (1971, 6) conjecture quoted earlier in this chapter. Peltzman goes on to apply this type of analysis to the various industries that have been deregulated and finds that it fits some cases but not all. Perhaps the most prominent of the latter cases is the role of rents accruing to organized labor in industries like trucking, where such rents were relatively large and the recipient group was politically powerful (apparently to no avail).

All that one can do at this stage is agree with Peltzman, who argues for further research on this issue. Peltzman, however, has pointed in a useful direction. Namely, if wealth transfers are the basis of regulation, they are surely also the basis of its decline.

Loose Ends

First, one should not confuse interest-group theory with Marxism. Simple-minded Marxism suggests that capital always wins over labor in the legislative process. Interest-group theory stresses the costs and benefits of organization and lobbying. Any group can win benefits from the state in interest-group theory. Moreover, there is ample evidence that labor, the elderly, small business, and so on benefit from regulation.

Second, the theory of economic regulation is a positive theory that, following Peltzman, implies an equilibrium price between the perfectly competitive and pure monopoly levels. The welfare analysis of the social costs of monopoly, however, does not mirror the positive analysis of regulation. Following Harberger (1954) and Tullock (1967), the welfare costs of monopoly are still estimated as if one is comparing a pure monopoly outcome with a perfectly competitive outcome, all else being equal. The social costs of monopoly are, thus, a trapezoid composed of the Harberger triangle and the Tullock rectangle. Peltzman's analysis suggests that actual instances of regulated prices will rarely correspond to the model used to estimate the welfare costs of such policies. Obviously, some work needs to be done to make the welfare economics of monopoly and regulation more congruent with positive economics of the same phenomena.[17]

Third, a closely related point is that the theory of rent seeking (Tullock 1967) is a very close cousin to the interest-group theory of government. The formal developments in rent-seeking theory have to do with the nature and costs of competition for governmental favors. Empirical episodes of rent seeking are the same thing as instances of economic regulation and wealth transfers. The two literatures should thus be considered one and read accordingly.[18]

---

17. For efforts in this direction, see Baysinger and Tollison 1980; Rowley and Tollison 1986; Wenders 1987.

18. For surveys of the theory of rent seeking, see Tollison 1982 and 1987. For collections of rent-seeking literature, see Buchanan, Tollison, and Tullock 1980; Rowley, Tollison, and Tullock 1988.

Concluding Remarks

A lot of ground has been covered since Stigler 1971 and Posner 1974. In fact, one might say that opposing theories of regulation have been pretty thoroughly driven from the scene. Mathematical economists still spin out complex considerations of optimal regulation and so on, but the workers who toil in the empirical field of regulation and governmental behavior know better. The impact of interest groups on the economy is a fascinating problem, as scholars such as Becker (1983) and Olson (1982) have shown. A whole new type of political economy is emerging from this work that will become the dominant paradigm in political economy because it is grounded in positive economic methodology.

REFERENCES

Anderson, G. M.; Rowley, C. K.; and Tollison, R. D. 1988. "Rent Seeking and the Restriction of Human Exchange." *Journal of Legal Studies* 17 (January): 83–100.

Anderson, G. M.; Shughart, W. F., II; and Tollison, R. D. 1989. "On the Incentive of Judges to Enforce Legislative Wealth Transfers." *Journal of Law and Economics* 32 (April): 215–28.

Anderson, G. M., and Tollison, R. D. 1983. "The Myth of the Corporation as a Creation of the State." *International Review of Law and Economics* 3 (December): 107–20.

Anderson, G. M., and Tollison, R. D. 1984. "A Rent-Seeking Explanation of the British Factory Acts." In *Neoclassical Political Economy*, ed. David C. Colander, 187–201. Cambridge, Mass.: Ballinger.

Anderson, G. M., and Tollison, R. D. 1985. "Ideology, Interest Groups, and the Repeal of the Corn Laws." *Journal of Institutional and Theoretical Economics* 141 (June): 197–212.

Anderson, G. M., and Tollison, R. D. 1986. "Luddism as Cartel Enforcement." *Journal of Institutional and Theoretical Economics* 142 (December): 727–38.

Anderson, T. L., and Hill, P. J. 1980. *The Birth of a Transfer Society*. Stanford, Calif.: Hoover.

Ault, R. W.; Ekelund, R. B. Jr.; and Tollison, R. D. 1987. "The Pope and the Price of Meat." *Kyklos* 40 (fasc. 3): 399–413.

Bartel, A. P., and Thomas, L. G. 1987. "Predation through Regulation." *Journal of Law and Economics* 30 (October): 239–64.

Baysinger, B., and Tollison, R. D. 1980. "Evaluating the Social Costs of Monopoly and Regulation." *Atlantic Economic Journal* 8 (December): 22–26.

Becker, G. S. 1976. "Comment." *Journal of Law and Economics* 19 (August): 245–48.

Becker, G. S. 1983. "A Theory of Competition Among Pressure Groups for Political Influence." *Quarterly Journal of Economics* 98 (August): 371–400.

Bentley, A. F. 1908. *The Process of Government*. Chicago: University of Chicago Press.

Buchanan, J. M.; Tollison, R. D.; and Tullock, G., eds. 1980. *Toward a Theory of the Rent-Seeking Society*. College Station: Texas A&M University Press.

Buchanan, J. M., and Tullock, G. 1975. "Polluter's Profits and Political Response: Direct Controls versus Taxes." *American Economic Review* 65 (March): 39–147.

Crain, W. M.; Davis, M. N.; and Tollison, R. D. 1990. "An Economic Theory of Redistricting." In *Predicting Politics*, ed. W. M. Crain and R. D. Tollison, 183–96. Ann Arbor: University of Michigan Press.

Crain, W. M.; Leavens, D. R.; and Tollison, R. D. 1986. "Final Voting in Legislatures." *American Economic Review* 76 (September): 833–41.

Crain, W. M., and McCormick, R. E. 1984. "Regulators as an Interest Group." In *The Theory of Public Choice—II*, ed. J. M. Buchanan and R. D. Tollison, 323–37. Ann Arbor: University of Michigan Press.

Crain, W. M.; Shughart, W. F., II; and Tollison, R. D. 1988. "Legislative Majorities as Nonsalvageable Assets." *Southern Economic Journal* 55 (October): 303–14.

Crain, W. M., and Tollison, R. D. 1979a. "Constitutional Change in an Interest-Group Perspective." *Journal of Legal Studies* 8 (January): 165–75.

Crain, W. M., and Tollison, R. D. 1979b. "The Executive Branch in the Interest-Group Theory of Government." *Journal of Legal Studies* 8 (June): 555–67.

Easterbrook, F. H. 1983. "Antitrust and the Economics of Federalism." *Journal of Law and Economics* 26 (April): 23–50.

Ekelund, R. B., Jr.; Hebert, R. F.; and Tollison, R. D. 1989. "The Medieval Church and Vertically Intergrated Monopoly: Church Interests and the Doctrine of Usury." *Journal of Law, Economics, and Organization* 5 (Fall): 307–31.

Ekelund, R. B., Jr., and Tollison, R. D. 1981. *Mercantilism as a Rent-Seeking Society*. College Station: Texas A&M University Press.

Faith, R. L.; Higgins, R.; and Tollison, R. D. 1984. "Managerial Rents and Outside Recruitment in the Coasian Firm." *American Economic Review* 74 (September): 660–72.

Faith, R. L., and Tollison, R. D. 1983. "Voter Search for Efficient Representation." *Research in Law and Economics* 5:211–24.

Fleisher, A. A., III, and Tollison, R. D. 1988. "A Capture Theory of the NCAA." Metropolitan State College, Denver, CO.

Harberger, A. C. 1954. "Monopoly and Resource Allocation." *American Economic Review* 44 (May): 77–87.

High, J. C. 1990. "Can Rents Run Uphill?" *Public Choice* 65 (May): 229–37.

High, J. C., and Coppin, C. A. 1988. "Wiley and the Whiskey Industry." *Business History Review* 62 (Summer): 286–309.

Hirshleifer, J. 1976. "Comment." *Journal of Law and Economics* 19 (August): 241–44.

Hughes, J. S.; Magat, W. A.; and Ricks, W. E. 1986. "The Economic Consequences of the OSHA Cotton Dust Standards: An Analysis of Stock Price Behavior." *Journal of Law and Economics* 29 (April): 29–60.

Jarrell, G. A. 1978. "The Demand for State Regulation of the Electric Utility Industry." *Journal of Law and Economics* 21 (October): 269–96.

Kimenyi, M. S.; Shughart, W. F., II; and Tollison, R. D. 1988. "An Interest-Group Theory of Population Growth." *Journal of Population Economics* 1 (October): 131–39.

Kolko, G. 1965. *Railroads and Regulation, 1877–1916*. Princeton: Princeton University Press.

Landes, W. M. and Posner, R. A. 1975. "The Independent Judiciary in an Interest-Group Perspective." *Journal of Law and Economics* 18 (December): 875–901.

Lindsay, C. M., and Maloney, M. T. 1988. "Party Politics and the Price of Payola." *Economic Inquiry* 26 (April): 203–22.

McChesney, F. S. 1987. "Rent Extraction and Rent Creation in the Economic Theory of Regulation." *Journal of Legal Studies* 16 (January): 101–18.

McCormick, R. E. 1984. "The Strategic Use of Regulation: A Review of the Literature." In *The Political Economy of Regulation: Private Interests in the Regulatory Process*, 13–32. Washington, D.C.: Federal Trade Commission.

McCormick, R. E., and Tollison, R. D. 1980. "Wealth Transfers in a Representative Democracy." In *Toward a Theory of the Rent-Seeking Society*, ed. J. M. Buchanan, R. D. Tollison, and G. Tullock, 293–313. College Station: Texas A&M University Press.

McCormick, R. E., and Tollison, R. D. 1981. *Politicians, Legislation, and the Economy: An Inquiry into the Interest-Group Theory of Government*. Boston: Martinus-Nijhoff.

Mackay, R. J.; Miller, J. C., III; and Yandle, B., eds. 1987. *Public Choice and Regulation*. Stanford, Calif.: Hoover.

Maloney, M. T., and McCormick, R. E. 1982. "A Positive Theory of Environmental Quality Regulation." *Journal of Law and Economics* 25 (April): 99–124.

Maloney, M. T.; McCormick, R. E.; and Tollison, R. D. 1984. "Economic Regulation, Competitive Governments, and Specialized Resources." *Journal of Law and Economics* 27 (October): 329–38.

Marvel, H. P. 1977. "Factory Regulation: A Reinterpretation of Early English Experience." *Journal of Law and Economics* 20 (October): 379–402.

Mueller, D. C., ed. 1983. *The Political Economy of Growth*. New Haven: Yale University Press.

Olson, M. 1982. *The Rise and Decline of Nations*. New Haven: Yale University Press.

Pashigian, P. 1984. "The Effects of Environmental Regulation on Optimal Plant Size and Factor Shares." *Journal of Law and Economics* 27 (April): 1–28.

Pashigian, P. 1988. "Why Have Some Farmers Opposed Futures Markets?" *Journal of Political Economy* 96 (April): 371–82.

Peltzman, S. 1976. "Toward a More General Theory of Regulation." *Journal of Law and Economics* 19 (August): 211–40.

Peltzman, S. 1989. "The Economic Theory of Regulation after a Decade of Deregulation." In *The Brookings Papers on Economic Activity*, ed. Martin Neal Baily, and Clifford Winston, 1–41. Washington: Brookings Institution.

Posner, R. A. 1974. "Theories of Economic Regulation." *Bell Journal of Economics and Management Science* 5 (Autumn): 335–58.

Rowley, C. K., and Tollison, R. D. 1986. "Rent-Seeking and Trade Protection." In *Protectionism and Structural Adjustment*, ed. H. Hauser, 141–66. Grusch: Verlag Ruegger.

Rowley, C. K.; Tollison, R. D.; and Tullock, G. eds. 1988. *The Political Economy of Rent Seeking*. Boston: Kluwer.

Schwert, G. W. 1981. "Using Financial Data to Measure Effects of Regulation." *Journal of Law and Economics* 24 (April): 121–58.

Shughart, W. F., II, and Tollison, R. D. 1981. "Corporate Chartering: An Exploration in the Economics of Legal Change." *Economic Inquiry* 23 (October): 585–99.

Shughart, W. F., II, and Tollison, R. D. 1986. "On the Growth of Government and the Political Economy of Legislation." *Research in Law and Economics* 9 (1986): 111–28.

Shughart, W. F., II; Tollison, R. D.; and Goff, B. L. 1986. "Bureaucratic Structure and Congressional Control." *Southern Economic Journal* 52 (April): 963–72.

Shughart, W. F., II; Tollison, R. D.; and Kimenyi, M. S. 1986. "The Political Economy of Immigration Restrictions." *Yale Journal on Regulation* 4 (Fall): 79–97.

Stigler, G. J. 1971. "The Theory of Economic Regulation." *Bell Journal of Economics and Management Science* 2 (Spring): 3–21.

Stigler, G. J. 1985. "The Origin of the Sherman Act." *Journal of Legal Studies* 14 (1985): 1–12.

Stigler, G. J., and Friedland, C. 1962. "What Can Regulators Regulate? The Case of Electricity." *Journal of Law and Economics* 5 (October): 1–16.

Tollison, R. D. 1982. "Rent Seeking: A Survey." *Kyklos* 35 (fasc. 4): 575–602.

Tollison, R. D. 1987. "Is the Theory of Rent Seeking Here to Stay?" In *Democracy and Public Choice*, ed. C. K. Rowley, 143–57. Oxford: Blackwell.

Tollison, R. D. 1988. "Public Choice and Legislation." *Virginia Law Review* 74 (March): 339–71.

Truman, D. B. 1951. *The Government Process: Political Interests and Public Opinion*. New York: Knopf.

Tullock, G. 1967. "The Welfare Costs of Tariffs, Monopolies, and Theft." *Western Economic Journal* 5 (June): 224–32.

Weingast, B. R., and Moran, M. J. 1983. "Bureaucratic Discretion or Congressional Control? Regulatory Policymaking by the Federal Trade Commission." *Journal of Political Economy* 91 (October): 765–800.

Wenders, J. T. 1987. "On Perfect Rent Dissipation." *American Economic Review* 77 (June): 456–59.

CHAPTER 3

Halfway Home: U.S. Telecommunications (De)Regulation in the 1970s and 1980s

Robert W. Crandall

Since the breakup of the Bell System, there has been considerable popular dissatisfaction with the changes that have occurred in the U.S. telephone industry. Because of federal deregulation, one frequently hears, we have lost the benefits of the best telephone network in the world. Consumers have been faced with such a confusing array of vendors that they do not even know whom to call when they lose telephone service, need a new line, or encounter a faulty telephone receiver. And, most important, telephone rates have risen dramatically because of federal deregulation. Bring back the old, regulated AT&T, and we will return to the era of low rates and assured service.

There is much to fault with this popular analysis, but perhaps the most serious error is the assumption upon which it is based—namely, that telephone service has been deregulated. Since the late 1950s, the Federal Communications Commission (FCC) has, indeed, pursued a program of liberalizing entry into telephone service and telephone equipment sales or rentals. But with one exception, the provision of terminal equipment, there has been no deregulation in this industry. Long-distance services are still regulated by federal and state authorities. Local service continues to be regulated at the state level. Spectrum assignments are still tightly controlled by the FCC. And Bell operating companies must petition not only federal and state regulators, but even a federal district court judge, if they want to offer a new service.

It is true that AT&T has been broken up by a consent decree and that scores of service providers have replaced the dominant telephone monopolist, AT&T. Thus, simply put, the telephone industry has been transformed from a regulated monopoly to an industry of regulated competition. Given previous experiences with regulated competition in transportation or financial markets, one might reasonably question whether this transformation is likely to enhance economic welfare, but it is inaccurate to attribute whatever one views as the current ills of the industry to deregulation.

In this chapter, I shall argue that liberalization of entry has, at least, created the pressures to eliminate some of the worst distortions of the old regulatory regime in the telecommunications sector. Unfortunately, this transformation is apparently occurring too slowly to prevent large telecommunications users from fleeing the public network, even though the changes have been too rapid for many politicians. More disturbing, perhaps, is the fact that regulators and politicians apparently have no clear road map for phasing out rate and entry regulation where competition is a feasible alternative. Nor do they have a plan for eliminating the restrictions under which the divested Bell operating companies operate.

An Unnatural Monopoly

For all we know, the provision of telephone service may be a "natural" monopoly. That is, the cost of providing data and voice signals to about 125 million access lines nationwide may potentially be lower if offered by a single carrier than if offered by numerous carriers. There are no dispositive studies of the economies of scope in telecommunications, and even the studies of scale economies are rather flawed because they cannot accurately capture the effects of technical progress.[1] But to say that telephone service exhibits cost subadditivity with currently available technology is not to say that it will still be a natural monopoly tomorrow.

Whatever the economies of scale or scope in telecommunications, AT&T's monopoly did not evolve naturally from this technology. In the early part of this century, entrants appeared at the local level, and AT&T attempted to repulse them by denying them access to its long-distance circuits.[2] A threatened antitrust suit ended this practice, as AT&T agreed to submit to government regulation rather than face a Sherman Act suit. AT&T subsequently bought up a large share of the new, independent local companies after Congress passed a law exempting telephone company mergers from the antitrust laws. As a result, by the 1930s, AT&T had about 80 percent of the local telephone circuits and all of the long-distance market, and for the next twenty-five years there was little evidence that entry into either market was feasible.

In the 1950s and 1960s, microwave replaced copper wires for long-distance transmission. Satellites were also developed for certain telecommunications uses. The economies of scale or scope in long-distance were surely altered by these dramatic new technologies. As these new technologies developed, the FCC began to feel the pressure to allow firms other than AT&T to build long-distance transmission facilities.

At first, in the late 1950s, these new entities were simply large users who

1. See Leonard Waverman, "U.S. Interexchange Competition," in *Changing the Rules: Technological Change, International Competition, and Regulation in Telecommunications*, ed. Robert W. Crandall and Kenneth S. Flamm (Washington, D.C.: Brookings Institution, 1989).

2. Gerald Brock, *The Telecommunications Industry* (Cambridge, Mass.: Harvard University Press, 1981).

wanted to build their own microwave circuits to avoid AT&T's high tariffs. The FCC began to license private (non-AT&T) microwave circuits in 1959. Soon thereafter, it received a petition from a new firm seeking common carrier status. In 1963, MCI petitioned for the right to build microwave capacity to offer dedicated (private-line) circuits to businesses whose communications needs were too limited to allow them to build their own microwave capacity. After a six-year battle with AT&T before the commission, MCI was finally successful in gaining a license to offer these dedicated circuits, but it was not authorized to offer general, switched long-distance service.

Other specialized carriers followed in the 1970s, but none was licensed to offer regular long-distance service. The FCC apparently believed that switched long-distance service was a natural monopoly that was to be guaranteed to AT&T. Nevertheless, MCI soon began to lease local circuits from Bell operating companies and to offer switched long-distance service in 1974 to its private-line customers, without FCC permission.

The FCC attempted to block MCI's new long-distance service, first through an administrative order and then by federal court action. However, because the commission had never provided a coherent reason for its limitations upon MCI's license, the courts refused to allow the FCC to deny MCI the right to offer the service.[3] Thus was the competitive long-distance market born. Had the FCC done its homework more carefully, AT&T might still have a long-distance monopoly today—perhaps not "naturally" but unnaturally protected by FCC regulation.

If there is some doubt about whether telephone service is a natural monopoly, there can be no similar doubts about telephone equipment manufacture. Yet, until the mid-1970s, AT&T produced virtually all of its own equipment and required that customers lease only AT&T (Western Electric) terminal equipment. In the 1970s, the FCC began to question this latter requirement, eventually forcing the states to allow customers to connect any certified equipment to local telephone company lines.[4] By 1978, the telephone company monopoly on terminal equipment had ended as hundreds of new competitors began offering consumers telephone handsets, cordless phones, modems, and answering machines to connect to their telephone outlets.

In the 1980s, all terminal equipment was "detariffed"—removed from the rate base—when AT&T was broken up by an antitrust decree.[5] Today, customers may still lease equipment from AT&T, but they are free to buy their own equipment from among literally hundreds of suppliers. Telephone equip-

3. MCI Telecommunications Corp. v. FCC, 561 F.2d 365 (D.C. Cir. 1977).

4. The courts repulsed state challenges to the FCC's authority to require that competitive equipment be allowed on local (intrastate) telephone circuits. See North Carolina Utilities Commission v. FCC, 552 F.2d 1039 (1977).

5. The Bell operating companies' equipment was detariffed immediately; the independents' equipment was phased out of the rate base over a number of subsequent years.

ment has now become so competitive that AT&T has had to resort to the same strategy as other U.S. consumer electronics producers—namely, the filing of massive antidumping suits against "unfairly" traded imports from Korea, Japan, Singapore, and other countries.

Regulatory Distortions

Students of regulation know quite well that the objective function of regulators is rarely the simple pursuit of efficient (or quasi-efficient) pricing. Political pressures assure that distortions in rates and services will arise. Rural customers are treated differently than urban customers. Business users face different rates than those offered to residential customers. Poor customers may gain preferential rates. Incumbent carriers are often protected from competition from new carriers or new services.

In telecommunications, regulators have been particularly careful to maintain the appearance of fair, reasonable rates by keeping rural rates artificially low, by keeping long-distance rates high relative to incremental costs, and by attempting to maintain uniform rates within each mileage band regardless of the density of traffic. The results have been that urban consumers subsidize rural consumers; consumers with intense long-distance use subsidize those who use little long-distance service; and business costs in telecommunications-intensive industries are artificially increased to subsidize residential consumers.[6]

Much of the distortion in telephone rates did not appear in earnest until the 1960s, when a joint board of state and federal regulators began allocating an increasing share of the costs of providing local circuits to interstate long-distance service. Surprisingly, AT&T did not object to this change in policy, even though competition was on the horizon in long-distance services. By the early 1980s, fully 28 percent of all local circuit (nontraffic-sensitive) costs were being recovered from long-distance charges even though interstate long-distance calls only accounted for 8 percent of the minutes of use and despite the fact that these long-distance calls did not add to the cost of a local circuit.

The regulatory distortions obviously invited competition. Had regulators allowed real long-distance rates to fall as rapidly as costs and to vary inversely with the density of the route, the entry by MCI and, later, the other long-distance competitors might have been postponed for a substantial time. Moreover, the regulators' current problems might have been much less severe if they had endeavored to keep rates reasonably in line with their best estimates of costs. Instead, they invited entry into long distance, and this entry, in turn, created a host of regulatory problems that are still not fully resolved.

6. By *subsidize*, I refer to a regulatory-induced distortion in pricing. I do not necessarily imply that rates for some services are raised above stand-alone costs, although they may have been.

First, as a result of competitive entry, the FCC now has to contend with determining the reasonableness of individual tariffs. Until the 1960s, the commission rarely investigated AT&T's individual service tariffs—switched long-distance, private lines, radio and television network connections, etc.—preferring, instead, simply to insure that AT&T remained within its rate of return constraint. Now, the commission is forced to examine every tariff filed by AT&T.[7]

Second, the FCC had to begin to deal with an increasing number of tariffs filed by AT&T in response to the new competition. Some of these tariffs were designed to provide discriminatory discounts to the customers most affected by the new private microwave services or by MCI's private-line competition. Other tariffs represented an attempt to set rates more in line with costs, inhibiting further entry on dense routes.

Third, the commission was placed in the position of having to regulate the rates at which AT&T operating companies supplied circuits to MCI and the other entrants to connect their calls to their customers. The new carriers had to use the local franchised lines (monopolies) to reach their customers, and their principal rival, AT&T, owned 80 percent of these circuits.[8]

Finally, the FCC was faced with the necessity of establishing ground rules for AT&T (and other carriers) to prevent cross-subsidization from monopoly to competitive services. This was a curious problem, given that the FCC and state regulators had been pushing subsidies in the other direction—from long-distance to local services since the early 1960s. Now that long-distance and terminal equipment are becoming competitive, the commission has to assure the new competitors that regulators would not be fooled by any potential AT&T attempt to assign the costs of these competitive services to local monopoly services, thereby allowing them to slash rates for competitive services and raise rates for monopoly services.[9]

The regulators were thus under pressures that they had not anticipated when they cautiously began to admit entry. By the late 1970s, the barriers to entry into long-distance and terminal equipment had completely fallen, and the regulatory problems had become quite acute. Political pressures kept regulators from simply eliminating their carefully crafted system of cross-subsidies, but market pressures would make continuation of these subsidies very difficult.

---

7. There is a long history of FCC futility in this regard, beginning with the TELPAK tariff investigation that was launched in 1962 and essentially limped to an end in 1979 without an FCC determination that any tariff was lawful.

8. This resulted in a hastily crafted ENFIA access tariff for the new carriers that offered connections at rates as much as 65 percent lower than the rates implicitly charged AT&T by its operating companies.

9. There have been three major FCC decisions in this matter: *Computer I*, *Computer II*, and *Computer III*, requiring various degrees of accounting separations or separate subsidiaries for competitive and monopoly services.

Antitrust

The FCC was not the only venue in which the new competitors could shop for protection from AT&T's competitive response. Throughout the early 1970s, MCI complained of AT&T's unwillingness to provide access to its local circuits for connecting MCI's private lines (and, later, switched long-distance calls). Failing to gain full satisfaction from the FCC, MCI eventually succeeded in persuading the Justice Department to bring a 1974 antitrust suit against AT&T, seeking the breakup of the company.[10] This suit was settled in 1982 with the divestiture of the Bell operating companies (BOCs) from AT&T. The divestiture was consummated on January 1, 1984.

The decree entered in the AT&T case is based upon the theory that the local exchange is a "bottleneck" monopoly whose services are required to deliver other services.[11] The local companies own the wires that connect subscribers to a local switch and, therefore, to the networks. All other services are assumed to be potentially competitive, including the supply of telecommunications equipment. For these reasons, local service was divorced from interstate long distance and from the manufacture of equipment.

The AT&T decree also bars the divested BOCs from offering long-distance services or "information" services and from engaging in the manufacture of equipment. It also required the BOCs to install equal access capability in their switches, so that interexchange carriers may be treated equally.[12] Theoretically, this equal access provision should render long-distance services outside the BOCs' local access and transport areas (LATA) competitive.

The Results of Divestiture and Liberalization

The results of the FCC's liberalization of long-distance services and terminal equipment markets and of the AT&T antitrust decree are in at least one sense quite obvious: these markets are far more competitive today than in previous decades.[13] But the continuation of regulation in both local and long-distance

10. See Gregory Coll, *The Deal of the Century: The Breakup of AT&T* (New York: Athaneum, 1986), for a sometimes hilarious account of the decision to press this action.

11. The decree is called the Modified Final Judgment, or MFJ, and is found in U.S. v. AT&T, et al., 552 F.Supp 131 (D.D.C. 1982). See Robert W. Crandall, "The Role of the Local Operating Companies," in *Changing the Rules*, ed. Robert W. Crandall and Kenneth S. Flamm (Washington, D.C.: Brookings Institution, 1989).

12. Prior to the decree, subscribers could only gain access to a long-distance competitor of AT&T by dialing a long access-code. Moreover, these new competitors could not obtain the complete array of services available to AT&T—such as call-completion information and billing information.

13. The subsequent material is summarized from my recent book, *After the Breakup: U.S. Telecommunications in a More Competitive Era* (Washington, D.C.: Brookings Institution, 1991).

services may limit the benefits of these dramatic changes. Before providing a summary of some of the more important changes in the various markets, therefore, it is useful to provide a brief review of the continuing political pressures to retain regulation of basic telephone services in the United States.

The Continuation of Regulation

Unfortunately, the FCC has not been able to deregulate telecommunications services in the manner in which the 1982 AT&T antitrust decree anticipated. Long-distance rates remain regulated. Every new long-distance tariff offered by AT&T is challenged by the new competitors.[14] Even attempts to change the mode of regulating long-distance rates has been mired in controversy.[15]

Nor has the commission been able to establish ground rules for allowing the providers of other "information" services to gain access to local connections. Fearing that the BOCs will eventually be relieved of the decree's prohibition on offering these services, information service providers have complained bitterly about the BOCs' "open architecture" plans invited by the FCC in its *Computer III* ruling.[16]

The judge administering the decree, Harold Greene, has been quite clear, stating that he intends to keep the restrictions on the BOCs as long as these companies control the access to local subscribers. However, this control is regulated by state commissions, not the FCC. Some state commissions have begun to experiment with various forms of regulatory flexibility, and a few are even beginning to be receptive to competitive entry in local services, but most of this entry is for services to large, concentrated customers, not to the dispersed smaller customers who account for most of the telephone access lines.[17]

Unfortunately, the only real hope for competition in local telephone service derives from mobile (cellular) technology; the FCC has only allocated sufficient spectrum for two modestly sized cellular systems in each metropolitan area, and one of these allocations has been reserved for the established local telephone company. The other cellular system in each area simply does not have the capacity to reach a large share of subscribers in the larger cities. Unless there are technological breakthroughs in the spectrum used for cellular telephone or changes in the FCC's allocation of the electromagnetic spectrum, cellular cannot become the competitive threat that Judge Greene requires for the relaxation of the decree's restrictions on the BOCs.

---

14. There is some progress in this regard. The FCC has recently opined that AT&T may offer large customers reduced rates in response to competitors low rates in the *Tariff 15* matter.

15. See the subsequent discussion of price caps.

16. FCC, *Third Computer Inquiry* (*Computer III*), released February 18, 1988.

17. See the periodic tabulations published in Capitol Publications, Inc., *State Telephone Regulation Reports*.

Reform of Pricing

The inefficiency of earlier telephone regulatory decisions has not been lost on the current FCC, but the commission's hands have been tied by political forces and by the federal system of regulation. In 1976, the FCC ruled that AT&T must allow the resale of its discounted (WATS) long-distance service offerings.[18] This decision eliminated a substantial amount of the price discrimination in AT&T tariffs as AT&T moved to end the opportunities for arbitrage.

More recently, the commission attempted to phase out the policy of assigning 28 percent of nontraffic-sensitive local circuit costs to interstate long-distance calls. It proposed to begin substituting a fixed monthly "subscriber line charge" (SLC) for the access charges levied upon long-distance calls. This SLC would rise to $6 or $7 per month, eliminating all interstate long-distance access charges.[19] Unfortunately, the political backlash against this inherently sensible proposal has been so strong that the commission has been forced to delay its implementation and to cap the SLC at $3.50 per month for residential subscribers.

Even the $3.50 monthly SLC represents substantial progress. The previous practice of assigning a substantial share of the fixed (nontraffic-sensitive) costs of local circuits to long-distance rates in the form of carrier access charges induces uneconomic reduction in the number of long-distance calls completed. Moreover, it induces long-distance companies to search for other, less efficient technologies to originate or terminate their calls.

The shift to a fixed monthly SLC to replace at least part of the carrier access charge has allowed interstate long-distance rates to fall rapidly since 1983, obviously at the expense of local rates (table 1). The FCC has no jurisdiction over intrastate rates; therefore, there has been a slower rate of decline in intrastate long-distance rates than in interstate rates. However, even some states are beginning to realize that using intrastate toll charges to subsidize local service is of dubious value.

Obviously, the problems of rate regulation extend beyond the deliberate distortions that arise because of political pressures. Rate of return regulation creates little incentive for carrier efficiency, induces uneconomic substitution of capital for labor, and provides inadequate rate increases during a period of inflation. Perhaps just as important, rate regulation in the current telecommunications market requires regulators to measure the costs of a large number of services provided under conditions of joint and common costs.

The FCC has been somewhat schizophrenic about rate regulation in the current environment. On the one hand, it has continued a futile process, begun twenty-five years ago, of attempting to allocate carrier costs across a

18. 60 FCC 2d 261 (1976).

19. FCC, CC Docket no. 78–72.

TABLE 1. The Trend in Real Consumer Price Indexes for Telephone Service, 1964–89 (1977 = 100)

Year	All Telephone Service	Local Service	Interstate Toll	Intrastate Toll
1964	152.2	N.A.	N.A.	N.A.
1965	147.4	N.A.	N.A.	N.A.
1966	140.4	N.A.	N.A.	N.A.
1967	138.2	N.A.	N.A.	N.A.
1968	132.7	N.A.	N.A.	N.A.
1969	127.5	N.A.	N.A.	N.A.
1970	121.8	N.A.	N.A.	N.A.
1971	122.5	N.A.	N.A.	N.A.
1972	125.2	N.A.	N.A.	N.A.
1973	121.0	N.A.	N.A.	N.A.
1974	13.6	N.A.	N.A.	N.A.
1975	107.4	N.A.	N.A.	N.A.
1976	105.2	N.A.	N.A.	N.A.
1977	100.0	100.0	100.0	100.0
1978	93.9	94.0	92.1	93.1
1979	84.2	84.0	82.2	84.5
1980	76.0	77.4	73.4	73.4
1981	75.0	78.2	72.1	68.5
1982	77.8	82.1	74.8	69.0
1983	80.3	86.1	74.0	71.5
1984	83.4	94.2	69.4	72.3
1985	83.7	98.0	64.1	70.4
1986	86.2	106.0	58.6	69.1
1987	82.6	107.4	48.2	65.4
1988	79.0	104.6	44.4	60.9
1989	76.1	103.5	41.0	55.5
	Average Percentage Change			
1977–83	−3.7	−2.5	−5.0	−5.6
1983–89	−0.9	+3.1	−9.8	−4.2

Source: Bureau of Labor statistics.
Notes: N.A. = not available. All indexes are CPI indexes deflated by CPI-U.

broad array of services.[20] On the other hand, it has recently proposed substituting a series of price caps for rate regulation of interstate services.[21] These price caps would allow carriers some discretion in raising or lowering rates as long as the overall rate of increase did not exceed a rate equal to the difference between the national inflation rate and the assumed rate of growth in productivity.

20. FCC, CC Docket no. 86–111.
21. FCC, CC Docket no. 87–313.

There are a number of difficult theoretical and practical problems with rate caps. At what rate level does the process begin? What is the industry's productivity growth rate? Can the price cap formula be adjusted periodically? If so, is the price cap system not simply rate of return regulation with regulatory lag? How are the weights on each rate category determined for the purpose of calculating the weighted average rate increase? Should these weights change with the changing importance of different service categories?

These conceptual and practical problems have made it difficult for the FCC to sell its rate cap proposal to Congress. It is easier to advance price caps as a transition to full deregulation of interstate long-distance rates than to extend the proposal to the interstate activities of the local telephone companies. Politicians worry that such a regulatory mechanism will allow carriers to compete vigorously for large business accounts while raising rates for residential customers. Nevertheless, the FCC has succeeded in imposing a highly constrained form of price caps on both AT&T and the local exchange companies' interstate activities.

There has been some progress in federal telephone rate regulation. The distortions that were built into the rate structure have been reduced due to the pressures created by competition and divestiture. Nevertheless, continued regulation by federal and state authorities does not augur well for the promotion of efficiency in telecommunications. With new fiber optics technology, economies of scale may be so great as to allow only one or two efficient national long-distance carriers, but the FCC will find it difficult to let most of the new entrants fail. As a result, long-distance rates are likely to be kept artificially high.

The Growth of Telecommunications in the 1980s

Despite the enormous technological breakthroughs in telecommunications, the rapid growth in the service sector of the U.S. economy, and the reforms in pricing regulated services, the growth of telecommunications carriers has slowed markedly in the 1980s. Throughout the rapidly growing 1960s and the more lethargic 1970s, telecommunications carriers grew by about 8 percent per year. In the 1980s, this growth slowed to about 4 percent per year (table 2).

Part of the decline in growth is due to the detariffing of terminal equipment. Most subscribers now own their own telephone handsets, and—more important—most large businesses own their key telephone systems or PBXs. But even after accounting for the loss of telephone set rentals, the growth of telephone carriers has slowed markedly.

The slowest growing sector is quite obviously the local sector. With telephones now in 93 percent of homes,[22] there is little room for growth in

22. U.S. Bureau of the Census, *Current Population Surveys*, 1988.

TABLE 2. Telephone Industry Indexes of Industry Output, 1960–88 (1977 = 100)

Year	Industry Data (1)	BLS Index (2)	BEA Index (3)
1960	27.5	27.4	29.0
1961	29.1	29.1	30.4
1962	31.1	31.2	32.9
1963	33.3	33.5	36.0
1964	35.9	36.1	38.8
1965	39.1	39.4	42.3
1966	43.1	43.5	46.6
1967	46.4	47.2	50.6
1968	50.8	51.0	55.0
1969	56.2	56.6	60.5
1970	60.6	60.4	66.9
1971	64.1	63.4	70.2
1972	69.3	69.2	76.9
1973	76.1	76.2	83.1
1974	81.7	81.8	87.3
1975	85.6	84.8	90.7
1976	91.2	90.8	94.2
1977	100.0	100.0	100.0
1978	111.0	110.8	110.4
1979	123.2	122.2	118.4
1980	134.9	133.2	129.4
1981	142.5	140.7	136.7
1982	146.5	144.2	140.6
1983	149.9	146.6	151.5
1984	149.3	149.1	151.1
1985	156.6	153.7	156.1
1986	167.9	159.8	162.4
1987	183.8	167.9	177.5
1988	194.6	177.4	N.A.

Sources: Column 1: author's calculation, based on data from U.S. Telephone Association; FCC, *Statistics of Common Carriers;* Annual reports of OCCs and Western Union; for 1960–72, Christensen et al., "Total Factor Productivity in the Bell System, 1987–89." Column 2: U.S. Bureau of Labor Statistics, Office of Productivity. Column 3: U.S. Department of Commerce, Bureau of Economic Analysis, National Income and Product Accounts, table 6-2.

Note: N.A. = not available.

traditional residential, local exchange service. Since the subscriber's telephone sets are not generally leased from the telephone company, there is little prospect for growth in residential equipment rental. And since this equipment is offered for sale by thousands of competitive retail stores, telephone companies will not be able to grow noticeably by retailing such equipment.

In the future, the most important source of telephone company growth is likely to be in offering new services other than the standard voice and data circuits to customers. However, the political concern for fairness and for the preservation of competition has prompted the antitrust courts to be very wary in allowing local telephone carriers (the BOCs) into such services. And if

TABLE 3. Consumer Spending on Telephone Service, 1965–88 (in billions of dollars)

Year	Personal Consumption Expenditures on Telephone Service	Common-Carrier Telephone Revenues	Consumer Share
1965	6.5	13.3	0.49
1966	7.0	14.7	0.48
1967	7.7	15.7	0.49
1968	8.3	17.2	0.48
1969	9.3	19.2	0.48
1970	10.1	20.9	0.48
1971	11.0	22.9	0.48
1972	12.4	25.9	0.48
1973	14.1	29.2	0.48
1974	15.5	32.5	0.48
1975	17.7	36.0	0.49
1976	19.8	40.7	0.49
1977	21.5	45.4	0.47
1978	23.9	51.3	0.46
1979	25.8	57.4	0.45
1980	27.8	64.4	0.43
1981	31.2	73.8	0.42
1982	35.6	82.5	0.43
1983	37.9	87.6	0.43
1984	39.8	89.4	0.45
1985	40.4	96.0	0.42
1986	42.7	101.7	0.42
1987	44.1	105.4	0.42
1988	47.2	107.4	0.44

Sources: U.S. Department of Commerce and author's calculations.

these services require custom-designed equipment, the BOCs are further hampered by the manufacturing prohibition in the antitrust decree.

The major growth in telecommunications demand comes from the business sector, not the residential sector (table 3). Moreover, a large share of the business demand originates from a small number of businesses. The large national customers are particularly important to telecommunications vendors, but the BOCs have a considerable handicap in dealing with them because the AT&T decree limits their ability to offer the full range of services and equipment.

Similarly, AT&T is handicapped by regulation because of its need to tailor service offerings and rates to individual customer demands. Each new offer of a special package for a large customer invites a filing before the FCC from competitors claiming that such a package is "discriminatory." To its credit, the FCC has thus far resisted the entreaties from the new long-distance competitors that AT&T's rates be kept uniform and high.

TABLE 4. U.S. PBX Market Shares by Lines Shipped, 1976–89 (in percentages)

Company	1976	1978	1980	1982	1984	1986	1989
AT&T	50	48	46	23	20	22	28
Northern Telecom	13	9	8	13	20	23	23
Rolm	4	7	10	13	14	16	12
Mitel	0	0	7	12	10	10	9
NEC	5	3	3	5	8	8	7
GTE	1	7	6	5	5	4	—
Siemens	0	1	4	5	4	4	5
Others	27	25	16	24	19	13	16

Sources: Richard H. K. Vietor and Davis Dyer, *Telecommunications in Transition*, 62; "PBX Market Analyses," *Teleconnect* (September 1, 1985): 90; Huber Report, table PX.4; and *Communications Week* (January 8, 1990): 28.

Equipment Markets

One reason for the slow growth of regulated telephone companies has been the development of vigorous competition in the telecommunications equipment market. AT&T no longer controls the market for terminal equipment, switches, or transmission equipment. As a result, telephone subscribers now are much less likely to rent equipment from telephone companies, and the largest businesses may even own a few large switches.

AT&T's loss of market share in terminal equipment markets began in the 1970s, as the FCC began to require that telephone companies allow the connection of "foreign" terminal equipment to telephone company lines as long as it was certified as posing no danger to the network. AT&T's share of the ordinary telephone set and PBX markets has fallen dramatically since the mid-1970s. For example, AT&T had only 22 percent of the important PBX market in 1986 (table 4), a substantially smaller share than in the mid-1970s. Its share of key telephone systems, a somewhat less sophisticated business product, had also fallen to less than 25 percent, and its share of the ordinary handset market was also about 35 percent in 1986–87.[23]

Since divestiture, AT&T has lost a substantial share of the market for other telephone equipment, such as transmission and switching devices, largely because its divested operating companies no longer are compelled to buy from AT&T. By 1987, AT&T's equipment sales were at least $3 billion less than they would have been had AT&T not been broken up by the antitrust courts.[24]

Nevertheless, AT&T remains a potent force in the large switching sys-

23. These data come from a variety of sources, including the U.S. Department of Justice and *The Geodesic Network: 1987 Report on Competition* (the Huber Report).

24. Data from author's analysis of AT&T Annual Reports, 1970–87.

TABLE 5. U.S. Digital Switch Market, by Lines Placed in Service, 1982–86 (in percentages)

	1982	1984	1985	1986
AT&T	< 1	22	39	49
Northern Telecom	66	42	44	35
GTE[a]	3	28	13	10
Others	31	8	4	6

Sources: Jacquie McNish, "Digital Switch Business Sees More Competition," *Wall Street Journal*, January 22, 1986, 26; Huber Report, table CO.4.

[a]GTE has recently formed a joint venture with AT&T for the production of central office switches (*Telephony*, January 9, 1989, 10–11).

tems, despite an early setback at the hands of Canada's Northern Telecom. Between them, Northern Telecom and AT&T continue to control more than 80 percent of the digital switch market in the United States (table 5).

Long-distance Service

The rapid decline in interstate long-distance rates have propelled a substantial acceleration in the rate of growth of this service. Between 1972 and 1983, interstate long distance grew at an annual real rate of 7.2 percent per year. Since 1983, this growth has exceeded 12 percent.

As the demand for long-distance service has grown, new carriers have begun to make serious inroads into AT&T's once impregnable position. Today, these new carriers have more than 30 percent of the interexchange market, and their share is growing rapidly as they rush to complete enormous fiber-optic networks (table 6).

Despite the rapid expansion of new competition from other common carriers, regulators are unwilling to propose total rate deregulation because there are many routes on which AT&T is the only direct carrier. The other carriers or resellers may serve many of these markets, but only by leasing AT&T circuits. Moreover, there is a widespread fear that overcapacity already exists on the major routes and that deregulation would trigger a price war that AT&T would win. The parallels with railroad and trucking regulation of 100 and 50 years ago, respectively, are obvious.

Information Services

There are now a host of potential services that could be offered via the telecommunications network that involve more than the mere transmission of data or voice signals. These include protocol conversion for dissimilar computer systems, videotext, voice storage, transaction services, home telemeter-

TABLE 6. Market Shares of U.S. Interexchange Revenues (in percentages)

							Non-LEC Share			
	1978	1982	1985	1986	1987	1988	1985	1986	1987	1988
AT&T	99.4[a]	96.5[a]	67.2	63.7	60.8	57.5	86.3	81.9	79.1	75.4
Local Exchange Carriers (LECs)			22.1	22.2	23.1	23.8				
MCI	0.3	1.8	4.2	5.9	6.8	7.9	5.5	7.6	8.8	10.4
Sprint	0.2	0.9	2.8	3.7	4.5	5.5	3.5	4.8	5.8	7.3
Others	<0.1	<0.8	3.7	4.5	4.8	5.3	4.7	5.7	6.3	6.9
Total	100.0	100.0	100.0	100.0	100.0	100.0	100.0	100.0	100.0	100.0

Sources: FCC, *Statistics of Communications Common Carriers;* AT&T, *Bell System Statistical Manuals.*
[a]Includes all LEC interexchange shares prior to 1984.

ing, financial data services, database retrieval services, and many more. Many or all of these services could be provided at least as efficiently, and perhaps more efficiently, by telephone companies than by outside vendors.

The strictures in the AT&T decree prevent the divested BOCs—or 80 percent of the local telephone service industry—from participating in most of these "information services" markets. Judge Greene has relaxed this restriction marginally—for gateways to videotext and for voice storage services—but the BOCs are otherwise forbidden to compete in these markets.

Because the local telephone companies are still largely franchised monopolies, the FCC has struggled with potential rules that would allow all outside vendors equal access to the local phone circuits for accessing customers. In terminal equipment and long distance, such equal access provisions have worked well. In information services, however, the requirements of current and potential services are so varied that specifying "open network architecture" has become an issue over which the various interests have collided. Whether such open architecture rules can work remains unknown, but it is quite clear that Judge Greene will not relinquish his stranglehold on BOC participation in these markets until this issue is resolved.

Private Networks

The continuing regulation of the telecommunications network by fractious federal and state regulators as well as Judge Greene has resulted in a series of product offerings and regulated rates that are not efficient. Long-distance rates have not been allowed to fall to costs. Local telephone companies are constrained in their product offerings. Urban areas are subject to discrimination. Large users have had some difficulty in gaining discounted rates for the tailored services offered them by AT&T.

With entry liberalized and rate/service options in the regulated sector still distorted by politically sensitive regulators (and the district court), large private users have the option of simply constructing all or part of their own networks. Since the mid-1970s, when access to terminal equipment was liberalized, the purchase of telephone and nonbroadcast communications systems by firms other than regulated common carriers has soared. Capital spending by telephone companies has been remarkably stagnant despite the enormous outlays on fiber optics and the huge expenditures by BOCs to convert their central office switches to equal access. Indeed, since 1983, the last year before the AT&T breakup, the capital stock of the telephone industry has only grown by 1.8 percent per year.[25]

Perhaps the best indicator of the flight of investment to private users is a comparison of growth rates in real investment for telephone carriers with the growth in total telephone and nonbroadcast communications equipment consumption in the United States. Prior to 1977, virtually all telephone investment was undertaken by regulated telephone carriers. Indeed, more than 85 percent of it was undertaken by AT&T. Since 1977, total investment in telephone equipment has grown much more rapidly than investment by telephone companies. In 1987, roughly one-third of all telecommunications investment was undertaken by firms other than telephone companies.[26]

Since 1980, telephone company spending on capital equipment has increased at only a 0.8 percent annual rate. By contrast, total consumption of telephone and nonbroadcast communications equipment has increased at a 3.4 percent rate. Obviously, someone other than the telephone company is buying this equipment. Once again, the flight to private carriage is reminiscent of an earlier era in surface transportation, when shippers shifted to private carriage to avoid the excessive rates permitted by the ICC.

Have Liberalization and Divestiture Improved Economic Welfare?

It is, perhaps, still too early for precise measurement of the welfare effects of liberalization. Constructing a telephone network is a very complex matter. Developing new generations of equipment requires hundreds of millions of dollars and several years' lead time. We are only fourteen years into terminal equipment liberalization and only nine years past the AT&T antitrust decree.

It is already clear, however, that the principal benefits from liberalization/divestiture will come from innovation in equipment and services as well as from repricing of telephone service. Unfortunately, as we have seen, fully

25. Author's calculation from company data.

26. This result is obtained by comparing all telephone company capital spending with data on telephone (SIC 3661) and nonbroadcast communications systems (SIC 36621) consumption published by the U.S. Bureau of the Census.

rational repricing has been prevented by political forces in a still heavily regulated industry. I estimate that the repricing that has already occurred has improved economic welfare by about $1 billion per year (in 1987 dollars).[27] Others have suggested that truly efficient pricing might yield as much as $12 billion in welfare improvements.[28] Of course, it is naive to assume that optimal pricing and efficient service delivery can ever occur in a regulated monopoly.

Liberalization of terminal equipment markets and the divestiture of Western Electric (AT&T's manufacturing subsidiary) from the BOCs have created a much more dynamic market in all varieties of telephone equipment. Freeing the design and production of equipment from a sluggish monopoly regulated by politically sensitive regulators is likely to be the most important source of potential gains in economic welfare from liberalization. For example, customers may now purchase a wide variety of terminal equipment at highly competitive prices. These options were simply unavailable fifteen years ago.

The sluggishness in telephone-industry innovation is probably best illustrated by the modest rate of improvement in central-office switching equipment prior to divestiture. Studies of the rate of improvement in large central-office switches suggest a 5 percent average real annual gain. During the past twenty years, the computer industry has realized a rate of improvement of 20–25 percent per year. Since a large central-office switch is largely a computer with a great deal of software, there are obviously much more rapid rates of improvement possible.

Every telephone equipment supplier in the world has, until recently, had a captive market in its national telephone monopoly. Most often, this monopoly has been a state-owned PT&T. As the United States, Japan, the United Kingdom, and potentially even Western Europe begin to liberalize and open up their markets for telephone equipment, we should witness an explosion in technology far greater than that which has already occurred. Unfortunately, the AT&T divestiture and the liberalization in Japan and the United Kingdom are too recent to allow us to measure their effects on central-office equipment innovation. There is, however, fragmentary evidence that switch prices have begun to fall more rapidly in the post-1984 period than in previous years.[29]

One further piece of evidence that the divestiture has improved efficiency may be found in its effect upon employment. Until 1982, employment in the

---

27. By *repricing*, I mean the reduction in interstate long-distance rates at the expense of higher local access rates, principally through the subscriber line charge. This calculation is based upon research reported in *After the Breakup*.

28. John T. Wenders and Bruce L. Egan, "The Implications of Economic Efficiency for U.S. Telecommunications Policy," *Telecommunications Policy* (March 1986): 33–40. (Their estimate is 11 billion in 1983 dollars.)

29. Data supplied by New York Telephone to the New York Public Service Commission; Kenneth S. Flamm, "Technological Advance and Costs: Computers Versus Communications," in *Changing the Rules*, ed. Robert W. Crandall and Kenneth S. Flamm.

telephone sector had increased more or less steadily. Since 1982, however, employment has fallen by 5.4 percent per year. Part of this decline may be attributed to the slowdown of demand growth for regulated services. But the sharp downturn that occurred after 1982 must reflect, in part, the enormous rationalization of service delivery within the BOCs and AT&T. For example, the independent telephone companies have lost only 2.2 percent of their employees per year, while the BOCs and AT&T have shed 6.4 percent of their employees per year between 1982 and 1988.

Summary

No one familiar with the history of regulation in inherently competitive industries could possibly be sanguine about the development of regulated competition in the telephone sector. Regulators have admitted new players, but they and the legislators who oversee them are unwilling to let all of the players compete freely. In part, this reluctance is due to a fear that competition is not truly sustainable in many telephone services. However, it also reflects a desire by some of these politicians to protect as much of the remaining cross-subsidies as possible.

The artificial constraints placed on the divested Bell operating companies by the AT&T antitrust decree may be sacrificing economies of scope and potential sources of competition in many markets. These constraints will not be released by the court administering the decree unless competition develops at the level of the local exchange, an unlikely prospect given past state and federal regulatory decisions and the apparent technological options.

At this juncture, the most serious causes for concern in the current telecommunications regulatory environment are the potential for cartelization of long-distance services and the flight of business users to their own networks. If there are, indeed, economies of scale or scope beyond the level of most of these private users' demands, such private networks may be creating a large welfare loss. If, on the other hand, the economies of scale and scope are more modest, the private networks are simply adding competitive force to an industry that was once a lethargic giant impacted by a monumental change in technology. That the government has attacked this giant and roused it from its slumber can hardly be all bad.

CHAPTER 4

Entrepreneurship and Competition in Bureaucracy: Harvey Washington Wiley's Bureau of Chemistry, 1883–1903

Clayton A. Coppin and Jack High

> Perhaps the single most promising area for the application of REMM [resourceful, evaluative, maximizing man], however, is to government. It seems to me that it is here that a major change is called for in the resourcefulness attributed to the participants.—(William H. Meckling, "Values and the Choice of the Model of the Individual in the Social Sciences," *Schweizerische Zeitschrift für Volkswirtschaft und Statistik* 112 [1976]: 557)

Harvey Washington Wiley was appointed chief of the Bureau of Chemistry in 1883. He took over a small group of ten professional employees and a budget of under $50,000. When he resigned in 1912, the bureau employed over 600 and its budget exceeded $1,000,000.

The growth of Wiley's bureau was not an isolated case. Between 1897 and 1913, the Department of Agriculture, of which the Bureau of Chemistry was a part, grew from 2,400 employees and a budget of $3.6 million to 13,800 employees and a budget of $21.0 million.

Had such growth taken place in the market, these organizations would be regarded as highly successful enterprises, and the individuals who built them would be heralded as astute and able entrepreneurs. Yet we rarely think of bureaus and bureaucrats in this light.

Near the end of his study of three successful public figures, Eugene Lewis coined the term *heroic bureaucrat.* This oxymoron calls to mind a salient feature of U.S. bureaucracy. For all their dull routine, bureaucracies often display fierce rivalry and dynamic growth, commanded by individuals of unusual talent and dedication. Enterprising bureaucrats have changed U.S. social life. They have influenced the food we eat, the clothes we wear, the

The authors gratefully acknowledge that a grant from the Earhart Foundation supported the research for this chapter.

environment we work in, the schools our children attend, the terms we trade on, and our political processes. They have built huge organizations with budgets that run into the hundreds of millions, and with control over land, labor, and capital that rival the most successful of business leaders. The bureaucratic entrepreneur is no less a force of U.S. life than the business entrepreneur.[1]

The bureaucrat has not been much studied as an entrepreneur, especially in that quarter of academia where they should naturally command attention—the economics department. Modern economic theory is almost devoid of entrepreneurship. As Baumol has said, "Look for him [the entrepreneur] in some of the most noted of recent writings on value theory, or in neoclassical or activity analysis models of the firm. The references are scanty and more often they are totally absent. The theoretical firm is entrepreneurless—the Prince of Denmark has been expunged from the discussion of Hamlet."[2]

Economists have developed a large and impressive literature on bureaucracy without much explicit attention to entrepreneurs. Yet bureaucratic entrepreneurship is central to the origin and growth of bureaus. Frolich, Oppenheimer, and Young call it the "missing link" in analyzing the evolution of bureaucracy.[3] Certainly the history of American bureaucracy cannot be fully understood apart from the competitive process set in motion by entrepreneurs within the political system.

Entrepreneurship in Bureaucracy

Bureaucratic Entrepreneurship Defined

Entrepreneurship means "acting man exclusively seen from the aspect of uncertainty inherent in every action."[4] In economic theory, entrepreneurship refers not to particular individuals, but to an aspect of action or decision. It emphasizes the complexity and uncertainty that surround action and the eco-

1. See Eugene Lewis, *Public Entrepreneurship: Toward a Theory of Bureaucratic Political Power* (Bloomington: Indiana University Press, 1980), 228.

2. William J. Baumol, "Entrepreneurship in Economic Theory," *American Economic Review* 58 (May, 1968): 66. See also James Buchanan, "What Should Economists Do?" *Southern Economic Journal* 30 (January, 1964): 213–22; Israel Kirzner, *Competition and Entrepreneurship* (Chicago: University of Chicago Press, 1973), 8; Robert Hebert and Albert Link, *The Entrepreneurs* (New York: Praeger, 1982), 51–52; Mark Casson, *The Entrepreneur* (New York: Barnes and Noble, 1982), 9–13.

3. Norman Frolich, Joe A. Oppenheimer, and Oran Young, *Political Leadership and Collective Goods* (Princeton: Princeton University Press, 1971), Robert Salisbury, "An Exchange Theory of Interest Groups," *Midwest Journal of Political Science* (1969): 21. Besides Salisbury, the relevant works on bureaucratic entrepreneurship also include Richard Wagner, "Pressure Groups and Political Entrepreneurs," in *Papers on Non-Market Decision Making*, ed. Gordon Tullock (Charlottesville: University of Virginia Press, 1966), 161–70; Albert Breton and Raymond Breton, "An Economic Theory of Social Movements," *American Economic Review* (1969): 198–205; Eugene Lewis, *Public Entrepreneurship*.

4. Ludwig von Mises, *Human Action* (New Haven: Yale University Press, 1966), 253.

nomic advantage of foresight. "Entrepreneurial talent consists in peering into an unknown future and arriving at an assessment of the relevant features of that future."[5]

Entrepreneurship has, of course, been mainly studied as it applies to the theory of markets. The pursuit of entrepreneurial profit sets in motion a competitive process that, taken as a whole, determines the production, allocation, and consumption of economic goods. Yet the meaning of entrepreneurship does not tie it to any particular economic system. Schumpeter points out that private property is not essential to entrepreneurial activity. Frolich, Oppenheimer, and Young develop a theory of public or political entrepreneurship, as does Eugene Lewis. Casson points out that the meaning of entrepreneurship is "institution free," and Mises says, "In using this term [entrepreneurship] one must never forget that every action is embedded in the flux of time and therefore involves a speculation." Entrepreneurship is present in the actions of politicians and bureaucrats as well as those of businessmen.[6]

Bureaucratic entrepreneurs are appointed government officials who exercise creativity, alertness, and judgment in attempting to increase their control over scarce resources. This definition emphasizes that, although bureaucrats operate in a world of rules and routine, they need not passively accept their environment. They can actively try to change the law to increase the bureau's budget and their control over it.[7] Government officials, as McChesney notes, are not "mere brokers redistributing wealth in response to competing private demands, but . . . independent actors making their own demands to which private actors respond."[8]

The definition also emphasizes that entrepreneurship can fail as well as succeed. Bureaus can diminish as well as expand, bureaucrats can fall as well as rise. The very complexity that makes alertness and judgment valuable implies that some failure is inevitable. Some will expand their control over

5. Israel Kirzner, *Discovery and the Capitalist Process* (Chicago: University of Chicago Press, 1985), 110.

6. Joseph Schumpeter, *The Theory of Economic Development* (Cambridge: Harvard University Press, 1934), 93–94; Casson, *The Entrepreneur*, 24–25; Mises, *Human Action*, 253. Frolich, Oppenheimer, and Young write, "At the most general level, an entrepreneur can be defined as an individual who seeks to make a profit from the supply of some good to members of a group" (*Political Leadership*, 57). These goods can be either public or private, supplied by either the market or the state. Lewis says, "A public entrepreneur may be defined as a person who creates or profoundly elaborates a public organization so as to alter greatly the existing pattern of resource allocation of scarce public resources" (*Public Entrepreneurship*, 9). See also William J. Baumol, "Entrepreneurship: Productive, Unproductive, and Destructive," *Journal of Political Economy* 98 (October, 1990): 893–921.

7. Mises writes, "Bureaucratic management means, under democracy, management in strict accordance with the law and the budget" (*Bureaucracy* [New Haven: Yale University Press, 1944], 43).

8. Fred S. McChesney, "Rent Extraction and Rent Creation in the Economic Theory of Regulation," *Journal of Legal Studies* 16 (January, 1987): 102. See also Thomas DiLorenzo, "Competition and Political Entrepreneurship," *Review of Austrian Economics* 2 (1987): 66.

resources, and some will lose their control. Although a bureau does not operate according to monetary profit and loss, as a business firm does, bureaus are nevertheless subject to a principle of survivorship within the competitive process.

Competition within Bureaucracy

In order to increase the resources under their control, bureaucratic entrepreneurs must win the approval of legislators. The immediate source of the bureau's funds, in the U.S. system at least, is the legislature. Legislators provide the immediate demand for the activities of bureaus, in the sense that they raise and allocate tax funds. But legislators themselves are only intermediaries. They require the votes of their constituents to hold office. Raising and allocating taxes ultimately requires approval of the electorate. Demand for the services of the bureau runs from the voters through politicians (especially those whom the actions of the bureau can help or hurt) to the members of the bureau.[9] The bureaucratic entrepreneurs can increase their budgets by influencing voters or elected officials, or both.

The same reasoning applies to the rules and regulations that govern the activities of the bureau. Elected officials pass the laws that create bureaus and their missions, but these officials must do so with an eye to their constituencies. If bureaucratic entrepreneurs want to change the rules that govern them, they must influence voters and/or elected officials.

The hierarchy of bureaus will often create chains of officials who influence the allocation of resources. Although decisions within the hierarchy will usually be vital to the entrepreneur's success, the principles determining success or failure remain the same. Ultimately, it is the voters, through elected officials and possibly higher-level appointed officials, who determine the rules and budgets that govern bureaus.

The ability of bureaucratic entrepreneurs to influence voters, while not always essential to success, can be a powerful weapon. As Becker notes, ". . . voter preferences are frequently not an *independent* force in political behavior. These 'preferences' can be manipulated and created through the information and misinformation provided by interested pressure groups, who raise their political influence partly by changing the revealed 'preferences' of enough voters and politicians."[10]

The opportunities to influence preferences will usually be greater in political than in commercial life. For one thing, voters have less incentive to

9. See William A. Niskanan, *Bureaucracy and Representative Government* (Chicago: Aldine-Atherton Press, 1971); Barry R. Weingast and Mark J. Moran, "Bureaucratic Discretion or Congressional Control?" *Journal of Political Economy* 91 (October, 1983): 765–800.

10. Gary S. Becker, "A Theory of Competition Among Pressure Groups for Political Influence," *Quarterly Journal of Economics* 98 (August, 1983): 392.

be informed than consumers, because each vote has only a minor influence on the outcome.[11] For another, the truth or falsity of particular claims are more difficult to ascertain in political life than in private.[12] Influencing public opinion is often an important part of the competition among bureaus.

The competitive process within bureaucracy differs from the market process in other respects that will not concern us here.[13] We simply want to emphasize that entrepreneurs in a bureau will simultaneously, as rivals, strive to increase their control over scarce government resources. Whether they are motivated by public purpose or private gain, these entrepreneurs will produce a process marked by creativity, alertness, success, and failure.

This concrete historical process, as manifested in the actions of Harvey Wiley and his competitors, is the focus of this study. In the period under consideration, 1883–1903, Wiley was not very successful. Nevertheless, the episode deserves scrutiny for several reasons. First, entrepreneurship does not always succeed immediately, and sometimes does not succeed at all. Second, it was during this period that Wiley laid the foundation for his spectacular success of later years. Third, Wiley's repeated failures demonstrate the overriding influence of the competitive process over the formulation of policy. Wiley's competitive strategy from 1883 to 1903 was logically sensible, but it was not politically compelling. His failure to comprehend this continually hampered Wiley's efforts to build his bureau. We cannot understand the Wiley episode without studying his failures and successes.

Sweet Politics with Lumps: Wiley Cultivates the Sugar Industry

From 1877 to 1883, the Division of Chemistry was headed by Peter Collier. A chemist trained at Yale, Collier vocally promoted the production of sugar from sorghum. He claimed that sorghum would soon supply all the nation's sugar needs and, perhaps, even become an export crop.

Collier's enthusiasm for sorghum sugar was shared by William Le Duc, the commissioner of agriculture during the 1870s. But when George Loring

---

11. See Anthony Downs, *An Economic Theory of Democracy* (New York: Harper and Row, 1957); Becker, "Competition Among Pressure Groups."

12. In *Capitalism, Socialism, and Democracy* (New York: Harper and Row, 1942), Schumpeter says,

> The picture of the prettiest girl who ever lived will in the long run prove powerless to maintain the sales of a bad cigarette. There is no equally effective safeguard in the case of political decisions. Many decisions of fateful importance are of a nature that makes it impossible for the public to experiment with them at its leisure and at moderate cost. Even if that is possible, however, judgment is as a rule not so easy to arrive at as it is in the case of a cigarette, because the effects are less easy to interpret. (263)

13. See Richard Wagner, "Agency, Economic Calculation, and Constitutional Construction," in *The Political Economy of Rent Seeking*, ed. Charles Rowley (Boston: Kluwer Academic Publishers, 1988), 423–45.

replaced Le Duc as commissioner of agriculture in 1882, Collier ran into trouble. Loring thought Collier's claims were excessive, and Loring replaced him with Harvey Washington Wiley, whose views were closer to Loring's, in 1883.[14]

Wiley was a chemist at Purdue University. At the time of his appointment, he had achieved some national recognition for his work on sugar. He believed the United States should be self-sufficient in sugar, but he had more modest views than Collier on what could be accomplished with sorghum. He advocated a broader base of production, which included cane and beets as well as sorghum.

Wiley favored a tariff to protect the industry from the cheap sugar produced in tropical areas. He believed that sugar production would be a great boon to U.S. farmers, who were in constant danger of failure. People in the tropics, according to Wiley, could lie on the beaches and eat coconuts and bananas and still survive, but the U.S. farmer would freeze and starve if he failed.[15]

Wiley believed that sugar consumption marked the degree to which a country was civilized. He thought it was an appropriate part of all U.S. diets, particularly children's. "Childhood," he said, "without candy would be Heaven without harps." Wiley's attitudes toward sugar consumption reflected the growing importance of sugar in European and U.S. diets throughout the nineteenth century.

To Commissioner Loring, who shared many of Wiley's views, Wiley seemed an ideal replacement for the difficult Collier. Loring hoped Wiley's appointment would diminish the opposition of the sorghum advocates, who supported Collier.[16]

Loring's hopes were short lived. Farm journals used Collier's dismissal as an excuse to attack Loring, whom they opposed anyway. Meanwhile, Collier organized for an all-out assault on Loring and Wiley. Collier attacked Wiley's professional competence and started a battle that would last for ten years, during which time Wiley would never be secure as chief of the chemistry division. Between battles with the Collier faction and the uncertainty created by changing political administrations, Wiley's job required continued political vigilance.

Upon taking office, Wiley turned to the Louisiana Sugar Producers Association to cultivate political support. He involved them in decision making and wisely used his appointive powers for jobs in his division to cement alliances.

Government help in developing the sugar industry involved more than

14. John Alfred Heitmann, *The Modernization of the Louisiana Sugar Industry, 1830–1910* (Baton Rouge: Lousiana State University Press, 1987), 123.

15. Oscar Anderson, *The Health of a Nation* (Chicago: University of Chicago Press, 1958), 35–37. The best coverage of Wiley's early years is William Fox, *Harvey W. Wiley: The Formative Years* (Ph.D. diss., George Washington University, 1960).

16. Anderson, *Health*, 28.

just scientific research; it involved a mixture of politics and science. Wiley developed his skills at both and learned that politics can triumph even when science has not.[17] Soon after he took over, Wiley changed the direction of the division's research by adopting European methods. The sugar beet industry had developed successfully in Europe, and Wiley turned there to learn new methods of manufacturing. For the next several years, he conducted a series of experiments in Kansas and Louisiana, all of which were unsuccessful except one, and even that one involved a process that soon was abandoned as too costly. Throughout this period, Wiley continued to support a high tariff to encourage development of the domestic sugar industry.[18]

These early experiments by Wiley were attempts to adopt the diffusion process of removing sugar by osmosis from both sorghum and sugar cane. It also involved various methods to economically refine the syrup and remove impurities. Wiley employed a number of competent chemists to assist him in the experiments. Among them was M. A. Scovell, who had failed at a sugar-making venture and was looking for employment. Scovell was a valuable employee and Wiley assisted him in becoming the director of the Kentucky Agriculture Experiment Station. M. A. Scovell would later play an important role in Wiley's campaign for a national pure food law.[19]

Wiley relied heavily on the Louisiana sugar producers to fend off the attacks of Peter Collier and to survive a change in administration. When the Democrats took over in 1885, Wiley, a good Republican, managed to keep his position by working to have Norman Jay Coleman appointed commissioner of agriculture. Coleman wrote Wiley, asking him if he could help in getting the support of the sugar producer. Wiley evidently did so, and left Coleman in his debt.

Wiley needed Coleman's backing, because a full-scale attack on his professional abilities, the accuracy of his reports, and even his honesty was launched by J. Floyd King, a representative from northern Louisiana.[20] King attacked Wiley's competence, both in the press and from the floor of Congress. King was particularly irritated by Wiley's trips to Europe and his attempts to transfer European technology to U.S. sugar production. An anti-European bias was common in the United States at the time, but King's attacks on Wiley were frequently personal. Fortunately, Wiley enjoyed Commissioner Coleman's support as well as the backing of powerful Democratic leaders of the Louisiana Sugar Producers Association.[21]

King's attack, much of which was unfounded, was less serious than the criticism of W. P. Kirchoff, a sugar chemist who observed the experiments

17. Heitmann, *Sugar*, 125.

18. Heitmann, *Sugar*, 125.

19. Harvey Washington Wiley, *An Autobiography* (Indianapolis: Bobbs-Merrill, 1930), 176.

20. Heitmann, *Sugar*, 136–38.

21. Heitmann, *Sugar*, 145–46.

that Wiley conducted at Ft. Scott, Kansas, for the Louisiana Sugar Producers Association in 1886. Kirchoff was one of three observers sent by the association to witness the experiments. The other two observers concurred with Wiley's conclusions, and their reports were accepted by the association. Kirchoff's report was at first suppressed, and when it was published, it disputed the accuracy of Wiley's analysis and his yield calculations. The criticisms were apparently well founded. Wiley responded with a personal attack on Kirchoff and his professional standing in the U.S. agricultural community. He never adequately answered Kirchoff's criticisms.[22]

Despite the criticism, Wiley retained his post, and in the fall and winter of 1887, he conducted his first successful experiment in Louisiana. Wiley discovered a diffusion process that increased the amount of sugar extracted from cane. Ultimately the discovery was insignificant. Wiley's new process required large amounts of water that had to be evaporated after diffusion. The quantity of fuel necessary for evaporation made the process too costly for commercial use, and Wiley eventually abandoned it. But in the short run he was able to claim success. He chose that moment to extract the Division of Chemistry from experimenting in large-scale manufacturing processes. Although his association with the Louisiana Sugar Producers Association had helped him weather some severe criticism, he lacked the engineering knowledge to advance commercial production. He decided to change his tactics, saying, "For my part I do not pretend to be a mechanical engineer and I do not see how I can do any further good in this matter. I propose hereafter to stick strictly to chemistry."[23]

Status Building in the Bureau

Although Wiley's early political and professional activities revolved around sugar, he never gave either himself or his bureau completely over to the sugar industry. Wiley had come to Washington from the academy, and he looked upon his bureau much as he would an academic department. He saw the Division of Chemistry as a group of professionals with the expertise to conduct all chemical analysis within the Department of Agriculture. He worked to enhance the professional status of chemists, especially agricultural chemists, and repeatedly stressed the necessity of competent analysis within the department.

Wiley's determination to build his bureau around the discipline of chemistry was, in retrospect, a misjudgment that hindered the growth of his bureau for many years. Nevertheless, the plan seemed reasonable, and his attempts to raise the status of chemists provided a solid organization that would later help him launch his successful crusade for a pure food law.

22. Heitmann, *Sugar*, 159–60.
23. Heitmann, *Sugar*, 166.

In the late 1800s, the chemistry profession was beginning to develop specialties. Although the full impact of these specialties was not felt until after the turn of the century, the reasons for them were present in Wiley's attempts at sugar production. It was one thing to be an analytical chemist working in a laboratory, and another to build a factory using chemical processes. Within private industry these differences produced two types of chemists—analytical chemists, who performed chemical analyses and worked mostly in quality control, and production chemists, who designed and built machinery for chemical processes.[24]

Production chemists had two models to follow. In the German model, chemists work with engineers and other necessary professionals to build the processing equipment. In the U.S. model, chemists also learned engineering, which created the chemical engineering profession. The U.S. model channeled analytical chemists into routine jobs in quality control. They did not have the training to design and supervise production projects.[25]

Wiley was an analytical chemist, but his involvement in the experiments of large-scale sugar production required him to either cooperate with a knowledgeable engineer or become one himself. He did neither. Instead, he attempted his experiments without an adequate knowledge of engineering. The result was a series of delays, mistakes, and failures. Had he devoted the whole of his department's resources to aiding sugar production, which meant that his bureau would have evolved toward chemical engineering, Wiley might have succeeded with his experiments, developed a constituency, and expanded his bureau.[26]

The other problem, which appeared at the same time for analytical chemists, was a decline in their status. As the work became more standardized and the analyses more routine, less and less actual chemical knowledge was necessary to accomplish the work. Analytical chemists were not held in high regard, and this was reflected in the lower wages they received in industrial positions. The decline reached the point in 1905 where a starting analytical chemist in industry would receive approximately $700 per year, compared to $1,200 per year for a skilled artisan.[27]

The Association of Official Agriculture Chemists was founded in 1884 to advance the professional standing of analytical chemists working in agriculture. As their first official task they undertook the standardization of methods for analyzing and classifying fertilizer. Although they succeeded in formulating standards acceptable to the fertilizer industry, they also set in place routine procedures that lowered the skill necessary to perform analytical tasks. Less

24. Terry S. Reynolds, "Defining Professional Boundaries: Chemical Engineering in the Early 20th Century," *Technology and Culture* 27 (October, 1986): 699–701.

25. Reynolds, "Professional Boundaries," 700–701.

26. Heitmann, *Sugar*, 151–53.

27. Reynolds, "Professional Boundaries," 702–3.

skill meant diminished status, even in the eyes of the agricultural chemists themselves.[28]

Wiley was a leading figure in the association. He served as its president in 1886–87, and remained the permanent secretary until he left government service in 1912. Although the original charter of the organization dedicated it to establishing uniform fertilizer standards, the association almost immediately expanded its activities to other agricultural products.[29]

The Department of Agriculture allowed the association to use its facilities and published the proceedings of its annual meetings. As early as 1885, the association expressed interest in chemically analyzing adulterated foods. Commissioner of Agriculture Coleman encouraged the interest.

In 1886, W. O. Atwater, a member of the association, suggested they examine the chemistry of human nutrition. He received little response to his suggestion, probably because chemists lacked the knowledge and skills to understand the subject. For several years the organization had studied animal feed. Despite careful analysis, the results did not distinguish between what was nutritious and what was not. In an address to the organization, Steven M. Babcock pointed out that, despite their studies, they were unable to tell the difference between what an animal ate and what it excreted. Chemical analysis showed the same constituent elements.[30]

Nevertheless, analytical chemists could identify many food adulterants. Wiley had been interested in the adulteration of foods when he arrived in Washington in 1883, but the demands of the sugar research kept him from devoting much time to the examination of foods. When Commissioner Coleman took charge of the department, he encouraged the Chemistry Division to step up the investigation of food adulterations. Coleman was concerned about the adverse economic impact that adulteration could have on producers, and he wanted the matter studied. Wiley welcomed Coleman's interest, and after 1886, when the sugar research was toned down, Wiley increased his study of food impurities.[31]

In 1887 the first parts of Bulletin 13, a detailed study of food adulterations by the Division of Chemistry, were published by the Department of Agriculture. (The final part of this study was not published until 1907, a year after the Pure Food and Drugs Act was passed.) The first three parts of

28. Alan I. Marcus, "Setting the Standard: Fertilizers, State Chemists, and Early National Commercial Regulation, 1880–1887," *Agricultural History* 1 (1987): 60, 71; Kenneth Helrich, *The Great Collaboration* (Arlington, Va.: Association of Official Agricultural Chemists, 1984), 1–16; see also Charles E. Rosenberg, "Rationalization and Reality in Shaping American Agricultural Research, 1875–1914," *Social Studies of Science* 7 (November, 1977): 401–22.

29. Helrich, *Great Collaboration*, 11–15.

30. Anderson, *Health*, 71–73. The proceedings of the Association of Official Agricultural Chemists were published annually as Bulletins of the Bureau of Chemistry until 1913, largely due to Wiley's support.

31. Anderson, *Health*, 71–73.

Bulletin 13 were on Dairy Products, Spices and Condiments, and Fermented Alcoholic Beverages. These were followed in 1889 with part 4, Lard and Lard Adulterations, and part 5, Baking Powders. In 1889, Congress appropriated $5,000 for further studies of "the adulteration of food, drugs, and liquors," but Wiley did not investigate drugs. He concentrated on food and liquor.

The association gained a reputation for respectable research in food adulteration, and used its reputation to endorse the need for pure food legislation. The standards it set for the fertilizer industry served as a model for regulating the food industry.[32] As Alan I. Marcus has written of the association, "Basing their claim for distinctiveness on the possession of a technical competence—a dubious contention at best—chemists created for themselves a governmental connection, labored to acquire that technical competence, and finally traded on it to redefine and expand their social role."[33] But in 1887, when the association published its first studies on food, cashing in on their technical competence was nearly twenty years away. Meanwhile, Wiley was trying to establish his bureau as the sole supplier of chemical analysis to the Department of Agriculture. For fifteen years, he would continue his attempts with precious little success.

Swimming against the Democratic Tides, 1893–97

During the next decade, from 1887 to 1897, the Division of Chemistry continued to work on sugar production, but on a smaller scale than previously. The division also continued its work on food adulteration. It published parts 6 and 7 of Bulletin 13 in 1892, and published part 8 in 1893. Together, these made a substantial contribution to the study of foods, but did little to increase the size or influence of the chemistry division.[34]

Meanwhile political and, especially, organizational changes in the Department of Agriculture were working against Wiley. In 1889, Coleman stepped down as Secretary of Agriculture. His replacement, Jeremiah Rusk, supported Wiley's work on food adulteration, but Wiley did not have the close personal association with "Uncle Jerry" that he had had with Coleman.

Even worse for Wiley was the election of Grover Cleveland in 1892. Cleveland appointed Julius Sterling Morton secretary of agriculture. Morton believed in limited government, with the emphasis on limited. He did not like paternalism. He thought that most government activity bestowed special favors to particular groups and that most government officials were corrupt.

32. For a similar view on the abilities of early food chemists, see Mitchell Okun, *Fair Play in the Market Place* (DeKalb, Ill.: Northern Illinois University Press, 1986), x–xi.

33. Alan I. Marcus, "Proceedings of The Tenth Annual Convention of The Association of Official Agricultural Chemists," *Chemistry Bulletin* 38 (Washington, D.C.: Department of Agriculture, 1893).

34. Part 6 studied "Sugar, Molasses and Sirup, Confections, Honey and Beeswax"; part 7 studied "Tea, Coffee, and Cocoa Preparations"; and part 8 studied "Canned Vegetables."

Morton sought to limit the growth of the department. At the end of his term, he recommended that the department be abolished.

The years under Morton were rough ones for the Department of Agriculture. The appropriation for the department was cut and the Division of Chemistry was not exempted. Although the change in the political environment was bad for Wiley, changes in the organization of bureaucracy, while more subtle, were worse.

The Bureau of Animal Industry exemplifies the organizational changes that were taking place in the Department of Agriculture. Congress created the bureau in 1884 to check the spread of animal diseases. Organized to solve a particular and visible problem, the bureau brought together experts from a variety of specialized backgrounds, including its own chemists. With the power to study a problem and to take regulatory action to ameliorate it, this kind of organization brought with it a built-in political constituency. As a consequence, the Bureau of Animal Industry, unlike the Chemistry Division, grew rapidly in the 1880s and 1890s. By the turn of the century, it was the largest bureau in the Department of Agriculture.[35]

Wiley's bureau found it difficult to compete with other bureaus. In 1894, a Division of Soils was created under the supervision of Milton Whitney. The Division of Chemistry had begun analyzing the chemistry of soils in 1887, shortly after it scaled back sugar research. Whitney was supposed to study the physical characteristics of soil, and Wiley the chemical, but it was not long before a dispute erupted into an all-out battle for control over the study of soils. Wiley fought hard to keep the chemical analysis of soils in his division, but he eventually lost.

A similar pattern occurred with nutritional studies. In 1895, Secretary Morton got an appropriation from Congress to study nutrition. Instead of placing this work in the Division of Chemistry, which had a long record of studying food adulteration, Morton gave it to the Office of Experiment Stations. These stations, one in each state, had been created in 1887 by the Hatch Act to aid agricultural research and production. Wiley fought to retain this work for his division, but to no effect.[36]

Wiley attributed his troubles to political differences with Secretary Morton, a Democrat, and Morton's assistant secretary in charge of scientific investigation, Charles W. Dabney. Dabney had been the director of the Agricultural Experiment Station in North Carolina and then president of the University of Tennessee. He had been one of the founders of the Association of Official Agricultural Chemists and had known Wiley for years. Wiley initially thought that this would benefit him, but was soon disillusioned. In the sum-

35. Alfred C. True, *A History of Agriculture Experimentation and Research in the United States, 1607–1925*, U.S. Department of Agriculture misc. pub. no. 251 (Washington, D.C.: GPO, 1937).

36. Anderson, *Health*, 86–97.

mer of 1895, Wiley complained to his former student, employee, and friend, G. L. Spencer, that he expected to be dismissed any day. He went on to accuse Dabney of being a traitor who supported Morton's attempts to destroy the department and was only interested in increasing his (Dabney's) own power. Dabney, said Wiley, favored only his friends—Galloway, Whitney, and Scribner.[37] Dabney was actually interested in reorganizing the scientific sections around specific problems, but, to Wiley, such a reorganization was tantamount to destroying his bureau.

Swimming against the Republican Tides, 1897–1903

Wiley was delighted when, in 1896, the Republicans under William McKinley came back into to power. He felt a great burden had been lifted from the country.[38] Wiley still had to survive the final days of Morton, and he was worried that the appropriation for the Division of Chemistry would be cut even further. He contacted Senator William B. Allison of Iowa to get appropriations restored to his budget. He also took the opportunity to tell Allison the damage that had been done to the Chemistry Division because of Morton's dislike for him, which Wiley believed resulted from their political differences.[39]

McKinley appointed James Wilson of Iowa as Secretary of Agriculture. Wilson was born in Ayrshire, Scotland, in 1835. He came with his parents to the United States in 1851, and settled in Iowa, where he was a successful farmer, in 1855. He would serve from 1873 to 1877 and again from 1883 to 1885 in the U.S. Congress. From 1891 to 1897, he was professor of agriculture and director of the Agriculture Experiment Station in Ames, Iowa. He would serve for sixteen years as secretary of agriculture, overseeing the growth of the department into a major scientific and regulatory agency.[40]

Wiley was sure things would be better under a Republican. He felt that the Republicans in power would bring back the protective tariff on sugar, which would mean additional appropriations for investigation of sugar, provided Wilson was not too frugal a Scotsman.[41]

Because he thought the decline of the Chemistry Division was due to parisian politics, Wiley perceived the change in administrations as an opportunity to regain control over all chemical investigations. He even thought that

37. Wiley to G. L. Spencer, July 28, 1895, Wiley Papers, box 5, Library of Congress.

38. Wiley to Blanch M. Thayer, November 5, 1896; Wiley to G. L. Spencer, November 5, 1896; WP, box 5.

39. Wiley to William B. Allison, February 3, 1897, WP, box 5.

40. Earley Vernon Wilcox, *Tama Jim* (Boston: Stratford Company, 1930).

41. Wiley to Herbert Marlick, February 3, 1897, WP, box 5. Secretary Wilson was not frugal when it came to departmental appropriations, but he did live a very frugal personal life. He spent little on lodgings or entertainment and saved nearly half of his salary. See David Houston, *Eight Years with Wilson's Cabinet, 1913–1920* (New York: Doubleday, 1926).

he might be able to take over direction of all scientific investigations conducted by the department.

Through political contacts, Wiley informed Wilson that he, Wiley, was the good Republican among the heads of the scientific sections of the department. He claimed that "10 of the 13" heads had been appointed by the outgoing administration, and that Wiley alone among them was a strong protectionist. He also let Wilson know how his division had suffered under Morton and Dabney. The only way to make up for what had happened, Wiley wrote, would be "the utter uprooting of the last vestige of that hateful period."[42]

In a confidential letter sent to Assistant Secretary Dabney, he attacked the work on food and nutrition being done by W. O. Atwater for the Office of Experiment Stations. He claimed that the recent Bulletin 34 on carbohydrates in wheat was full of "errors of the most dangerous character and statements which are calculated to bring the scientific work of this department into disrepute and ridicule." Wiley went on to tell the assistant secretary that, by law and custom, control over work belonged under the supervision of the Chemical Division and he did not understand why it was ever given to the Office of Experiment Stations, whose director did not even pretend to be a chemist. Wiley ended with the comment, "The fact that it is possible for such crude and misleading statements to be published by and with the authority of the Department of Agriculture, is one of the most striking arguments which has come to my attention for the necessity of a directorship of the Scientific Division."[43]

Wiley followed this letter with one to Congressman Long, a member of the Agricultural Committee, complaining about Bulletin 34 and the disrepute it would bring to the department. In the letter to Long, he denigrated the chemical work being done in the Soils Division. To make sure that the public would take notice, Wiley sent his old friend G. L. Spencer a copy of the bulletin marked with Wiley's own criticisms for Spencer to use in a review for *Popular Science*.[44] Shortly after they met, Wiley continued his campaign with a long letter directly to Wilson. Wiley detailed his complaints and asked that all chemical work be supervised by the Division of Chemistry. With the Republicans back in power, Wiley obviously felt he could capture chemical investigations for his division.

On his arrival, Wilson had made a tour of the department and was impressed with the competency of most of the bureau chiefs, particularly

42. Wiley to C. I. Long, February 13, 1897; Wiley to Henry T. Oxnard, February 9, 1897; Wiley to Henry Casson, March 27, 1897; all WP, box 5.

43. Wiley to Assistant Secretary Dabney, February 12, 1897, WP, box 5.

44. Wiley to C. I. Long, February 13, 1897; Wiley to G. L. Spencer, February 20, 1897; WP, box 5.

Beverley Galloway of Plant Industries, Willis Moore of the Weather Bureau, Daniel Salmon of Animal Industry, and Milton Whitney of Soils. Wiley was conspicuously absent from the list of chiefs who impressed Wilson. Wiley's complaints over control of chemical investigation could well have gotten him off on the wrong foot with the new secretary.[45] To make matters worse for Wiley, Wilson decided to keep Charles Dabney as a special agent in charge of scientific and statistical investigations. The job was a plum, paying $4,500 per year, the second highest in the McKinley administration that did not require Senate approval.

Wilson intended from the beginning that Dabney would only hold the position temporarily while Wilson learned the ropes for himself. Nevertheless, it caused an uproar among the Republicans, and Wiley contributed substantially to the noise. Wiley wrote numerous letters complaining about the situation; he even resorted to waving the "bloody shirt" by denouncing Dabney as an "unreconstructed Johnny" who had Wilson completely under his influence. He wrote of the poor morale in his division, saying only those who were Dabney's friends could expect promotion. He lashed out bitterly at Wilson, complaining the secretary should be called the minister of foreign affairs because of all the foreign-born people who worked there.[46]

Wilson soon dismissed Dabney and took over supervision of the scientific activities himself, but the change did not benefit Wiley.[47] Apparently slighting Wiley, Wilson appointed C. F. Saylor of Iowa as sugar beet commissioner. Saylor's assignment was to foster the sugar beet industry. He was directed to gather the necessary information on producing sugar from beets, and to make the information available to any interested party. He was responsible for an annual sugar beet report at the end of each year.[48]

Wiley was outraged. He had been the dominant figure in sugar investigations since his arrival at the Department of Agriculture in 1883. He wrote to his friend, G. L. Spencer, "The beet sugar work of the department has been taken away from me and given to Dabney and a special agent who has just been appointed and who never saw a beet field or factory and is absolutely ignorant of the whole business."[49]

45. Willard Lee Hoing, "James Wilson as Secretary of Agriculture, 1897–1913," (Ph.D. diss., University of Wisconsin, 1964), 23.

46. Hoing, *James Wilson*, 29–30; Wiley to E. B. Cowsill, March 27, 1897; Wiley to A. M. Todd, April 22, 1897; Wiley to Albert R. Leeds, April 24, 1897; Wiley to G. L. Spencer, May 6, 1897; Wiley to Henry Houston, April 21, 1897; Wiley to G. L. Spencer, May 10, 1897; Wiley to John McElroy, undated (circa May 11–12, 1897); all WP, box 5.

47. Wiley to Henry Casson, March 27, 1897; Wiley to Secretary of Agriculture Wilson, April 19, 1897; WP, box 5.

48. Hoing, *James Wilson*, 37.

49. Wiley to G. L. Spencer, May 6, 1897, WP, box 5; Anderson, *Health*, 106; Hoing, *James Wilson*, 37.

Wiley continued to complain about the chemical work being done on nutrition in the Office of Experiment Stations, and he vented his frustration in a letter to Secretary Wilson. On Wilson's suggestion, a meeting was held between Wiley, A. O. Atwater, the special agent in charge of the nutritional investigations, and A. C. True, the head of the Office of Experiment Stations. If Wilson had hoped that the problem could be resolved amicably, he was immediately disappointed. Wiley began the meeting by attacking the integrity of the studies done under Atwater's direction, even suggesting that a southern influence was at work. Why, Wiley wanted to know, was work given to Professor Mallet of the University of Virginia, who was still a British citizen, and who had made gunpowder for the South during the war. Wiley claimed the nutrition work had been originally given to his division, and in an act of highway robbery, Morton had removed it and given it to the Office of Experiment Stations. He saw this as egregious discourtesy; to allow the Office of Experiment Stations "to conduct scientific investigation is to sap the life blood of the other divisions." Wiley claimed that, by right of legislation and seniority, the old Divisions of Chemistry, Entomology, and Botany had priority. The right of research remained in these divisions.

Wiley did not question Wilson's intentions, but warned him that a precedent was being set for "when a scientific Sampson in the desperate exercise of a futile strength, may gather in his arms the pillars of the agricultural Temple and end his career by its destruction."[50]

Wilson, frustrated with the continual problems Wiley created with the other bureau chiefs, said of Wiley, "If anybody here gets too big for his trousers, we shall have to give him the privilege of going where trousers of larger dimensions are furnished."[51]

Nevertheless, food adulteration concerned Wilson because he thought it damaged the reputation of U.S. agricultural products, which would diminish exports. He encouraged Wiley to investigate food adulteration, but he did not want the reputations of U.S. products damaged by excessive claims.[52]

The effect on American exports of the embalmed meat scandal, which occurred after the Spanish-American War, concerned Wilson more than did the conditions of the soldiers. He worried that the three official investigations of the charges were inflaming European opinion against U.S. meats, so he began his own investigation with the objective of clearing the good name of U.S. meats. Wiley played a significant role in the investigation. He obtained canned meats from the open market and analyzed them. His findings met Wilson's hopes; Wiley testified that he found no samples in poor condition

50. Wiley to Secretary of Agriculture, April 19, 1897; Wiley to Secretary of Agriculture, "Memorandum Relating to Conference Between Dr. H. W. Wiley and Doctors Atwater and True," June 19, 1897; WP, box 5.

51. Hoing, *James Wilson*, 101–2. The quotation is from a letter in the Wilson papers to John Myers, March 15, 1899.

52. Hoing, *James Wilson* 60.

and no trace of any preservatives, except a small amount of saltpeter in corned and luncheon meat.[53]

Secretary Wilson wrote to his brother William, who lived in Chicago and was connected to the meat packers, that the report did not contain all of the evidence: Wilson had gone out of his way to make U.S. meats look as good as possible. The degree to which Wiley knowingly participated in this with the secretary is not known, but there was nothing in his testimony or later in the portion of Bulletin 13 on preserved meats, published in 1902, that challenged Wilson's public position.[54]

For whatever reason, Wiley emerged after the investigations of preserved meats on much better terms than he had been in 1897. After his initial attempts to influence the secretary to adopt his position on the role his division should play in the scientific work of the department, Wiley devoted more of his time to his personal and business affairs.[55]

In 1901, things improved somewhat for the Division of Chemistry. It was raised to bureau status in 1901 and it received new assignments. But the improvements were more superficial than real. Wiley wrote to Secretary Wilson in July, saying, "for reasons not necessary to discuss . . ." the Bureau of Chemistry's appropriation had not been increased since Wilson had taken charge, while "[all] the other bureaus and divisions have grown steadily in their appropriations."[56]

Convinced that Wilson tacitly supported his cause, Wiley sought outside support. He wrote professor N. S. Shaler, dean of the Lawrence Scientific School at Harvard University, pleading for support. He outlined the problem, saying, ". . . there is a tendency in the Department to establish independent chemical and physical laboratories for each of the bureaus and divisions. This tendency is opposed by the secretary who believes that all work should be concentrated under one direction. The influences which are brought to bear upon him, however, for the establishment of the separate laboratories are very strong, and gradually these laboratories are gaining a foothold."

He went on to explain that there were now three new, separate laboratories. Besides the older ones in the Bureaus of Chemistry and Animal Industry, there were now laboratories in the Office of Experiment Stations, the Bureau of Plant Industry, and the Bureau of Soils. The Bureau of Animal Industry was expanding beyond its original assignment and had recently taken the analysis of dairy products from the Bureau of Chemistry. Wiley claimed that "The avowed object is to break up the Bureau of Chemistry and to distribute it

53. Hoing, *James Wilson*, 59–61; Anderson, *Health*, 123; Senate Document 141, 56th Cong., 2d. sess.; for the story of the embalmed meat scandal, see Margaret Leech, *In The Days of McKinley* (New York: Harper Brothers, 1959).

54. Hoing, *James Wilson*, 60–61. Anderson, *Health*, 128.

55. Boxes 6–8 of the WP contain detailed information on Wiley's activities outside the department. Also see Anderson, *Health*, chap. 6.

56. Wiley to Secretary of Agriculture, July 30, 1901; WP, box 7.

piece by piece in other quarters. The bureau seems to be a veritable Gaul to some of these men and three, at least, are determined to divide it into three parts, if not more, thus out Caesaring Caesar."[57]

Wiley realized that he needed more than tacit support from the secretary. He needed to have Congress assign duties to the Bureau of Chemistry. He received permission from Secretary Wilson to take his case directly to Congressman James Wadsworth, the chairman of the Agricultural Committee. He met with Wadsworth and had some success. Besides increasing Wiley's salary, the Agriculture Committee passed a resolution that all chemical work in the department should be under the direction of the Bureau of Chemistry. However, the resolution was later rescinded in order to preserve peace in the department.[58]

Wiley's attempts to obtain outside support for the preeminence of his bureau were only mildly successful. The tides were against him. His weak strategic position is evidenced in his dispute with the Bureau of Soils. When the bureau published Bulletin 22, which Wiley believed to be scientifically unsound, Wiley enlisted Eugene W. Hilgard of the University of California, to criticize the Bulletin in *Science*.[59] Even criticism by a world renowned soil scientist in a respected publication could not arouse public opinion or convince those in power. Wiley's efforts produced a minor brouhaha, but no tangible results.[60]

Nevertheless, Wiley continued to fight for his conception of chemistry as the leading science in agriculture. He presented his position to the Committee on Organization of Government Scientific Work, formed in March, 1903, to improve efficiency. B. T. Galloway, in a memorandum to the committee, challenged Wiley, saying the old organization around a discipline had worked in the past, but that it was "now antiquated." In response to Wiley's claim that the Bureau of Chemistry would do better scientific work, Galloway wrote, "Now as a matter of fact, the average analytical chemist knows little about the chemical problems which confront physiologists and pathologists and could care less, and even then if work submitted to him were done properly it would be only in the most perfunctory and unsatisfactory manner . . . . When it is a question of ordinary routine analyses, which any chemist can perform, they are always glad to turn the matter over to the Bureau of Chemistry."

57. Wiley to N. S. Shaler, January 7, 1902, WP, box 7; also see Wiley to E. W. Hilgard, February 15, 1902, WP, box 7.

58. Wiley to Clifford Richardson, January 6, 1902; Wiley to James Wadsworth, December 27, 1901, and January 30, 1902; WP, box 7. Wiley to E. W. Hilgard, November 3, 1903, WP, box 8.

59. Anderson, *Health*, 108–9. Wiley to E. W. Hilgard, November 3, 1903, WP, box 8. Hilgard, as head of Experiment Stations in California, had his own disputes with the Department of Agriculture. See Ronald L. Nye, "Federal vs. State Agricultural Research Policy: The Case of California's Tulare Experiment Station, 1889–1909," *Agricultural History* 57 (October, 1983): 436–49.

60. See Anderson, *Health*, 108–12.

To Galloway, the whole dispute seemed like a tempest in a teapot. The work done in the Bureau of Chemistry "should be on problems, the same as in the other great Bureaus of the Department." He closed with a piece of advice for the Bureau of Chemistry:

> There is an imminent field for such a Bureau in the single item of the consideration of the multitudinous and constantly increasing adulterations of food products. There is enough work in this single line to keep 100 men employed. This would be putting the Bureau on specific problems rather than confining it to one narrow method and would do much to increase its usefulness.[61]

Galloway's opinion carried the day. The committee recommended to President Roosevelt that the the Road Material Lab in the Bureau of Chemistry be transferred to a new Road Division in the Geological Survey, that the Dendro Chemistry Lab be transferred to the Forest Service, and that the Soil Analysis Lab be transferred to the Bureau of Soils.[62]

Wiley would make similar arguments in 1905 to the Keep Commission, but his arguments had little effect on the trend toward problem-oriented bureaus. Gifford Pinchot later wrote that Wiley's idea to centralize chemistry was "about as reasonable as to confine all typewriting in a single bureau."[63]

The one area where the Bureau of Chemistry went unchallenged by other chiefs in the Department of Agriculture was the examination of foods for adulteration. The Bureau of Chemistry had begun to publish investigations in Bulletin 13 in 1897. The bulletin established the bureau as experts in the area and as leaders in the battle to stop adulteration. As chief, Wiley had directed the research and had become increasingly interested in the subject. As interest in national legislation grew, Wiley's primary problem, as always, was to keep control within his bureau.

Charting a Successful Strategy

The National Food and Drug Congress met in 1898, thanks to the efforts of a Virginia farm journal editor, Alexander J. Wedderburn, who called together a group that included citizens, grocers, journalists, farmers, state officials, and chemists to discuss the need for legislation. Congress would soon split over

61. Galloway's memorandum, dated July 10, 1903, is in the Gifford Pinchot Papers, box 599 Manuscript Division, Library of Congress.

62. Pinchot Papers, July 17, 1903, box 602.

63. For information on the Keep Commission, see Pinchot Papers, boxes 598–603: see also Harold T. Pinkett, "The Keep Commission, 1905–1909: A Rooseveltian Effort for Administrative Reform," *Journal of American History* 47 (1965): 297–312. Forest Service, RG 75, entry 28, National Archives; Gifford Pinchot, *Breaking New Ground* (Washington, D.C.: Island Press, 1987), 311. For a summary of Wiley's view, see "Report of the Bureau of Chemistry for the period Begun July 1, 1897 and Ending June 30, 1905," WP, box 199.

how the bill should be administered. Wiley and his supporters wanted the administration to be in the Bureau of Chemistry. Wedderburn and others wanted a new organization set up with an appointed food commissioner in charge.[64]

Wiley, working with his old friend William Frear of Pennsylvania, quickly moved to isolate Wedderburn and insure that the administration of the bill would be in his hands. The battle Wiley would fight over the next several years would be to promote the passage of a bill and, at the same time, to insure the control would end up in the Bureau of Chemistry. In many ways, this was a life or death struggle for the Bureau of Chemistry. A new bureau headed by a food official would soon have followed the pattern established by the other bureaus in the Department of Agriculture in establishing its own laboratories.

Wiley was confronted with multiple struggles: against those who opposed any pure food legislation, against those who only wanted a law that would outlaw their competition or place a special tax on products they competed against, and, most important, against those who wanted a national law administered outside of the Bureau of Chemistry.

There were a number of episodes over who should administer the law. Some involved personal attacks on Wiley, some involved special interest groups that hoped to benefit from a new organization, and some originated from the legitimate belief that a new organization was the best way to administer the law.[65]

In 1902, the possibility that a law would pass seemed likely to Wiley. He was extremely concerned about the position the National Association of State Dairy and Food Departments, an organization of state officials who had organized in the hope of obtaining uniformity among state laws. Experienced in enforcing food laws, these officials were well aware of many of the shortcomings of various state statutes. They complained about stores that demanded they put out of business peddlers who sold products from carts or hand baskets. They recognized that many of the food laws were instruments of special interests rather than protection for the public. Many state officials thought the Department of Agriculture represented only the interests of agriculture, and advocated an independent, national agency that would represent the consumer, manufacturer, and distributor as well as the farmer.[66]

In January, 1903, officials of the association testified before Senator McCumber of South Dakota, one of the sponsors of the pure food bill during

---

64. Wiley, *Autobiography*, 214; Anderson, *Health*, 123; Wiley to William Frear, March 12 and 16, 1898, WP, box 5; Wiley to A. J. Wedderburn, March 20, 1899, WP, box 6.

65. Wiley to William Frear, March 12 and 16, 1898, WP, box 5; Wiley to F. N. Barrett, December 1, 1901; February 15, 1902; June 17, 1902; all WP, box 7.

66. See Herbert B. Meyers, ed. *Journal of the Proceedings of the National Association of State Dairy and Food Departments, 1898–1904* (Chicago: National Association of State Dairy and Food Departments, 1898–1904). Proceedings after 1904 were published in The National Food Journal.

that session. Wiley favored the McCumber bill, which would place authority for administration in the Bureau of Chemistry. The delegation was split, with R. M. Allen of Kentucky speaking for and Professor Hamilton of Pennsylvania against. Wiley wrote his supporters that Hamilton had made a poor impression and Allen had made a good one. The bill did not pass, however, and Wiley was not sure why. He did not think the opposition from the Association of Dairy and Food Departments was the reason, but it remained the only group in favor of a national law opposing the Hepburn and McCumber bill. Wiley hoped to change their position.[67]

Wiley knew the secretary of the organization, R. M. Allen of Kentucky. Allen was an employee of M. A. Scovell, an old friend and associate. Allen, looking for support to publish the Annual Proceedings of the association's convention, inquired of Wiley about possible support from the Department of Agriculture. Wiley told him it would require more cooperation on the food law from his association: ". . . cooperation in regard to food legislation has never yet been secured. If your officials would come into harness and work for the pure food law without insisting on another particular form of legislation the way would be clear."

Wiley went on to explain his position. "There is a great danger in organizing a separate bureau of a political or semi-political nature where the incumbent would would be tempted, as is the case in some states, to magnify the importance of his office by unnecessary prosecutions. . . . I believe that if your organization could be brought to the patronage of the secretary much could be done to unify those who are in favor of a pure food bill." It is not clear if Secretary Wilson had approved this offer of patronage, but Wiley was secure enough to make a similar offer to the president of the State Food and Dairy Association.[68]

Allen was sure he could get the backing of the Executive Committee, but suggested that Wiley attend the July convention in St. Paul, Minnesota, with as many supporters as possible. Wiley quickly picked up on the suggestion and began to organize a group of supporters to attend. He planned to have himself appointed as the official delegate of the Department of Agriculture, which would make him a voting member. Wiley was taking no chances; he was expecting a fight at the convention. Among the scheduled speakers was Henry C. Adams, the recently elected representative from Wisconsin, whom Wiley knew would oppose him.[69]

To counter the opposition, Wiley wrote detailed letters to supporters,

67. Wiley to M. N. Kline, January 26, 1903; Wiley to F. N. Barrett, June 17, 1902; Wiley to M. A. Scovell, January 23, 1903; Wiley to Len. M. Frailey, May 21, 1903; Wiley to William Frear, January 16, 1903; all WP, box 7.

68. Wiley to R. M. Allen, April 2, 1903; Wiley to J. W. Bailey, April 2, 1903; WP, box 8.

69. Wiley to R. M. Allen May 1, 1903; May 9, 1903; July 6, 1903; July 8, 1903; Wiley to F. N. Barrett, May 9, 1903; Wiley to Len. M. Frailey, May 21, 1903; Wiley to J. N. Hurty, May 23, 1903; Wiley to P. J. McCumber, May 23, 1903; Wiley to W. P. Hepburn, May 23, 1903; all WP, box 8.

outlining and numbering the arguments to bring the organization behind the McCumber bill. Among the arguments he suggested were: (1) the Department of Agriculture is already fully organized and equipped with machinery for enforcing the law; (2) establishment of a separate bureau would involve an additional expenditure of public money, both for official salaries and for the establishment of chemical laboratories; (3) the Secretary of Agriculture now has full authority and equipment to execute the food law; (4) under the Hepburn and McCumber bill it will be the intention of the department to cooperate with various state officials; (5) the Hepburn and McCumber bill has the support of all the great interests in the distribution, wholesaling, and retailing of food; and (6) Congress has already approved the administrative features. From the effort Wiley put into the convention, it is easy to see how much importance he attached to administering a pure food law himself.[70]

The convention wasted no time getting to the main issue. Congressman Adams spoke dramatically about the need for a national food law and he did not skirt the issue of administration. He called for a pure food commissioner to be appointed by the president and to serve under the general supervision of the Secretary of Agriculture. He said, it was "an executive position and the law should not be drawn that the incumbent of some other office must inherit this office." He went on to say that it was not an attack on Wiley personally; he recognized the great contribution the Bureau of Chemistry under Wiley had made to the cause of pure food.

However, he added, "A chemist might be the best man in the world for an executive office, but his scientific training, as a rule, develops him in other directions. The head of the pure food bureau will have under his control chemists, detectives, lawyers, and hundreds of agents all over the United States. It is a position for an active man of affairs rather than a scientist."

Wiley and his supporters were prepared. R. M. Allen spoke about the need for the law and the success of the Hepburn and McCumber bill in passing the House in the last session. Allen claimed that Congress would oppose the establishment of a new bureau, and that to insist on one would cause the failure of any food bill.

Wiley spoke next. He said that he would support any pure food bill that came before Congress, but that he favored the Hepburn and McCumber bill. He cautioned against changing the bill in any form, saying it was a compromise of many interests, and that to change it could cause opposition of groups now supporting the bill. He said that he did not care about the administrative features of the bill, but that Secretary of Agriculture Wilson did, and without Wilson's support there would be no chance of passing the bill. Wiley carefully played the role of the public servant who was above the political squabbles surrounding the future administration of a bill.

70. Wiley to William Frear, to M. A. Scovell, to Len. M. Frailey, to Morrison, all June 30, 1903, WP, box 8.

William Frear and M. A. Scovell spoke in support of the Hepburn and McCumber bill, but did not address the administrative features. L. M. Frailey, representing Campbell Preserve Company and the Association of Manufacturers and Distributors of Food Products, supported the passage of the Hepburn bill. However, he misstated one of the arguments Wiley had sent him, saying ". . . those who are called upon to enforce the law should have the least to say in regard to its making."

This caused an uproar among the the state food officials, who thought their expertise should be central to the framing of any food law. Wiley came to Frailey's defense, saying he believed that the words were meant to apply to the national law and, particularly, to himself, and he agreed with Frailey that it was not his job to tell Congress what bill to pass. Wiley, of course, had every intention of using all his influence to secure the bill he wanted.[71]

Many attending the convention were unaware of the significance of the debate over how a food law would be administered and wondered why so much time was being taken up on the issue. This attitude was reflected by R. J. Mauck, a state chemist from Ohio, who said, ". . . so far as the [administrative] details are concerned I know nothing of them and am not interested. If the Department of Agriculture wants the work, let them have it, if the Department of Commerce wants it, let them have it, but for God's sake, rather give it to the Department of Navy than not get it at all."

The convention did not unanimously support the Hepburn and McCumber bill. Instead they passed a resolution that left it to the Executive Committee to do what was advisable to them. Wiley's supporters dominated the Executive Committee, so that support for his position was assured.[72]

Wiley emerged from the the St. Paul convention triumphant. No organized group any longer opposed his version of a national food bill. Wiley believed the way was now clear for the passage of a national food law that would be administered by his bureau in the Department of Agriculture.

Summary and Conclusion

The triumph of the problem approach in the Department of Agriculture, fed by large appropriations for research, had signaled the end for the old system, in which the Bureau of Chemistry had been the premiere scientific agency. Wiley at first tried to use his bureau's expertise in chemical analysis to combat the new organization. This strategy failed, partly because of mediocre results with sugar production, partly because analytical chemistry was itself a declin-

71. Herbert B. Meyers, ed., *Journal of Proceedings of the Seventh Annual Convention of the State Dairy and Food Departments*, (Chicago: National Association of State Dairy and Food Departments, 1904), passim.

72. Herbert B. Meyers, ed., *Journal of Proceedings of the Seventh Annual Convention of the State Dairy and Food Departments*, passim.

ing profession, and partly because mere technical competence in a scientific field could not stimulate the imagination of the public and politicians sufficiently to create a constituency.

The examination of food for adulteration, and the setting of standards for testing and purity, held the possibility of avoiding these causes of strategic failure. Food analysis did not require a knowledge of engineering. Agricultural chemists could adequately examine food, and a national food law would increase the demand for and restore the prestige of their skill. Finally, ensuring the purity of food was an issue that could excite and attract a constituency.

Once Wiley devoted his entrepreneurial abilities to securing passage and administration of a pure food law, his career and his bureau blossomed. He became a nationally respected figure, the "father of pure food" in the United States.

Despite the success that followed, it is doubtful that Wiley ever consciously decided to build his bureau around a problem rather than a discipline. As late as 1905, he was still fighting to keep chemical analysis within his division. It was the competitive bureaucratic process that finally led him to crusade for pure food.

Changing competitive strategies did not gurarantee success. The passage of a national pure food law could insure the continuation of the Bureau of Chemistry as a significant part of the Department of Agriculture, but the establishment of a new bureau to administer such a law would be fatal to the Bureau of Chemistry. In order to prosper, the Bureau of Chemistry would have to administer the act, even if this involved the Bureau in regulatory activities far beyond its chemical expertise.

Initially, administrative control by the Bureau of Chemistry was opposed by a significant number of state food officials through the Association of State Dairy and Food Departments. Wiley, through careful planning, maneuvered the organization into supporting his position.

Having triumphed in this area, the way was clear to fight for the passage of a national pure food law. In the process, however, he made alliances and public statements that would result in new opposition to the passage and enforcement of a law. Wiley's competitive struggle to succeed within the bureaucracy was far from over.

CHAPTER 5

The Baseball Anomaly and Congressional Intent

Jerome Ellig

> I want to say parenthetically that I have never known, in my 35 years of experience, of as great a lobby that descended upon the House than the organized baseball, and football, lobby that waylaid—and I use the word 'waylaid' advisedly—the Members of Congress, during the days this bill was being considered. They came upon Washington like locusts. They were in every nook and cranny—baseball players, the owners, and their cohorts. Some day it might be well for somebody to stage an inquiry as to the operations of this huge lobby, the likes of which I have never seen in my life.
>
> —Representative Emmanuel Celler (D-N.Y.)

Organized baseball is the only professional sport enjoying a blanket exemption from antitrust prosecution, the result of a 1922 U.S. Supreme Court decision (*Federal Baseball Club of Baltimore v. National League* 1922). The court subsequently refused to grant similar immunity to other professional sports. This situation is known as the "baseball anomaly."[1] Judicial attitudes have embroiled league officials, players, and interested observers in a controversy over congressional intent for, though Congress has frequently taken up sports antitrust issues since 1950, it has enacted no comprehensive legislation either repealing baseball's exemption or extending it to other sports.

Debates over congressional intent usually focus on the stated intentions of legislators gleaned from statutory language, floor debates, committee hearings, and committee reports. Economic analysis of political behavior offers an alternative means of ascertaining congressional intent by interpreting legislative action as a response to political incentives. From this perspective, con-

I am indebted to Jack High, Bill Shughart, Bob Tollison, and members of the weekly Center for the Study of Market Processes seminar for comments on earlier drafts of this chapter.

1. Equally anomalous is the fact that organized baseball, alone among industries exempt from antitrust, is under the review of no federal, state, or local regulatory body.

gressional failure to alter organized baseball's differential antitrust treatment arises because its large number of teams and highly integrated structure give it a comparative advantage in political lobbying over other professional sports. As a result, an economic theory of regulation combined with attention to institutional detail yields a consistent explanation for what appear to be inconsistent federal policies.

Sports, Courts, and Congress

Organized baseball survived its first antitrust challenge before the Supreme Court in 1922.[2] In 1913, a group of wealthy promoters had organized the eight-team Federal League with plans to lure players from the two major and top minor leagues and claim major league status. The Federal League opened the 1914 season with franchises in Cleveland, Chicago, St. Louis, Pittsburgh, Indianapolis, Kansas City, Baltimore, and Buffalo. The Indianapolis team moved to Newark in 1915. The Federals faced major league competition in the first four cities and minor league competition in the rest.

The Federal League was an Indiana corporation owned by the individual team backers, each of whom served on its board of directors. Each owner's stock in the league, as well as his team's player contracts and stadium leases, were assigned back to the league as a pledge "for faithful performance of the obligations of its franchise" (*Federal Baseball Club of Baltimore* 1921, 79). According to its president, James Gilmore, "The majority vote of our entire board of managers gave us the right to do anything" (1921, 382).

The majority's desire to dissolve the league after 1915 provoked the famous suit in which the Supreme Court ruled that organized baseball is exempt from antitrust laws. By the winter of 1915, five of the six owners of solvent franchises decided to let organized baseball pay them more than $2 million to go out of business and drop an antitrust suit they had instituted against organized baseball (1921, 228–29). Several owners bought National or American League teams. Baltimore's owners received no compensation, and they sued both organized baseball and the rest of the Federal League for conspiring to put them out of business.

However, Justice Holmes's majority opinion held that baseball is not subject to the Sherman and Clayton Acts because it is not interstate commerce:

> The business is giving exhibitions of base-ball, which are purely state affairs. It is true that, in order to attain for these exhibitions the great popularity they have achieved, competitions must be arranged between

2. For a thorough summary of the history of sports law, see Sobel 1977.

> clubs from different cities and States. But the fact that in order to give the exhibitions the Leagues must induce free people to cross state lines and pay for their doing so is not enough to change the character of the business. (*Federal Baseball Club of Baltimore* 1922, 208–9)

Although the Supreme Court subsequently liberalized its definition of interstate commerce, it continued to uphold the baseball exemption in *Toolson v. New York Yankees* (1953) and *Flood v. Kuhn* (1972). The justices insisted that Congress, not the courts, should exercise authority in this area. The majority opinion's citation of the Court of Appeals in *Flood* illustrates judicial attitudes toward baseball: "If baseball is to be damaged by statutory regulation, let the congressman face his constituents the next November and also face the consequences of his baseball voting record" (1972, 268: citing 443 F.2d 264). This argument curiously overlooked the fact that the courts, not Congress, were the original source of baseball's exemption.

The Supreme Court refused to grant similar immunity to other sports. Since football, basketball, and hockey were involved in few significant antitrust cases until the 1950s, baseball's immunity was already regarded as an aberration when their day in court came. The first major sport to cite *Federal Baseball Club of Baltimore* in its defense before the Supreme Court was boxing, in 1955. Noting that television, radio, and movie receipts comprised 25 percent of defendants' business, the justices decided that prize fighting was interstate commerce (*United States v. International Boxing Club* 1955). Two years later, the court ruled that professional football, too, is subject to antitrust, stating that it upheld *Federal Baseball* in *Toolson* only because "it was concluded that more harm would be done in overruling *Federal Baseball* than in upholding a ruling which at best was of dubious validity" (*Radovich v. NFL* 1957, 450). "As long as Congress continues to acquiesce," the majority said, "we should adhere to—but not extend—the interpretation of the Act made in those cases" (1957, 451). From *Radovich* onward, it was clear that only baseball would enjoy a judicial exemption.

Legislators' failure to revoke baseball's exemption could be interpreted as acquiescence; courts have accepted this kind of interpretation in the past when faced with other issues (Sobel 1977, 67–68). On the other hand, Congress may simply regard other matters as more pressing (Noll 1982, 355).

However, Congress has enacted sports antitrust legislation from time to time. Baseball, football, basketball, and hockey have an express exemption allowing leagues to pool broadcasting rights for sale to networks. Congress passed legislation exempting the merger of the National and American Football Leagues in 1966, but it refused a similar request by the National and American Basketball Associations five years later. Legislation applying the antitrust laws to all sports, but exempting certain practices believed (by the bills' supporters) to be essential for the functioning of the league, has passed each house of Congress once. Significantly, no congressional committee has ever approved legislation merely repealing baseball's exemption.[3]

In light of these facts, economic analysis suggests that the extent and content of sports legislation at any given time depends on the particular political incentives Congress faces. In preserving the baseball anomaly, Congress may well be responding to differential effective demands from various segments of the sports industry. From a public choice perspective, the search for congressional intent thus becomes a search for the source of these differential demands rather than a search for the stated purposes of public sports policy.

The Sports Industry and Congressional Motivation

A useful beginning point for an interest-group theory of sports policy is the economic theory of regulation pioneered by Stigler (1971) and expanded upon by Peltzman (1976), McCormick and Tollison (1981), and Becker (1983). Becker presents a general equilibrium model of politics in which taxes and subsidies are a function of various interests groups' ability to produce political pressure. The aspects of this approach that are relevant to an analysis of the baseball anomaly can be summarized by a simple model of the market for wealth transfers (fig. 1) based on that developed by McCormick and Tollison.

Curve *D* is one coalition's demand curve for legislation, regulation, or some other form of wealth transfer. It represents the *net* benefit the group derives from government activity after deducting information and organization costs the group incurs in seeking legislation. These costs include those of discovering the effects of legislation, identifying political coalition partners, overcoming free-rider problems (McCormick and Tollison 1981, 16–17; Olson 1982, 39; Becker 1983, 377), and negotiating political alliances (cf. Peltzman 1976, 213; Buchanan and Tullock 1962, chap. 8). For ease of analysis, it is also assumed that groups demanding government action compensate the government for any administrative costs.

The government's supply-of-wealth-transfers curve, *S*, represents the opportunity cost to the government of acceding to an interest group's request. Specifically, it indicates the amount opposition interest groups are willing to spend to prevent passage. Like the demand curve, the supply curve indicates what interest groups will pay *over and above* their organization and information costs. If no interest groups organize on one side of an issue, either the

3. Maverick baseball executive Bill Veeck once commented, "With the Supreme Court beginning to look as if it may cop out on us at any time, baseball, which is no less alert to the Court's subversive tendencies than any hard-working Southern senator, has been pushing to get its exemption written into the law. And you can't blame us. After all, what faith can anyone have in a Supreme Court that doesn't know a business when it sees one?" (Veeck and Linn 1965, 78–79). He also noted, "The Supreme Court exemption was based upon its considered opinion that baseball is a sport rather than an entertainment, which would indicate that the Justices had done their research at Griffith Stadium" (81).

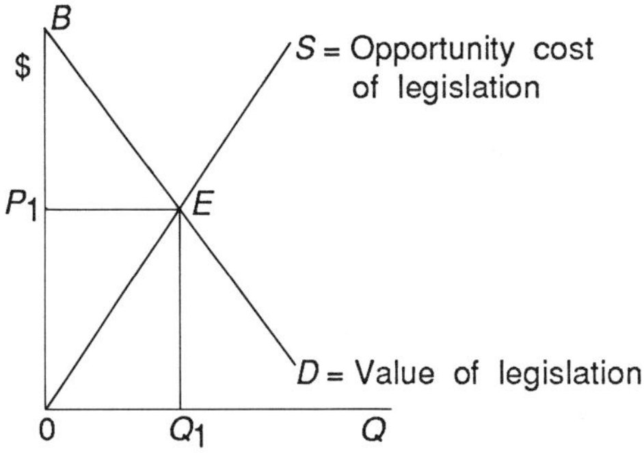

Fig. 1. A market for legislation

demand for legislation is zero at any price or the opportunity cost of legislation is zero at any quantity.

In figure 1, quantity Q_1 of legislation is enacted at "price" P_1. Politicians receive the area $0P_1EQ_1$ in cash or, more likely, in kind (votes, campaign volunteers, etc.), and "consumer surplus" is P_1BE. Opposition groups submit to a transfer of $0EQ_1$ because they would have to pay more than that amount to prevent passage of Q_1.

Since the curves represent what coalitions are willing to pay over and above what are here called organization and information costs, changes in these costs can lead to changes in the amount of legislation enacted. Figure 2 shows the effects of a cost-reducing change in political technology equally available to all coalitions. Such a change raises the net value of legislation to its proponents, shifting the demand curve out to D'. However, it also increases the amount the opposition is willing to pay to prevent legislation, thus increasing politicians' opportunity cost of legislation to S'. In this particular example, the change does not alter the amount of government activity but does increase politicians' share of the benefits.

The main implication relevant here, though, is that groups with lower information and organization costs will, ceteris paribus, demand more favorable legislation and/or supply more opposition to unfavorable legislation. A large number of factors can influence these costs. The sheer size of interest groups is, of course, one consideration: the smaller the group, the lower the costs of organization (Olson 1982, 41). Another important factor is the extent to which coalitions have already incurred some of the costs of organization for reasons unrelated to political activity. McCormick and Tollison state the point especially succinctly.

> . . . [O]rganization costs . . . are like start-up costs. Once they are borne, they do not affect marginal costs (though if the "firm" is to survive, they must be borne over time). Groups that have already borne these start-up costs, for reasons unrelated to lobbying, will have a com-

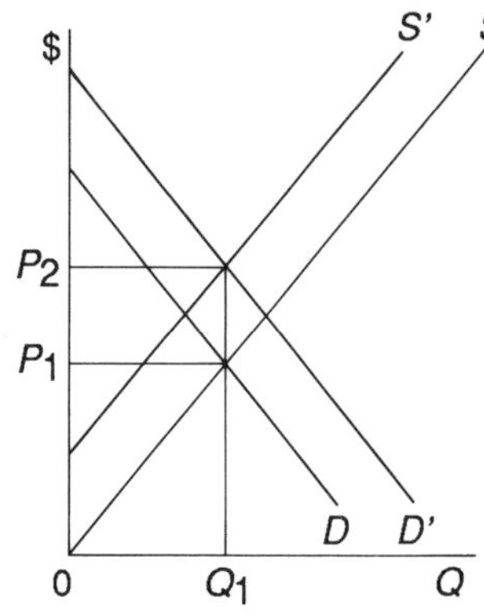

Fig. 2. Uniform reduction in lobbying costs

> parative advantage in seeking transfers and will therefore be more successful in producing transfers as a result. This is simply a point about jointness in production. Some groups will be able to produce political lobbying as a by-product of some other function, thereby avoiding start-up costs for lobbying. There are many examples of such groups in the economy, among which are labor unions, trade associations, corporations, and the like. (1981, 17)

Another group that could produce lobbying as a "by-product of some other function" is a vertically or laterally integrated industry. There are, of course, many economic explanations of vertical integration, many of which have been inspired by the work of Coase (1937). There can be degrees of integration that give one agent the right to direct another agent's activities to a greater or lesser extent. Perhaps it is terminologically more convenient to say that members of an industry who have strong institutional ties but are not jointly organized as a single firm share a common "governance structure" in Williamson's (1985) sense. Entities that share a common governance structure for economic reasons may also experience lower lobbying costs for reasons analogous to those responsible for their lower economic transaction costs.[4]

A vertically or laterally integrated industry may be able to take advantage of economies of scale in the analysis of pending legislation. At least, different elements of the political coalition have little incentive to conceal information from each other, since they need not strive for advantage over one another in assembling a legislative package. Coalition partners are already identified.

4. Of course, if the degree of vertical or lateral integration influences political success, it should be shaped by political as well as economic factors. This endogeneity problem, however, is outside the scope of this chapter. It is taken as given that the industrial structures of various sports take the forms they do primarily for economic reasons but, nevertheless, have political effects.

Common control of several stages of a production process attenuates free-rider problems and replaces conflict over political goals with agreement. It prevents, or at least sharply curtails, "holdout problems" associated with bilateral monopoly in the formation of political coalitions as well as in ordinary economic transactions.

More generally, common control over several components of a potential political coalition may make possible political cooperation that would not otherwise be feasible because the costs of writing and enforcing joint lobbying contracts would be prohibitive. The political advantages of vertical integration thus underscore Williamson's assertions about the importance of organizational forms. A common governance structure lowers an industry's lobbying costs, raising the net amount it will be willing to pay the government to enact or prevent any given piece of legislation.

According to this theory, then, those sports that share common governance structures should be more successful at obtaining favorable legislation and avoiding unfavorable legislation, ceteris paribus. Casual observation suggests that this view has some validity. Organized baseball is thoroughly integrated backward into player development, whereas football and basketball rely on the colleges for their talent. Former NFL commissioner Bert Bell is even on record stating that football did not want minor league affiliations. "I think if a kid can't make it in eight weeks' tryout after he has been to college," he said, "he ought to get a job elsewhere" (House Antitrust Subcommittee 1957, 2529). Hockey also operates minor leagues, but historically there have been relatively few minor league hockey teams and a substantial proportion have been located in Canada. Therefore, one would generally expect organized baseball to do better in obtaining favorable treatment, or avoiding unfavorable treatment, when Congress turns its attention to sports law.

Organized Baseball's Governance Structure

Each major league baseball team operates a large "farm system" of minor league teams. Some of these are wholly owned subsidiaries of major league clubs, but many are owned by local executives in small and medium-sized towns. These latter teams have "working agreements" under which major league clubs agree to provide them with players to be trained and tested for the majors.

The minor leagues are as old as baseball itself, since they are essentially made up of all of the leagues that have declined to call themselves "major league." Table 1 lists the number of minor leagues at the start and finish of each baseball season between 1903 and 1949. In 1903, the National and American leagues ceased their fierce economic competition and established the basic structure of organized baseball as it exists today.

In 1951, the first year in which Congress held hearings on professional sports legislation, there were 326 minor league clubs, the vast majority of

TABLE 1. Number of Minor Leagues, 1903–49

Year	Start of Season	End of Season	Failed During Season
1903	19	19	0
1904	23	23	0
1905	28	27	1
1906	28	27	1
1907	36	34	2
1908	32	32	0
1909	36	31	5
1910	46	42	4
1911	43	39	4
1912	48	36	12
1913	43	40	3
1914	40	37	3
1915	30	23	7
1916	24	22	2
1917	40	28	12
1918	9	1	8
1919	15	13	2
1920	22	21	1
1921	26	26	0
1922	30	29	1
1923	31	28	3
1924	28	25	3
1925	24	24	0
1926	28	28	0
1927	24	24	0
1928	25	23	2
1929	25	24	1
1930	23	21	2
1931	19	16	3
1932	18	13	5
1933	14	14	0
1934	19	19	0
1935	21	21	0
1936	26	26	0
1937	37	37	0
1938	37	37	0
1939	41	41	0
1940	43	43	0
1941	41	41	0
1942	31	26	5
1943	10	9	1
1944	10	10	0
1945	12	12	0
1946	42	42	0
1947	52	52	0
1948	58	55	3
1949	59	59	0

Source: Craig 1950, 66–77.

TABLE 2. Number and Ownership of Minor League Clubs, 1951

League Classification	Owned	Working Agreement	Independent	Total
Open	2	0	6	8
AAA	12	2	2	16
AA	8	6	2	16
A	12	11	9	32
B	15	22	25	62
C	6	31	45	82
D	12	44	54	110
Total	67	116	143	326

Source: House Antitrust Subcommittee 1957, 371.

which were located in the United States. Table 2 shows the number and ownership of minor league clubs in each classification in 1951. Minor league classifications (Open, AAA, etc.) are listed in descending order of their proximity to major league status. As table 3 indicates, the number of clubs had fallen to 151 by 1960, still a respectable number. Twenty-five percent fewer clubs existed in 1976 (table 4).

Agreements between all major and minor leagues obligate each club to respect other leagues' player eligibility rules and territorial rights in relation to both broadcasting and physical location of a team's home games (House Subcommittee on Monopoly Power 1952a, 1157–58). Elaborate rules govern the transfer of players from minor league rosters to major league teams or teams in higher minor league classifications. When a major league club moves into minor league territory, it must compensate both the displaced minor league club and the minor league itself. Minor league clubs must also compensate each other for an invasion of territory. Organized baseball has created a quasi-judicial structure, with the commissioner at its head, in order to enforce rules and settle disputes between separate clubs and separate leagues.[5] Other sports' experience suggests that many elements of this web of agreements and enforcement mechanisms could be challenged if baseball's antitrust exemption were removed.

5. When the Brooklyn Dodgers moved to Los Angeles in 1957, for example, they had to compensate the Pacific Coast League and the league's Los Angeles club. The league's Hollywood club had already been paying Los Angeles a percentage of its gross receipts as compensation for moving into its territory (House Subcommittee on Monopoly Power 1952a, 705). And when the Pacific Coast League, frustrated in its attempt to attain major league status, discussed seceding from organized baseball, the Hollywood club voiced opposition out of fear that a major league club would then be able to move into the Los Angeles metropolitan area without compensating anyone (1952a, 412). The records of congressional hearings, meanwhile, are replete with correspondence regarding disputes between players, owners, and leagues, all of which were ultimately settled by the commissioner or by agreement.

TABLE 3. Number and Ownership of Minor League Clubs, 1960

League Classification	Owned	Working Agreement	Independent	Total
AAA	8	15	1	24
AA	1	13	6[a]	20
A	6	8	0	14
B	0	18	2	20
C	0	20	0	20
D	1	33	14[b]	48
Rookie	5	0	0	5
Total	21	107	23	151

Source: Senate Antitrust Subcommittee 1960, 94.
[a] Includes five clubs in Mexican League.
[b] Includes six clubs in Mexico Center League.

Although the minor leagues were once financially independent, by the 1940s, they received ever-increasing subsidies from the majors. In the early 1950s, for example, the New York Yankees annually spent one-third of their budget, $1 million, on player development—their farm system ("Monopsony" 1953, 597). Senator Ed Johnson (D-Colo.), president of the Western League and perennial sponsor of sports antitrust exemption legislation, stated (in 1952) that the majority of clubs in his league could not afford to operate in the absence of subsidies (House Subcommittee on Monopoly Power 1952a, 380). Ninety percent of minor league clubs were reported to have operated in the red in 1957 (Senate Antitrust Subcommittee 1958, 209).

In the mid-1960s, each major league club explicitly agreed to subsidize five minor league clubs. (Voigt 1983, 280). Former Baseball Commissioner Bowie Kuhn estimated that minor league costs were over 25.0 percent of professional baseball's gross revenues between 1963 and 1967 and 21.8 percent between 1969 and 1973 (Senate Antitrust Subcommittee 1972, 184; House Select Committee 1976, pt. 2, 354). In 1980, major league subsidies to

TABLE 4. Number and Ownership of Minor League Clubs, 1976

League Classification	Owned	Working Agreement	Independent	Total
AAA	3	21	0	24
AA	4	19	1	24
A	4	37	4	45
Rookie	18	0	0	18
Total	29	78	5	11

Source: House Select Committee on Professional Sports 1976, 346–49.
Note: Figures do not include Mexican League (sixteen clubs), Mexican Center League (six clubs), Mexican Pacific League (eight clubs), and Gulf States League (six clubs).

the minors amounted to $40 million (House Subcommittee on Monopolies 1984, 427).

With financial assistance comes control. Baseball executive Bill Veeck complained, in the mid-1960s, that "company men" had taken over the minor leagues, removing "all the elements of free enterprise—initiative, imagination, and brigandry—that had made the minors great" (Veeck and Linn 1965, 175). Outgoing Baseball Commissioner A. B. "Happy" Chandler told a congressional subcommittee in 1951 that it would make no difference if minor league clubs were given a voice in the selection of the commissioner because the major leagues controlled them through working agreements anyway.[6] Senator Johnson described the majors' control in the following manner.

> Now, when the National Association of Professional Baseball Clubs [an organization made up of all the minor leagues] have an annual meeting, all the proposals that are to come before that meeting are submitted to the managers of the various clubs making up the league, and these managers go to the majors and say, well, how should I vote on this proposal? How should I vote on that proposal?
>
> In this way the major leagues completely dominate them. (Senate Antitrust Subcommittee 1958, 256)

Two years later, Branch Rickey, father of the farm system and an officer of a proposed third major league, said of the minors, "Their associations have been so long with the kindnesses and largesse from the major leagues that they are within the sphere of it. They couldn't imagine what will happen if they got outside it" (Senate Antitrust Subcommittee 1960, 69). As if to confirm Rickey's statement, one minor league president wrote to the National Association of Professional Baseball Leagues that 85 percent of minor league franchises were locally owned and that such owners had "neither the tools nor the inclination" to locate players for their own teams to take the place of those supplied by the majors (Senate Antitrust Subcommittee 1960, 136–37).

Economic interdependence of the major and minor leagues, coupled with a common governance structure, gives organized baseball a potent lobbying force. Many minor league clubs are owned by prominent local citizens whose political and financial support few aspirants to public office would intentionally ignore. In 1952, for instance, the vast majority of minor league officers and directors were owners of small businesses, business executives, baseball executives, doctors, lawyers, and similar professionals (House Subcommittee on Monopoly Power 1952b, 3). Markham and Teplitz (1981, 40)

6. Veeck, for his part, compared minor league meetings to an attempt to revive burlesque: "It isn't really a performance, it's a reproduction of a performance. It has no life of its own, no relevancy. Minor league meetings have been irrelevant for about twenty years" (Veeck and Linn 1965, 174).

report that, in the late 1970s, minor league clubs were frequently run by local auto dealers, store owners, or other executives as sidelines to their more conventional enterprises. Senator Johnson summarized the "civic pride" aspects of minor league ownership:

> Many chambers of commerce and public officials pass the hat and sponsor public drives to sell baseball attendance tickets to keep their minor league ball clubs operating. Very few of the minor league officials draw a salary. They are the men about town, the bankers and the preachers and the lawyers. For the good of the community they get out and they support minor league baseball . . . it is a business in which the communities have a tremendous interest and do take part in its promotion. (Senate Antitrust Subcommittee 1958, 230)

Some owners or league officials, like Colorado's Senator Johnson, may themselves serve in Congress. Representative Frank Horton (R-N.Y.), another frequent sponsor of sports antitrust exemption bills, spent eight-and-a-half years as president of the International League's Rochester Red Wings before running for Congress (Senate Antitrust Subcommittee 1972, 159–60). Representative Sid Herlong, who testified in favor of sports antitrust exemption legislation in 1951, was a former president of the Class D Florida State League (House Subcommittee on Monopoly Power 1952b, 2). Among legislators with less formal ties to organized baseball, future Ohio Senator John Bricker caught for the 1914 Ohio State University baseball team, whose pitchers included future NAPBL President George Trautman (Senate Antitrust Subcommittee 1958, 494). Trautman and other baseball officials lobbied Bricker and other legislators for favorable antitrust treatment in the late 1950s and early 1960s.

Some minor league clubs have been owned, in whole or in part, by local fans, a ready-made voting bloc. Representative Herlong, describing the financial plight of the Florida State League, noted,

> [A]nd if you look at the financial statements of these teams you will find some very interesting ways of keeping books. They will go out and sell, say, $10,000 worth of stock in the ball club to the fans. In other words, you are a part owner in the ball club. They put that $10,000 down as income because the man expects to lose it. So that is part of their income. It is a very interesting way of keeping books. (House Subcommittee on Monopoly Power 1952a, 453)

In 1957, the Indianapolis (AAA) club was owned by 6,672 shareholders, none of whom owned more than 100 shares. Buffalo (AAA) had also sold 182,000 one-dollar shares to 2,657 shareholders (House Antitrust Subcommittee 1957, 193–94). Occasionally, fans even took up a collection to reward a player who hit a game-winning home run (House Subcommittee on Monopoly Power 1952a, 452). It is probably safe to surmise that such fans may also devote more than the ordinary amount of resources to monitoring and lobbying their members of congress and senators when there is legislation under consideration that threatens baseball's antitrust exemption.

Lobbying Costs and Antitrust Asymmetries

Baseball enjoys an advantage over other sports in obtaining favorable legislation and avoiding unfavorable legislation because economic integration lowers its lobbying costs. The common governance structure lowers the cost of negotiating and enforcing political alliances between major leagues and minor leagues. In other sports, negotiating and enforcement costs are likely to be higher because the other professional leagues and the National Collegiate Athletic Association (NCAA) are legally separate entities.

The three major economic practices of professional sports leagues whose legality has been regarded as questionable under the antitrust laws are "reserve" rules and other restrictions by which clubs divide up the labor market, geographical market division, and restrictions on individual clubs' right to broadcast. Whether one believes these practices to be monopolistic or efficiency enhancing, there is no doubt that both major and minor league baseball benefited from them. The reserve system, which effectively gave a club that owned a player's contract an annual option to renew it, was the result of agreements among major and minor leagues, as were territorial restrictions. In addition, because the major leagues had an economic interest in the survival of at least some minor league baseball, they could arrange a joint, profit-maximizing mix of broadcasting restrictions and direct subsidies.

Professional football and basketball, of course, likewise have benefited from their own restrictive labor policies and sets of territorial rights. Geographical territorial rights are more or less a moot point for colleges, but the National Collegiate Athletic Association also has rules that limit compensation to student-athletes (Koch 1983). These rules have generally been regarded as immune from antitrust challenge because their stated purpose is to preserve the amateur status of collegiate athletics. Until 1984, the same was true of NCAA rules that prevented colleges from negotiating their own national broadcasting contracts (*NCAA v. Board of Regents* 1984).

The fact that collegiate athletics is officially amateur also serves to protect from antitrust professional leagues' decisions to refrain from broadcasting in competition with college programs. Since colleges are the main source of professional football and basketball players, the pros have the same kind of interest in their financial well-being that major league baseball has in that of the minors. Antitrust seems to pose no barrier to a package of professional broadcasting restraints and subsidization that jointly maximizes profits of colleges and professionals.[7]

Other professional practices that could be threatened by antitrust, however, seem to confer no positive benefits on the colleges and may actually harm them. When professional teams agree not to sign college athletes until graduation, labor market practices that hold down professional salaries make it more difficult for all colleges to attract quality athletes away from more profitable alternatives. Empirically, it does seem to be the case that "reserve" rules and drafting procedures help hold down professional salaries by curbing competition for players.[8] If territorial rights give rise to some type of efficiency, they make the professional leagues' product more competitive with that of the colleges by lowering its cost. The colleges, therefore, have little incentive to lobby for antitrust exemptions that benefit only professional leagues.[9]

The professional leagues could compensate the colleges for any damage and, perhaps, even offer them inducements to lobby for antitrust exemptions. Such payoffs could take at least four possible forms: direct subsidies, broadcasting restrictions over and above those necessary to preserve collegiate programs as training grounds, agreements not to sign college players until graduation, or other arrangements that lower colleges' player costs by restraining professional competition with colleges for players. But in contrast to the situation in baseball, such a contract for a political alliance would likely be unenforceable. After the subsidy, broadcast, or player agreement is publicly in place, the NCAA could simply renege on its commitment and lobby against the professionals' antitrust exemptions if it believes placing them under antitrust will benefit colleges on net. The professionals could then discontinue their part of the bargain, but such a threat is not likely credible because it would be publicly perceived as retaliation for the colleges' political position.[10] Even if an enforceable contract could be written, it would probably be at a higher cost than if the professional leagues and collegiate programs were under common ownership, for colleges have an ex-ante incentive to invest resources in strategic lobbying against antitrust in order to maximize the payment the professionals would be willing to offer.

7. It would appear that joint profit maximization in football and basketball requires a relatively greater amount of college broadcasting. College broadcasts thus displace some professional broadcasts; the fact that colleges train players at no charge to the professionals suggests that this is their way of compensating them for forgone broadcasting revenues.

8. See, for instance, Rottenberg 1966; Canes 1974; Scully 1974; Hunt and Lewis 1976; Medoff 1976; Holahan 1978; Sommers and Quinton 1982; Hill and Spellman 1983; Raimondo 1983.

9. Likewise, professional leagues would be better off if colleges attracted better athletes by permitting them to receive overt compensation for their performance.

10. In addition, the Federal Sports Broadcasting Act of 1961 prevents professional football from broadcasting in competition with college football.

The potential for opportunism is a direct result of the fact that professional and college football and basketball lack a common governance structure. If the two sports relied on minor leagues that were integrated with the major leagues, an antitrust exemption for professional sports would cover both majors and minors, protecting their common labor, territorial, and broadcasting practices, and removing the chance of opportunism. As it is, colleges' amateur status is a barrier to the creation of a more effective joint lobbying coalition.

This theory implies that certain patterns should be observed in various sports' lobbying efforts and elected representatives' response. One would expect major and minor league baseball to unite in support of antitrust exemptions. Colleges, on the other hand, are in a more ambiguous position relative to antitrust exemptions that cover only professional sports. If other opposition were roughly equal across sports, the structural differences between sports could explain their differential political success.

Congressional Testimony

Congressional hearings held between 1951 and 1985 provide a wealth of information on which private groups took which positions on sports antitrust issues.[11] Many of these hearings sought to evaluate proposed sports antitrust legislation, which was frequently introduced in response to major court decisions. Other events that have provoked hearings include football and basketball leagues' requests for antitrust exemptions shielding mergers in 1965 and 1972, the announcement of a proposed third major baseball league in 1959, the relocation of the Brooklyn Dodgers and New York Giants to the West Coast in 1958, and the Busch brewery's purchase of the St. Louis Cardinals in 1952.[12]

Major League Baseball

From the time of the first congressional baseball hearings in 1951, major league baseball quite naturally defended its antitrust exemption. In addition,

11. Johnson (1979) offers a summary of congressional activity up to 1978. The next hearings occurred in 1983–85 in response to a series of lawsuits surrounding the Oakland Raiders' move to Los Angeles.

12. The House of Representatives even established a Select Committee on Professional Sports in 1976, at the height of baseball's free agency turmoil and four years after the Washington Senators relocated to Arlington, Texas. John Y. Brown, former president of the American Basketball Association's executive committee, asked during one hearing, "Is the purpose of this hearing to explore all professional sports and problems as it relates to the fact . . . or it is to help get a team to Washington, or it is a multitude of different interests?" (House Select Committee on Professional Sports 1976, 459).

the majors frequently advocated similar exemptions for all professional team sports. Their position was and is remarkable for more than thirty years of consistency.

As recently as 1984, the baseball commissioner, Bowie Kuhn, stated that organized baseball's preferred resolution of the antitrust anomaly was legislation granting a blanket antitrust exemption to other sports (House Subcommittee on Monopolies 1984, 429). Traditionally, however, baseball had also strongly supported legislation that would place all sports under the antitrust laws but exempt professional league practices relating to:

1. the equalization of playing strengths;
2. the reserve clause, draft rules, and other employment relations;
3. the assignment of geographical territories;
4. regulation of telecasts and broadcasts; and
5. actions taken to preserve public confidence in the integrity of the sport.

Exemptions for 4 became law for all sports in 1961 as the Federal Sports Broadcasting Act (Sobel 1977, 586).

Kuhn told a House committee in 1972 that a bill sponsored by Representative Horton embodying 1, 2, 3, and 5 "is certainly a fair effort to deal with the problem and to protect from antitrust application the essential sports practices of the business and of all these businesses" (House Antitrust Subcommittee 1972, 188). In so doing, he merely echoed what his predecessors, other league officials, and club owners had been telling Congress for years. Ford Frick, for instance, commissioner of baseball from 1951 until 1964, said, in 1959, that baseball favored limited exemption legislation because it would clearly exempt "peculiar sports practices" for other sports, protect baseball from future Supreme Court reversals, allow baseball to protect the minor leagues from major league broadcasts, and relieve him of the obligation to attend congressional hearings (Senate Antitrust Subcommittee 1959, 52–53).

Prior to passage of the broadcasting exemption in 1961, protection of minor league teams from the effects of major league broadcasts and telecasts into their territory was a particularly prominent theme in congressional baseball testimony. Major-minor league rule 1(d), adopted in 1946, prohibited a ballclub from broadcasting or telecasting its games from a station located within fifty miles of another club's ballpark on the day that club was playing a game at home. In 1949, the Department of Justice, at the urging of some broadcasters, threatened organized baseball with antitrust prosecution because of the rule (Senate Subcommittee on S. 1396 1953, 4–5; House Antitrust Subcommittee 1957, 140; Senate Antitrust Subcommittee 1958, 105). The department contended that baseball's exemption included only items 1, 2, 3, and 5 in the preceding list (Senate Antitrust Subcommittee 1958, 114–15). Furthermore, the head of the department's Antitrust Division refused to approve a plan under which major league clubs proposed to share broadcasting revenues with the minors (1958, 215).

Major league officials, such as Frick, regularly blamed their clubs' broadcasts for "60 to 75 percent" of the reduction of fan interest in the minor leagues (Senate Antitrust Subcommittee 1958, 186, and 1959, 57). Between 1949 and 1960, the number of minor leagues fell from 59 to 21, and the number of teams fell from 444 to 150 (Senate Antitrust Subcommittee 1960, 139). A statement by Larry MacPhail, president of the American League, is illustrative of the majors' attitude: "You cannot go to Kalamazoo, Michigan, and sell everybody in Kalamazoo on major-league baseball and make them Dodger fans and make them Detroit fans or Red Sox fans and expect to build up any interest in the Kalamazoo club" (House Subcommittee on Monopoly Power 1952a, 1061). Even C. Leo DeOrsey, a former director of the Washington Senators who felt baseball should have no antitrust exemption, believed that Congress should enact rule 1(d) into law (Senate Antitrust Subcommittee 1958, 459–60).

Minor League Baseball

The vast majority of the time, positions taken by minor league baseball on legislation were virtually indistinguishable from those of the majors. Majors and minors both had dissident owners and former officials, but at any given time the twin baseball associations moved in lockstep. Over the years, legislators and committees regularly received wires and letters from minor league officials and owners supporting organized baseball's position. (See, for instance, Senate Subcommittee on S. 1396 1953, 194–204; Senate Antitrust Subcommittee 1958, 747 and 791; Senate Committee on the Judiciary 1960, 24.)

Like the majors, the minors vigorously supported the reserve system, which effectively prohibited players from negotiating with more than one club for their services. Representative Herlong stated in 1952 that "If a minor league club cannot keep some strings on their players after the season is over . . . it will be just a short time before minor league baseball disappears . . . (House Subcommittee on Monopoly Power 1952a, 454). Senator Johnson seconded his sentiments, asserting that his major concerns in sponsoring limited exemption legislation were preservation of the reserve system and territorial rights (House Subcommittee on Monopoly Power 1952, 380–88). George Sisler, president of the Class AAA International League, predicted in 1976 that the minor leagues would perish in the absence of the reserve system (House Select Committee on Professional Sports 1976, pt. 1, 312). He requested legislation that would affirm the legality of the reserve clause, protect minor leagues from major league broadcasts, and make it easier for minor league clubs to attain major league status (1976, pt. 1, 313).[13] Robert Bragan, president of the National Association of Professional Baseball Leagues in 1976, asserted that free agency (or, by implication, unrestricted sale of player contracts by club owners) would radically reduce major league assistance to the minors.

> If I have a chance, under the absence of the reserve system, to buy Reggie Jackson in October, or buy Joe Rudi, or buy Rollie Fingers, I have to make a choice between buying him for my big club—because he is available—and sending $150,000 to St. Petersburg, Florida, for an A club, I might be tempted to buy Reggie Jackson and eliminate the operation of that A club to strengthen my big club where the dollars are. (House Select Committee on Professional Sports 1976, pt. 1, 319)

Minor league representatives also defended restrictions on the physical location of clubs' home games. "The territorial rights rule," NAPBL President George Trautman stated in 1957, "is nothing more nor less than a recognition of the fact that it is far better that one club should be able to live within a given territorial limit than that two or more shall die attempting to operate within the same limit" (House Antitrust Subcommittee 1957, 185). On an earlier occasion, he told a House subcommittee that "The function of the rule is not to limit the amount of baseball which may be played in a given area but to insure that some baseball may be played" (Subcommittee on Monopoly Power 1952a, 196).

Of course, the minors supported rule 1(d). On several occasions, Trautman spoke in favor of legislation permitting organized baseball to restrict broadcasts and telecasts in order to spur minor league attendance and help minor league teams sell their games to broadcasters. (See House Subcommittee on Monopoly Power 1952a, 196; Senate Subcommittee on S. 1396 1953, 19; House Antitrust Subcommittee 1957, 191; Senate Antitrust Subcommittee 1958, 211.) William McCarthy, manager of the Class AA Nashville Vols, testified that major league radio broadcasts were harmful only when they allowed one major league team to build up a following in a minor league territory, although television may be more harmful (Senate Antitrust Subcommittee 1958, 264). A former owner of the Portsmouth, Virginia, club, oblivious to the Justice Department's role in emasculating rule 1(d), charged that the major leagues "have invaded the minor league territory by radio and television and have plundered the minor leagues just like the pirates of old, with the result that the major leagues through the violation of this rule have received millions of dollars from radio and TV in the last 10 years, and many

13. A labor arbitrator's 1975 decision resulted in a radical revision of the reserve system that nevertheless generally preserved it for the minor leagues. See Seitz 1975.

minor league clubs have perished" (Senate Antitrust Subcommittee 1959, 113). The president of the Cotton States League said broadcasts of major league games were partially to blame for the fact that attendance in his league declined from 437,000 in 1949 to 410,000 in 1952 (Senate Subcommittee on S. 1396 1953, 68). In 1953, a Senate subcommittee received letters in support of limited exemption legislation from eleven different minor leagues (Senate Subcommittee on S. 1396 1953, 194–204).

Hockey

Major and minor league hockey have presented a similarly united front before Congress. In fact, the president of the National Hockey League usually appeared representing the entire hockey structure, even though no major-minor agreement granted him the same kind of power over minor league hockey that the commissioner of baseball has over minor league baseball (House Antitrust Subcommittee 1957, 2994). During the 85th Congress (1957–58), NHL President C. S. Campbell said that broadcasting was not a particularly significant issue for hockey. However, other items proposed for exemption, such as reserve clauses, player relations, and territorial rights, were. He called a limited antitrust exemption "reasonable" but expressed a preference for a baseball-like blanket exemption in order to minimize the risk of litigation (House Antitrust Subcommittee 1957, 2986; Senate Antitrust Subcommittee 1958, 496–500).

As hockey's popularity grew, broadcasting became a more relevant issue. In 1976, Campbell requested an antitrust exemption for leaguewide sale of rights to cable television, because the NHL had no contract with a regular national television network (House Select Committee on Professional Sports 1976, pt. 1, 172).

One of the few minor league hockey officials to testify was William Beagan, commissioner of the International Hockey League. In 1976, he blamed the antitrust laws for the fact that NHL clubs had stopped financing the minor leagues. NHL clubs were faced with a free-rider problem: the rival World Hockey Association was signing players from NHL-subsidized teams (House Select Committee on Professional Sports 1976, pt. 1, 330).

Basketball

Professional basketball leagues were traditionally more concerned about preservation of territorial rights and player draft systems than broadcasting exemptions. "Professional basketball could not exist without territorial rights," NBA President Maurice Podoloff said in 1957 (House Antitrust Subcommittee 1957, 2853). He emphasized that basketball could not survive without the player draft (1957, 2895). When the NBA and ABA sought an antitrust exemption for their proposed merger in 1972, their principal economic argument was that a common draft would lower costs by ending intense competition for players (Senate Committee on Commerce 1973, 112–13). NBA Commissioner Walter Kennedy summed up their position on antitrust in general when he said, "You cannot have a league unless a group of men sit down at a single table and agree on how their businesses are going to be conducted. And once you acknowledge that difference, it seems to me that you cannot apply the antitrust laws to sports in the same way that those laws are applied to other businesses" (1973, 212).

Football

Like the hockey and basketball leagues, football leagues first appeared before Congress in 1957. At that time, NFL Commissioner Bert Bell expressed his concern that the player draft, reserve clause, territorial rights, and actions to discipline conduct detrimental to the sport receive antitrust exemptions (House Antitrust Subcommittee 1957, 2537). "I am convinced," he said, "that, in order to operate successfully and in the best interest of the public, every professional team sport must have some type of equalization, reserve clause, a commissioner with powers similar to those of the commissioner of the National Football League, and territorial rights" (House Subcommittee 1957, 2498). After two decades of occasional NFL efforts to obtain broad antitrust immunity, Commissioner Pete Rozelle was still favorably disposed but realistic. "I think it would be a very healthy thing for the sport," he declared in 1976, "and I also feel it would be impossible to attain" (House Select Committee on Professional Sports 1976, pt. 1, 95).

At the time Bell first testified, the NFL was less concerned about broadcasting because it had no minor leagues to protect and some of its broadcasting restrictions had already been found reasonable by a federal court in 1953 (Senate Antitrust Subcommittee 1958, 365; see also *United States v. NFL* 1953). Bell was even willing to support a bill, opposed by baseball, that would have simply subjected many league practices to the rule of reason rather than the per se test (Senate Antitrust Subcommittee 1958, 415).

In 1961, however, the same judge who rendered the 1953 decision declared that the NFL's broadcasting contract with CBS violated the antitrust laws (*United States v. NFL* 1961). The NFL argued that it needed to sell broadcasting rights to networks on a leaguewide basis in order to divide revenues equally and help equalize playing strengths. Representative John W. Byrnes of Wisconsin, whose district included Green Bay, stated the NFL's case quite succinctly: "The Green Bay Packers will be hit hard by this ruling, since they cannot, if forced to market their television rights alone, receive the television income they could anticipate by sharing the proceeds of a league-negotiated contract" (House Antitrust Subcommittee 1961, 71). The rival American Football League also supported the NFL's position, although AFL Commissioner Joe Foss did suggest that legislative language intended to protect college football from competition from professional telecasts was a bit restrictive (1961, 50–52).

Colleges

The National Collegiate Athletic Association (NCAA) took upon itself the task of representing the interests of collegiate athletics before Congress. Bud Wilkinson, head football coach at the University of Oklahoma and chairman of the NCAA's committee on athletic relations with professional football, enunciated (in 1958) some themes that would become mainstays of NCAA testimony. He attacked football's player draft because it gave rookies no option for where they would play. He opposed antitrust exemptions for professional sports in general, stating, "I don't think there is anything that peculiar about the operation of athletics that they should be entitled to exemptions that other people are not" (Senate Antitrust Subcommittee 1958, 428). But most of all, he complained about the effects of professional telecasts on collegiate games. He expressed outrage at the professional league's decision to telecast on a Saturday during the final college game of the 1957 season.

> The professional people felt that this was one Saturday beyond the traditional end of the college football season. They have refrained up to now, at least, from playing and televising in competition with college football on Saturdays, but their position was that the colleges had arbitrarily extended their season in order to have this game on TV . . . .
>
> The point at issue, though, is that the professional people arbitrarily decided when the collegiate season ended. They said it ended with the Army-Navy game and any college football after that was an extension of the season, and were the colleges to extend their season, that they would not recognize our traditional Saturday afternoon game. (1958, 434)

The NCAA took no position on the antitrust exemption portion of the 1961 broadcasting bill. However, Big Ten Commissioner William Reed, who was also chairman of the NCAA's Legislative Committee, urged "that the broad license for the televising of professional football contests contained in this bill be limited so as to preclude the televising of such events in direct opposition to the conduct of an intercollegiate football contest on any day other than Sunday, which by custom has been identified as a day for professional football events just as Saturdays traditionally have been college football days" (House Antitrust Subcommittee 1961, 66). Representative George Miller (R-Mich.), whose district included Ann Arbor, put his colleagues on notice that he was "very sensitive to the interests of the universities, the Big Ten, and college athletics generally" (1961, 38). The NCAA succeeded in its quest to restrict professional football broadcasts, and, in 1972, its executive director, Walter Byers, recommended that even if the broadcasting exemption were to be repealed, the protection of high school and college football from competing broadcasts should be retained (House Antitrust Subcommittee 1972, 270–71).

Byers also attacked professional drafts; sought legal penalties against teams, leagues, or third parties who tried, before the conclusion of the academic year, to solicit student commitments to play professionally; and called on Congress to bring all sports fully under antitrust.

> [T]he economic survival of interscholastic and intercollegiate athletics, is far more important to the national welfare than any interest advocated by professional sports. We further believe that such survival requires the rigorous application of the antitrust laws to professional sports, and that any action giving antitrust exemptions to any professional sports should be carefully measured as to the impact the exemption will have on interscholastic and intercollegiate athletic programs. (House Antitrust Subcommittee 1972, 269–71)

The NCAA's attorney, Philip Brown, was even more forceful during hearings on a proposed federal regulatory body for professional sports. "The NCAA believes that the most important point to be made is that there is ample evidence that the excessive power of professional sports interests must be controlled in the interests of amateur athletics, individual athletes, and of the fans and the general public," he said. Nevertheless, Brown favored antitrust prosecution, not federal regulation (Senate Committee on Commerce 1973, 49). He accused professional basketball clubs of "harassing" college basketball players (i.e., trying to sign them to contracts) during their playing season and academic year in an effort to pressure the NCAA into supporting the basketball merger (1973, 32). He also called on Congress to expand protection of college and high school football from professional broadcasts and to extend this protection to college and high school basketball as well (1973, 40–41).

The professionals were certainly not oblivious to the NCAA's presence. Jack Dolph, commissioner of the ABA, urged Congress not to confine its attention to professional sports.

> The amateur athlete may or may not be an amateur depending on what standards you apply, but I can tell you that amateur athletics is not amateur. It is very big business, with television and gate receipts.
>
> I think any exploration of professional sports should treat the possibility that amateur sports is also big business. (Senate Committee on Commerce 1973, 114)

Other Groups: The Ceteris Paribus

Only two other interest groups regularly appeared before Congress to share their views on sports antitrust questions: broadcasters and players.

As might be expected, broadcasters opposed any antitrust exemptions that would give leagues greater control over the number of games broadcast. Harold Fellows, president and chairman of the board of the National Association of Broadcasters (NAB), said in 1958 that "We do not believe that the public's interest is served by a blanket authorization for restrictive agreements limiting the radio and television broadcasting of these events which have such great appeal to the American public" (Senate Antitrust Subcommittee 1958, 486). In a letter to Senate Antitrust Subcommittee Chairman Estes Kefauver (D-Tenn.), the Station Representatives Association voiced opposition to any provisions in antitrust bills that would let leagues restrict broadcasts (Senate Antitrust Subcommittee 1958, 745). The NAB also opposed the 1961 exemption for leaguewide pooling of broadcasting rights (House Antitrust Subcommittee 1961, 52–53).

Players' views on antitrust exemptions changed over time as their unions organized and became more aggressive. Beginning with Ty Cobb, the Celler Committee's leadoff witness in 1951, individual baseball players as well as player representatives repeatedly asserted that some form of reserve clause was necessary for the survival of organized baseball, although they often sought modifications in the rule. Nevertheless, they supported antitrust immunity. (See House Subcommittee on Monopoly Power 1952a, 15; House Antitrust Subcommittee 1957, 1248–51 and 3148; Senate Antitrust Subcommittee 1958, 35–45, 298–301; Senate Antitrust Subcommittee 1965, 38.) Pitcher Bob Feller, president of the Major League Baseball Players Association, also defended territorial rights and broadcasting restrictions (House Antitrust Subcommittee 1957, 1231; Senate Antitrust Subcommittee 1958, 303). In the 1970s, though, the players' union sought to have the reserve clause declared subject to U.S. antitrust laws and, when that failed, to U.S. labor laws (*Flood v. Kuhn* 1972; Seitz 1975 and 1977). In 1983, the MLBPA's executive director said the union favored congressional action to remove baseball's antitrust exemption (Senate Committee on the Judiciary 1983b, 157).

The stated views of players in other sports followed a similar evolution. In the late 1950s, Creighton Miller, counsel to the National Football League Players' Association, decried the lack of competitive bidding between NFL clubs for players' services, but stated that NFL recognition of the union as a bargaining agent would give the players sufficient influence to redress grievances. He agreed with team owners that some restrictions on player mobility are necessary and echoed NFL Commissioner Bert Bell's call for legislation specifying that the legality of certain league practices be tested under the rule of reason rather than the per se standard (House Antitrust Subcommittee 1957, 2628–30 and 2662–63; Senate Antitrust Subcommittee 1958, 321). The NFLPA took a similar position in 1964 (Senate Antitrust Subcommittee 1965, 98–100).[14] By 1985, however, the union was firmly against antitrust

14. Interestingly, a 1972 poll of members of the National Football League Alumni Association, composed of players who retired before 1959, turned up strong opposition to government

exemptions for professional sports (Senate Committee on Commerce 1985, 112–13).

Representatives of basketball players have been less active at antitrust hearings. One exception was basketball players' vocal opposition to any antitrust exemption for the proposed NBA-ABA merger in 1972 that would allow the clubs to reduce competition for players. The NBA Players Association opposed legislative authorization of the merger itself out of fear that it would permit the two leagues to establish a "common draft" under which each player could negotiate with only one team (Senate Antitrust Subcommittee 1972, 230–46). The ABA Players Association favored the merger but was equally opposed to collusion in the labor market. Its president, Zelmo Beatty, told a Senate subcommittee, "Anything less than total elimination of restrictions on the player to freely sell his services is unacceptable" (Senate Antitrust Subcommittee 1972, 312). In contrast, back in 1957, veteran players Bob Cousey, Edward Macauley, and Robert Petit all voiced support for professional basketball's draft and option clause, which operated like baseball's reserve clause (House Antitrust Subcommittee 1957, 2897–2904).

Hockey players' unions have been the least active of all before Congress. The attorney for the National Hockey League Players Association in 1957 sided with team owners in favoring a limited antitrust exemption for all sports (House Antitrust Subcommittee 1957, 1255–56), a position consistent with that taken by other player unions at the time.

These brief excerpts of player testimony reveal that, although player attitudes changed markedly over time, they were not at any time substantially different between sports.

Conclusion

Congressional testimony of various sports officials strongly suggests that major and minor league baseball (and hockey), because they share a common governance structure, find it easier to reach agreement on common political objectives and then lobby for them than do major leagues and colleges in other sports. Collegiate testimony contrasts markedly in both tone and substance with that of minor league baseball. Compare, for instance, a statement by NAPBA President Trautman in 1953 on the broadcasting issue: "I am sure the major league people, if they had the right to do something about this whole program, would do it. They have a sympathy for our problem" (Senate Subcommittee on S. 1396 1953, 19). No doubt this sympathy was due largely to the fact that the majors, in one way or another, had to make good minor league losses if these training grounds for young players were to survive in the same form.

---

regulation of sports and strong support for the NFL's option clause in player contracts. See Senate Committee on Commerce 1973, 248–49.

In addition, both majors and minors benefit from territorial restrictions, draft rules, the reserve clause, and the commissioner's authority to "preserve the integrity of the game." While colleges and professional sports leagues also share common economic interests, the fact that they are distinctly separate entities that can be subject to differential antitrust treatment makes it more costly for them to reach agreement on common objectives. As a result, they frequently end up in conflict in the political arena.[15]

Baseball's lower organizational costs, combined with the sheer size of its minor league system, give it a comparative advantage in lobbying relative to other major sports. When the economics of public decision making are taken into account, congressional acquiescence in baseball's differential treatment under the antitrust laws may not be an anomaly at all.

REFERENCES

Articles and Books

Becker, Gary. 1983. "A Theory of Competition Among Pressure Groups for Political Influence." *Quarterly Journal of Economics* 98, no. 3 (August): 372–400.

Buchanan, James, and Tullock, Gordon. 1962. *The Calculus of Consent*. Ann Arbor: University of Michigan Press.

Canes, Michael E. 1974. "The Social Benefits of Restrictions on Team Quality." In *Government and the Sports Business*, ed. Roger Noll, 81–113. Washington: Brookings Institute.

Coase, Ronald. 1937. "The Nature of the Firm." *Economica* 56, no. 4 (November): 386–405.

Craig, Peter. 1950. "Organized Baseball: An Industry Study of a $100 Million Spectator Sport." Bachelor's thesis, Oberlin College.

Hill, James P., and Spellman, William. 1983. "Professional Baseball: The Reserve Clause and Salary Structure." *Industrial Relations* 22, no. 1 (Winter): 1–19.

Holahan, William L. 1978. "The Long-Run Effects of Abolishing the Baseball Player Reserve System." *Journal of Legal Studies* 7, no. 1 (January): 129–38.

Hunt, James W., and Lewis, Kenneth A. 1976. "Dominance, Contracting, and the Reserve Clause: Major League Baseball." *American Economic Review* 66, no. 5 (December): 936–43.

Johnson, Arthur T. 1979. "Congress and Professional Sports: 1951–1978." *Annals of the American Academy of Political and Social Science* 445 (September): 102–15.

Jones, J. C. H., and Davies, D. K. 1978. "Not Even Semitough: Professional Sport and Canadian Antitrust." *Antitrust Bulletin* 23, no. 4: 713–42.

15. The experience of Canadian antitrust law provides ambiguous evidence on these issues. Amateur sports are exempt, while agreements among professional teams that "unreasonably" restrict entry as either a player or an owner, impose "unreasonable" terms on industry participants, or "unreasonably" limit player mobility. Prior to 1976, all professional sports were exempt (See Jones and Davies 1978). Uniform treatment for professional sports could be interpreted as contradicting the differential lobbying strength hypothesis. On the other hand, the lobbying strength of various professional sports in Canada may simply not be that disparate, for most minor league and all but two major league baseball teams are in the United States.

Koch, James. 1983. "Intercollegiate Athletics: An Economic Explanation." *Social Science Quarterly* 64, no. 2 (June): 360–74.

Markham, Jesse W., and Teplitz, Paul V. 1981. *Baseball, Economics, and Public Policy*. Lexington, Mass.: D. C. Heath.

McCormick, Robert E., and Tollison, Robert D. 1981. *Politicians, Legislation, and the Economy*. Boston: Martinus Nijhoff.

Medoff, Marshall H. 1976. "On Monopsonistic Exploitation in Professional Baseball." *Quarterly Review of Economics and Business* 16, no. 2 (Summer): 113–21.

"Monopsony in Manpower: Organized Baseball Meets the Antitrust Laws." 1953. *Yale Law Journal* 62, no. 4 (March): 576–604.

Noll, Roger. 1982. "Major League Sports." In *The Structure of American Industry*, ed. Adams, 348–87. 6th ed. New York: Macmillan.

Olson, Mancur. 1982. *The Rise and Decline of Nations*. New Haven: Yale University Press.

Peltzman, Sam. 1976. "Toward a More General Theory of Regulation." *Journal of Law and Economics* 19, no. 2 (August): 211–40.

Raimondo, Henry J. 1983. "Free Agents' Impact on the Labor Market for Baseball Players." *Journal of Labor Research* 4, no. 2 (Spring): 183–93.

Rottenberg, Simon. 1966. "The Baseball Players' Labor Market." *Journal of Political Economy* 64, no. 2 (June): 242–58.

Scully, Gerald W. 1974. "Pay and Performance in Major League Baseball." *American Economic Review* 64, no. 6 (December): 915–30.

Seitz, Peter. 1975. "Professional Baseball Clubs." *Labor Arbitration and Dispute Settlement* 22:101.

Seitz, Peter. 1977. "Are Professional Sports Sports or Business, or How Much Would You Pay Catfish Hunter?" *Proceedings of the 29th Annual Winter Meeting*. Madison, Wis.: Industrial Relations Research Association Services.

Sobel, Lionel. 1977. *Professional Sports and the Law*. New York: Law-Arts Publishers.

Sommers, Paul, and Quinton, Noel. 1982. "Pay and Performance in Major League Baseball: The Case of the First Family of Free Agents." *Journal of Human Resources* 17, no. 3 (Summer): 426–35.

Stigler, George. 1971. "The Theory of Economic Regulation." *Bell Journal of Economics* 2, no. 1 (Spring): 3–21.

Veeck, Bill, and Linn, Ed. 1965. *The Hustler's Handbook*. New York: G. Putnam's Sons.

Voigt, David. 1983. *American Baseball*. Vol. 3. University Park: Penn State University Press.

Williamson, Oliver E. 1985. *The Economic Institutions of Capitalism*. New York: Free Press.

Court Cases and Records

Federal Baseball Club of Baltimore, Inc. v. National League of Professional Baseball Clubs. 1921. Transcript of Record, U.S. Supreme Court Docket no. 204 (October Term).

Federal Baseball Club of Baltimore, Inc. v. National League of Professional Baseball Clubs, 1922. 259 U.S. 200.

Flood v. Kuhn, 1972. 407 U.S. 258.

NCAA v. Board of Regents. 1984. 104 S.Ct. 2945.
Radovich v. NFL. 1957. 352 U.S. 445.
Toolson v. New York Yankees. 1953. 346 U.S. 356.
United States v. International Boxing Club. 1955. 348 U.S. 236.
United States v. NFL. 1953. 116 F. Supp. 319.
United States v. NFL. 1961. 196 F. Supp. 445.

Congressional Hearings and Reports

House Antitrust Subcommittee. 1957. *Organized Professional Team Sports, Hearings*. 85th Cong., 1st sess.

House Antitrust Subcommittee. 1961. *Telecasting of Professional Sports Contests, Hearing*. 87th Cong., 1st sess.

House Antitrust Subcommittee. 1972. *The Antitrust Laws and Organized Professional Team Sports, Hearings*. 92d Cong., 2d sess.

House Select Committee on Professional Sports. 1976. *Inquiry Into Professional Sports, Hearings*. Parts 1 and 2. 94th Cong., 2d sess.

House Select Committee on Professional Sports. 1977. *Inquiry Into Professional Sports*. 94th Cong., 2d sess. House Report 1786.

House Subcommittee on Monopolies. 1984. *Antitrust Policy and Professional Sports, Hearings*. 98th Cong., 2d sess.

House Subcommittee on Monopoly Power. 1952a. *Hearings: Part 6, Organized Baseball*. 82d Cong., 1st sess.

House Subcommittee on Monopoly Power. 1952b. *Organized Baseball*. 82d Cong., 2d sess. House Report 2002.

Senate Antitrust Subcommittee. 1960. *Organized Professional Team Sports, 1960 Hearings*. 86th Cong., 2d sess.

Senate Antitrust Subcommittee. 1965. *Professional Sports Antitrust Bill of 1965, Hearings*. 89th Cong., 1st sess.

Senate Antitrust Subcommittee. 1971. *Hearings on S. 2373*. Parts 1 and 2. 92d Cong., 1st sess.

Senate Antitrust Subcommittee. 1972. *Professional Basketball, Hearings*, Part 1. 92d Cong., 1st sess.

Senate Antitrust Subcommittee. 1958. *Organized Professional Team Sports, Hearings*. 85th Cong., 2d sess.

Senate Antitrust Subcommittee. 1959. *Organized Professional Team Sports, Hearings*. 86th Cong., 1st sess.

Senate Committee on Commerce. 1973. *Federal Sports Act of 1972, Hearings*. 92d Cong., 2d sess.

Senate Committee on Commerce. 1985a. *Professional Sports Community Protection Act of 1985, Hearings*. 99th Cong., 1st sess.

Senate Committee on Commerce. 1985b. *Professional Sports Community Protection Act of 1985*. 99th Cong., 1st sess. Senate Report 99–69.

Senate Committee on the Judiciary. 1960. *Professional Sports Act of 1960*. 86th Cong., 2d sess. Senate Report 1620.

Senate Committee on the Judiciary. 1983. *Professional Sports Antitrust Immunity*. 97th Cong., 2d sess.

Senate Subcommittee on S. 1396. 1953. *Broadcasting and Televising Baseball Games, Hearings*. 85th Cong., 1st sess.

CHAPTER 6

Regulation and Technology in the Electric Utility Industry: A Historical Analysis of Interdependence and Change

Richard F. Hirsh

The electric utility industry is currently in the throes of a radical restructuring movement. After more than a half century of benign regulation and cheap power, the industry now confronts deregulation of its generation activities and the introduction of new and unfamiliar players. Producing up to 5 percent of the nation's electricity needs are companies exempt from regulations governing traditional companies. As can be imagined, many utility managers are displeased by these developments, while entrepreneurial spirits rejoice.

The move toward partial deregulation of the utility industry has been discussed extensively during the last 1980s. But the central role played by technological change in the deregulation movement has not been widely acknowledged. This chapter serves as a preliminary effort to remedy that shortcoming. It begins with a background discussion of how, early in the century, new technology in the forms of the steam turbine, generator, and alternating current transmission systems permitted exploitation of large scale and high thermal efficiencies. At the urging of several utility managers, states agreed that electricity supply constituted an industry similar to the telephone and public works industries and should, therefore, be considered a natural monopoly. From the 1910s to the 1960s, generating technology improved incrementally, and all stakeholders (i.e., the people and institutions that held a stake in the production and use of electricity) appeared to benefit from the regulatory arrangement. By the 1970s, however, a series of events caused the standard technology to reach limits to improvement and productivity gains stalled. Unsettling economic crises of the decade added to utilities' woes, as did the creation of new public policy in 1978, which spurred a reexamination of the rationale for monopoly control. The availability of small-scale and efficient technologies used by nonutility companies in the 1980s challenged the rationale further, contributing to the move toward deregulation. In short, I will discuss how regulation and technology developed interdependently throughout much of the century: large-scale technology partially justified regulation of a natural monopoly while regulation spurred research and development (R&D) on big technology. I will also discuss how stagnation in traditional technology and advances in alternative power technology (along with new policy) destroyed the interdependent relationship and motivated a reexamination of the rationale for monopoly regulation. Unexpectedly, partial deregulation also provided incentives for R&D efforts in a way that will make a return to the former regulated structure almost impossible.

Origins of Regulation in the Electric Utility Industry

Electric utility regulation emerged as a managerial innovation coming largely from the industry itself. The main exponent (or at least the most vocal) of this regulation movement was Samuel Insull, the personal secretary of Thomas Edison who became president of the Chicago Edison Company in 1892. Though many companies competed in the Chicago area, Insull hoped his firm would eventually sell power to everyone in the city and the area surrounding it. In one approach that he took to achieve this goal, he experimented with new technology that he saw being used in Europe. Most important was the steam turbine, invented in 1884 by Charles A. Parsons. Parsons recognized that the standard reciprocating steam engine, one using a large piston that moved up and down in a huge cylinder, was approaching the limits of practical use. The machines had become so difficult to build and maintain, and their noise and throbbing motions so bothersome, that they could no longer be efficiently enlarged for more power output. Parsons' engine worked on radically different principles. Rather than reciprocal motion, the turbine produced rotary power directly as steam pressed against blades attached to a central shaft. Connected directly to a generator, the steam turbine could produce electricity from machinery taking up about 10 percent of the space of a similarly powered reciprocating machine and weighing about 12 percent as much. Moreover, because the turbine produced rotary motion directly, it operated smoothly and almost without noise and vibration outside the plant.[1]

Insull saw how even small turbines could produce as much power as did the most powerful reciprocating engines, and he pushed the U.S. manufacturer, General Electric, to build units that could yield 5,000 kilowatts (kw) of power. Though GE balked at first, arguing that it did not have the engineering expertise to do so, Insull encouraged the daring step by accepting the operating risk of using the units if GE would manage the manufacturing risk. The first unit was placed in service in 1903; three others were installed in

1. Much of the discussion of Insull and the early days of the utility industry comes from Thomas Hughes, *Networks of Power: Electrification in Western Society, 1880–1930* (Baltimore, Md.: Johns Hopkins University Press, 1983). A popularized history of the Parsons engine is in W. Garrett Scaife, "The Parsons Steam Turbine," *Scientific American* 252 (April, 1985): 132–39.

1905. Some problems existed with the units, but Insull felt encouraged by their performance, and he replaced them in 1911 with units that produced 12,000 kw each.[2]

The turbines exhibited great scale economies when enlarged. In other words, as the physical size of the machines increased, their power output increased even more. The major reason for this comes from simple geometrical extrapolation. By doubling the diameter (and circumference) of a steam delivery pipe, for example, the volume of the vapor contained is quadrupled. When constructing several other components of a power unit, the same principle applied. Namely, modest increases in material inputs produced disproportionately larger outputs. The "six-tenths" rule of thumb reflected this geometrical fact by approximating the added capital cost of capacity at 0.6 percent for each 1 percent of capacity increase.[3] In addition to scale economies stemming from geometry are economies derived from simplified organization. Construction of one large unit instead of two smaller ones requires only one foundation for a turbine, one control room, and less auxiliary equipment, thereby yielding lower capital costs per unit of capacity. Finally, utilities benefited from scale economies resulting from the reduced number of personnel required to operate a larger capacity unit. Since management of a large unit from a single control room did not differ significantly from management of a smaller unit, the company saved by having staff for only one control room.[4]

Insull also experimented with alternating current (AC) and high-voltage transmission of power as means to achieve his goal of consolidation. While

2. Samuel Insull, "Massing of Energy Production an Economic Necessity," in *Central Station Electricity Service: Its Commercial Development and Economic Significance as Set Forth in the Public Addresses (1897–1914) of Samuel Insull*, ed. William E. Keily (Chicago: private printing, 1915), 137–38; Thomas Hughes, "The Electrification of America: The System Builders," *Technology and Culture* 20 (1979): 124–61.

3. A 1.0 percent increment in a sphere's volume increases its surface area by about 0.6 percent. The rule holds if surface area is proportional to cost and if volume is proportional to output. See Robert J. Gordon, "The Productivity Slowdown in the Steam-Electric Generating Industry" (Northwestern University and National Bureau of Economic Research, February, 1983), 12. Also see F. T. Moore, "Economies of Scale: Some Statistical Evidence," *Quarterly Journal of Economics* 73 (1959): 232–45.

4. Aside from scale economies achieved by increasing the size of machinery, other scale economies are associated with increasing sales. As electricity sales increase with production coming from an existing plant, the cost per unit decreases because no extra investment of capital is expended. See Alfred E. Kahn, *The Economics of Regulation: Principles and Institutions* (New York: Wiley, 1970), 1:124–30. For economies of scale for a firm, not just a plant, see Paul Rodgers and Gordon L. Pozza, "Christensen and Greene's 'Economies of Scale in U.S. Electric Power Generation,'" National Association of Regulatory Utility Commissioners, Technical Economic Literature Review Series Paper no. 1 (July 27, 1979); Kenneth Jameson, "Economies of Scale in the Electric Power Industry," in *Values in the Electric Power Industry*, ed. Kenneth Sayre (Notre Dame, Ind.: University of Notre Dame Press, 1977), 115–48.

his Chicago firm originally used direct current (DC), the choice of Thomas Edison when he began the central station power business in New York City in 1882, other companies employed AC. When Edison first encountered competition from George Westinghouse and Elihu Thomson's AC systems, Edison maintained an advantage, since his opponents did not yet have AC electric motors. But by the 1890s, AC motors had become practical. Moreover, AC (unlike DC) could be transformed to high voltages and transmitted over long distances from the site of power production. This advantage allowed for sites of concentrated power production, using large machines that took advantage of economies of scale. After a vehement and colorful public fight over the various advantages of AC and DC systems (known as the "war of the currents"),[5] AC became the dominant approach by the late 1890s. Edison's company eventually succumbed, being absorbed by Thomson's in 1892 to form the General Electric Company. For Insull, the use of alternating current and steam turbines allowed him to sell growing amounts of electricity to a larger base of customers. He could even offer discounts to some customers, such as municipal railroad companies or electric ice makers, who used power during times when electric light use dwindled (such as during the day or late at night), thereby providing income from his investment in equipment and improving what became known as the "load factor."[6]

Insull realized that utility companies could take advantage of new developments in technology only if they could consolidate smaller firms and provide power to large geographical areas *without* encountering competition.[7] With several firms selling electricity in the same area, business would be fragmented, and none could use the biggest and most efficient equipment. Hence, companies would suffer along with customers, who would have to pay for more expensive power. Without saying so explicitly, Insull argued that the utility industry evidenced the most important features of "natural monopolies." As noted by historian Thomas K. McCraw in his description of regulation's origins in the United States, these features included, first of all, decreasing unit costs and economies of scale over a wide range.[8] With the use of

5. Theodore Bernstein, "A Grand Success," *IEEE Spectrum* (February, 1973): 54–58; Terry S. Reynolds and Theodore Bernstein, "The Damnable Alternating Current," *Proceedings of the IEEE* 64 (1976): 1339–43.

6. Load factor is the ratio of average daily (or yearly) use of electricity to the maximum load sustained during the same period. When use is distributed throughout a period without sharp peaks, the load factor increases, allowing for the most economical use of efficient "base-load" equipment. See John Hopkinson, "On the Cost of Electric Supply," in Edison Illuminating Company of Detroit *The Development of Scientific Rates for Electric Supply*, comp. (Detroit: private printing, 1915), 9; Samuel Insull, "Massing of Energy Production an Economic Necessity," in Keily, *Central Station Electricity Service*, 127–43; Samuel Insull, "The Production and Distribution of Energy," in Keily, *Central Station Electric Service*, 365.

7. Samuel Insull, "Standardization, Cost Control of Rates, and Public Control," in Ibid., 34–47.

8. Thomas K. McCraw, *Prophets of Regulation* (Cambridge, Mass.: Harvard University Press, 1984), 9–10.

increased sizes of steam turbine generators, capital costs decreased and scale economies seemed assured. Second, the industry appeared to experience a high ratio of fixed costs to variable costs in a way that necessitated large initial investments for entering a market. Quickly becoming the most capital-intensive industry in the country, the utility business certainly met this criterion. And as the scale of power plants increased, the amount of capital inputs into the production function increased at a much greater rate than did labor (and other) inputs, making entry into the business even more formidable.

This notion of natural monopoly deserves greater attention for our story. First of all, one could argue that large-scale enterprises, such as the major automobile and steel companies, evidenced similar characteristics of scale economies and investment requirements without leading them to natural monopoly status. The concept is clarified by James C. Bonbright, one of the most respected academic analysts of regulated utilities,[9] who argued that another standard required consideration. In addition to being a capital-intensive industry that yields decreasing unit costs, a natural monopoly also uses resources most efficiently in a restricted market:

> The familiar statement that a public utility is a "natural monopoly" is meant to indicate that this type of business, by virtue of its inherent technical characteristics rather than by virtue of any legal restrictions or financial power, cannot be operated with *efficiency* and economy unless it enjoys a monopoly of its market. So great are the diseconomies of direct competition that, even if it gets an effective start, the competition will probably not long persist if only because it will lead to the bankruptcy of the rivals. But even if the competition is long lived, as has occasionally happened when the rivalry has taken a restrained form, it is *wasteful of resources* because it involves unnecessary duplication of tracks, of cables, of substations, etc.[10]

In other words, a natural monopoly makes better use of resources in serving dense populations than would competitors who need to duplicate facilities or use equipment that could not (due to reduced demand) exploit scale economies or obtain high fuel efficiencies.[11] For similar reasons, the telephone, gas,

9. Bonbright's accomplishments are discussed in "James C. Bonbright's Contributions to Public-Utility Economics and Regulation," *Current Issues in Public-Utility Economics: Essays in Honor of James C. Bonbright*, ed. Albert L. Danielsen and David R. Kamerschen (Lexington, Mass.: Lexington Books, 1983), 3–21.

10. James C. Bonbright, *Principles of Public Utility Rates* (New York: Columbia University Press, 1961), 100; italics added.

11. Ibid., 11–13. Bonbright also points out that the efficiency criterion could apply to a natural monopoly whose incremental costs increased rather than decreased. For example, he points out that some utility systems, such as the Tennessee Valley Authority, exhausted their sources of cheap water power in the 1940s and then resorted to steam power. The incremental cost of power increased, but the authority still retained natural monopoly status because it could

and water industries had already won acceptance as natural monopolies by the end of the nineteenth century.[12]

Along with a few other like-minded entrepreneurs such as Detroit Edison's Alex Dow, Insull understood that he could exploit big technology and efficient transmission systems only if he held monopoly control of specific geographic regions. Of course, in an era of trustbusting and generally negative feelings toward monopolies, the public would not accept this managerial concept.[13] But as early as 1898, Insull advocated that private companies seek public regulation as a means to achieve legal and unequivocal monopoly status. In return for exclusive rights to produce and distribute electricity within a specific region, the utility would submit to regulatory oversight by a governmental body.[14] The utility would be regulated in such a way that it would earn a fair rate of return on the property used to provide the public service.[15] Meanwhile, as utility costs decreased, regulators would see that customer prices followed suit. (In 1944, the Supreme Court further established the criterion that utilities would be assured rates permitting them to expand, raise capital, and compensate investors for their risk in supplying capital.)[16] Like executives in other industries, Insull advocated regulation by proclaiming that it would be "in the public interest." He also realized that it would legitimate his business strategy that, among other things, allowed him to eliminate the competition.[17]

Because of political difficulties in Illinois, Insull initially had trouble swaying government officials to his point of view. But in other states, such as New York, Massachusetts, and Wisconsin, government regulation of utilities began in 1907, with Illinois following in 1914.[18] At that time, Insull had

---

produce the power for less than competing companies that also would have been forced to use steam power (Ibid., 15–16).

12. For discussions of natural monopolies, see also William W. Sharkey, *The Theory of Natural Monopoly* (New York: Cambridge University Press, 1982).

13. An alternative model for power production that frequently won popular acceptance was municipal ownership of power systems. A discussion of public power systems can be found in Richard Rudolph and Scott Ridley, *Power Struggle: The Hundred-Year War over Electricity* (New York: Harper and Row, 1986), 22–56; Thomas K. McCraw, *TVA and the Power Fight: 1933–1939* (Philadelphia: Lippincott, 1971), 1–25.

14. Forrest McDonald, *Insull* (Chicago: University of Chicago Press, 1962), 114.

15. This principle was established in the case of Smyth v. Ames, 169 U.S. 466 (1898).

16. Federal Power Commission vs. Hope Natural Gas Company, 320 U.S. 591 (1944).

17. In retrospect, it appears that Insull's company may have benefited in another way. According to at least one economist who deals with the political behavior of regulatory commissions, regulated companies often earned greater profits (due to high valuations of property) than did their unregulated, competitive counterparts. See Gregg A. Jarrell, "The Demand for Electric Utility Regulation," in *Electric Power: Deregulation and the Public Interest*, ed. John C. Moorhouse (San Francisco: Pacific Research Institute for Public Policy, 1986), 291–305.

18. A brief history of regulation is included in Richard Hellman, *Government Competition in the Electric Utility Industry: A Theoretical and Empirical Study* (New York: Praeger, 1972), 8–11.

already taken advantage of large-scale technology and AC transmission to make his company one of the most impressive in the country. Exclusively serving customers in Chicago and some rural communities surrounding it, Insull's firm (then known as the Commonwealth Edison Company) charged some of the lowest rates in the country while remaining financially secure and able to expand even more.[19] Obviously, Insull's use of efficient technology combined with regulatory oversight of an acknowledged natural monopoly proved to be a successful strategy.

Technological Innovation and Regulation

As I have documented, the utility industry benefited from incrementally improving technology until the 1960s or 1970s.[20] The major manufacturers of equipment, most notably General Electric and Westinghouse, took advantage of their first-mover status and produced steam turbines, generators, and transmitting technology that brought down the marginal cost of power largely through two means. First, economies of scale resulted when equipment was enlarged, when new metals were used that could withstand greater forces and temperatures, and when techniques were developed that permitted transmission at higher voltages and lower losses. Second, advances in metallurgy and engineering practice enabled utilities to eke out more electricity from each pound of coal or barrel of oil—in other words, to improve thermodynamic efficiency of the equipment.

The extent of gradual improvements in technology can be visualized dramatically by the following graphs. First, consider a graph of the power output of turbine-generator equipment over the years (fig. 1). As is clear, maximum output in megawatts (1 MW = 1,000 kw) increased dramatically from the early years of the century, rising from about 5 MW in 1903 to a temporary plateau in the 1930s of 208 MW for the most powerful unit. Because demand for electricity slowed during the Depression, utilities did not need to install many new plants (and certainly none of unprecedented capacity).[21] During World War II as well, large new units had to be postponed as the manufacturers instead produced turbines for naval needs.[22] But after the war, when demand skyrocketed (reaching about 10 percent per year for the decade after the war's end), utilities ordered and manufacturers produced

19. In 1914, the company earned 2.05 cents per kilowatt-hour of electricity, less than half of what utilities in Boston or New York City earned (Samuel Insull, "Centralization of Energy Supply," in Keily, *Central Station Electric Service*, 460).

20. See Richard F. Hirsh, *Technology and Transformation in the American Electric Utility Industry* (Cambridge: Cambridge University Press, 1989).

21. Consumption first declined, then rose again as industrial activity returned. Still, from 1929 to 1939, electricity growth increased only 38 percent (Edison Electric Institute, *Statistical Bulletin*, 1949, no. 17, Publication no. 50–2 [New York: Edison Electric Institute, 1950]).

22. "We Chose Ships," *Electrical World* 128 (November 22, 1947): 76.

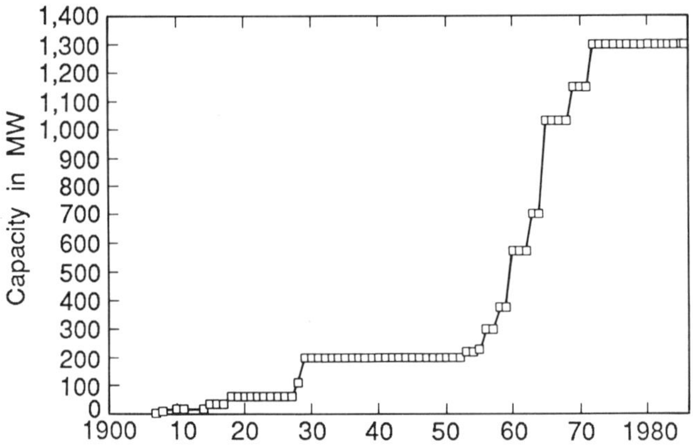

Fig. 1. Maximum capacity of power units, 1900–1986. (From Hirsh, *Technology and Transformation.* Reprinted with permission.)

increasingly powerful equipment: from around 200 MW for the largest unit in 1950, units grew to 1,000 MW in 1965.[23]

The great increases in scale helped depress the investment cost per unit of output. For the fifteen years before the Depression began, for example, the cost per kilowatt of capacity hovered around $100 as average unit output increased from 12.5 to 24.0 MW. Given that the consumer price index rose during this period, the real cost of capacity actually decreased about 70 percent.[24] A similar trend in capital costs existed after World War II. Despite tremendous cost increases in equipment and construction, the inflation-adjusted capital cost per unit of power dropped by more than 50 percent from 1929 through the 1960s.[25]

As capital costs declined in real terms, so did the energy cost of producing power because of increasing thermal efficiencies of plants. Edison's pioneering 1882 plant converted only 2.5 percent of raw fuel into electricity. But by 1940, average thermal efficiency of plants had advanced to about 20 percent.[26] By the early 1960s, further technical advances brought the average

23. Data from Edison Electric Institute, *Edison Electric Institute Pocketbook of Electric Utility Industry Statistics*, 27th ed. (Washington, D.C.: Edison Electric Institute, 1981), 17; "1957 Annual Statistical Report," *Electrical World* 143 (January 28, 1957): 133; "1966 Annual Statistical Report," *Electrical World* 165 (February 21, 1966): 89.

24. Cost per kilowatt data from L. W. W. Morrow, "Reduced Power Costs?" *Electrical World* 94 (September 28, 1929): 619. Average unit size data from U.S. Department of Energy, Generating Unit Reference File (February 24, 1987). Consumer price index data found in *Handbook of Basic Economic Statistics* (Washington, D.C.: Economic Statistics Bureau, 1986), 40:97–101.

25. Philip Sporn, *Vistas in Electric Power* (Oxford: Pergamon Press, 1968), 1:194.

26. Charles E. Neil, "Entering the Seventh Decade of Electric Power," *Edison Electric Institute Bulletin* 10 (September, 1942): 326; Edison Electric Institute, *Edison Electric Institute Pocketbook of Electric Utility Industry Statistics*, 30th ed. (Washington, D.C.: Edison Electric Institute, 1984), 21.

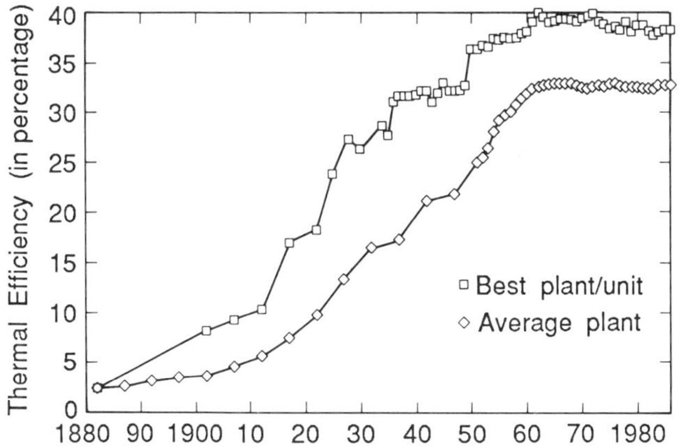

Fig. 2. Thermal efficiency of generating units, 1880–1986. (From Hirsh, *Technology and Transformation.* Reprinted with permission.)

rate up to about 33 percent (fig. 2), while the best new unit operated at about 40 percent efficiency.

Integral to the success of using new technology was the management approach of promoting electricity use among customers. Sometimes called "grow and build" by utility people, the strategy employed methods to encourage customers (industrial, commercial, and residential) to purchase more electricity. In the early part of the century, utilities spurred increased use by promoting home appliances and increased electric lighting. Following World War II (and after capacity shortages had been overcome in the late 1940s), the utility industry developed coordinated programs (such as the "Live Better Electrically" campaign) to promote use through "Gold Medallion, all-electric homes" and elsewhere. Many of these plans offered discounted rates for electricity if home owners, for example, installed electric water heaters or other high-usage appliances.[27]

In general, the public received these campaigns eagerly. From 1900 to 1920, electricity use advanced at about a 12 percent annual rate. From 1920 to 1973, with the exception of the Great Depression, electricity use grew 7 percent annually (a doubling period of only ten years), reflecting electricity's remarkable versatility for performing a plethora of tasks.[28] Utilities responded to increased demand by building new power plants that took advantage of incremental advances in technology. These new power plants generally cost less per kilowatt of capacity, meaning that as utilities sold more electricity and built new plants, their marginal and average costs decreased. As their loads grew even more, due partially to the impetus of lower rates, utilities needed to

27. See Hirsh, *Technology and Transformation*, 48–56.

28. Electricity consumption increased 4.0 to 5.5 times faster than the rate of all energy sources together from 1900 to 1960 (H. H. Landsberg and S. H. Schurr, *Energy in the United States: Sources, Uses, and Policy Issues* [New York: Random House, 1968], 63).

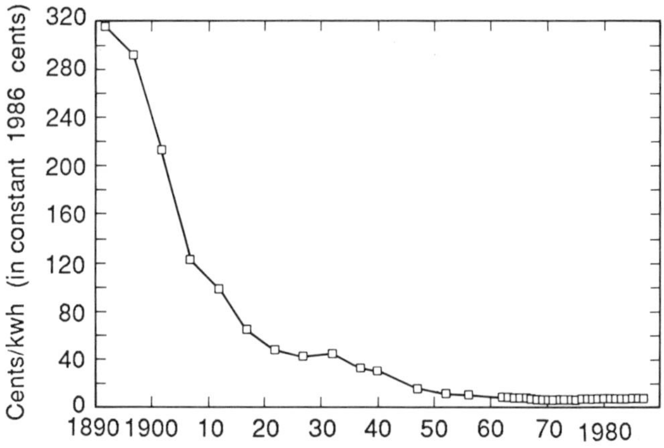

Fig. 3. Average price of electricity, 1892–1986, inflation adjusted in 1986 cents. (From Hirsh, *Technology and Transformation.* Reprinted with permission.)

build still more plants, which again lowered average costs. And thus the cycle continued.

Advantages of this grow-and-build technique accrued to utilities and their customers. First, since production costs could be spread over a greater number of kilowatt-hours (kwh) of electricity, utilities realized one form of scale economy. Reflecting part of the cost savings, prices fell, which encouraged further increases in use. Meanwhile, as new and lower cost plants went on line to meet growing demand, costs declined as well. Overall, the grow-and-build strategy, combined with incremental improvements in technology, enabled the utility industry to elevate its productivity dramatically. Between 1899 and 1953, the annual productivity growth rate of 5.5 percent proved higher than any other industry and was more than three times greater than the rate of the entire private domestic economy.[29]

These productivity improvements contributed to push down the unit cost of electricity. In 1892, residents paid about 92 cents per kwh (in adjusted 1967 terms). By 1967, the residential customer paid only 2 cents per kwh. (When adjusted in 1986 terms, the respective rates were 316 and 7 cents per kwh; see fig. 3.)[30] Accurately assessing the cause of this trend in its 1960 advertising, Duke Power Company proclaimed that "[y]our greater usage plus technological advances are responsible for the lower cost per kilowatt-hour."[31]

Regulation during this period did not directly focus on technology. In

29. John W. Kendrick, *Productivity Trends in the United States* (Princeton: Princeton University Press, 1961), 137–39. See also John W. Kendrick, *Postwar Productivity Trends in the United States, 1948–1969* (New York: Columbia University Press, 1973), 78–79.

30. Data are from Edison Electric Institute, *Pocketbook*, 30th ed. and "1988 Statistical Report," *Electrical World* 202 (April, 1988): 61.

31. *Charlotte Observer*, June 6, 1960.

fact, due to the nature of the mandates of state regulatory bodies, few discussions of specific technological systems arose at all. Rather, state regulation dealt largely with approving utility tariffs and earning the necessary rate of return on investments that would enable companies to produce adequate quantities of reasonably priced electricity. (In contrast, federal regulation dealt with financial concerns, the establishment of holding companies, securities arrangements, wholesale power transactions, and interstate transmission of power.)[32] To establish fair prices, regulators focused on the so-called rate base, which consisted of the sum of capital investments in equipment (minus depreciation) on which the utility would be permitted to earn a return from the customers. Customers had to pay their share of current expenses for fuel and labor, of course, but utilities could not charge more than they actually incurred. Though regulatory bodies in different states have various ways for determining the valuation of the rate base,[33] they generally permitted only capital expenditures to earn a return for the firms.

The significance of this type of regulation on utility strategies for deploying capital-intensive equipment was suggested by Harvey Averch and Leland Johnson in the early 1960s.[34] They pointed out that rate-of-return regulation promoted the use of expensive, large-scale technology whenever possible as a means for utilities to make greater profits (large scale has been seen as a proxy for technological advance in some studies).[35] Since labor costs could not earn returns for the utilities, the companies would eagerly purchase the largest scale equipment available that offered scale economies and reduced labor costs. This model helps explain, therefore, why utilities worked so well in concert with manufacturers to develop incrementally improving and growing equipment through the years. It also explains why the industry had such a high ratio of capital to labor expenses. Given the regulatory rules and constraints, utility managers followed a perfectly rational strategy.

Despite its apparent reasonableness, the Averch-Johnson hypothesis has been criticized as being less effective than expected for spurring capital investments in new technology. Some people argue that utilities' use of capital-intensive equipment may "pad" the rate base, but it may also yield counterproductive effects if the new technology lowers the cost of electricity. As regulated entities, utilities would be required to pass along savings to cus-

32. Claire Holton Hammon, "An Overview of Electric Utility Regulation," in Moorhouse, *Electric Power,* 43–44.

33. Randy A. Nelson and Walter J. Primeaux, Jr., "Rate Base Valuation Procedures and the Behavior of Regulated Firms," *Quarterly Review of Economics and Business* 24 (Winter, 1984): 72–81. Also see Frederic H. Murphy and Allen L. Soyster, *Economic Behavior of Electric Utilities* (Englewood Cliffs, N.J.: Prentice-Hall, 1983).

34. Harvey Averch and Leland L. Johnson, "Behavior of the Firm Under Regulatory Constraint," *American Economic Review* 52 (1962): 1052–69.

35. See John H. DeYoung, Jr., and John E. Tilton, *Public Policy and the Diffusion of Technology: An International Comparison of Large Fossil-Fueled Generating Units* (University Park, Pa.: The Pennsylvania State University Press, 1978), 8–11.

tomers in this case. Hence, new technology might not benefit regulated utilities as much as unregulated companies, which could earn greater profits from lower production costs. Others have noted, however, that utilities can benefit from lower costs when regulators delay rate reductions until well after lower costs are incurred. This often happens (and is known as regulatory lag) because regulatory bodies generally base future rates on costs incurred in an earlier "test period." Since costs tended to decline, utilities usually benefited from reduced costs before new rates were established.[36]

Whether or not the Averch-Johnson effect existed, regulation developed around a large-scale technological system that utility managers understood well and one in which they took great pride.[37] The system brought lower costs and an improved material standard of living as customers purchased more productivity-enhancing equipment and more leisure-enhancing appliances, such as air conditioners and televisions. What could have been better? Besides establishing the rules for this capital expansion during a long period of industry growth and prosperity, state regulators generally did not interfere much in the operation of utilities. Commissions generally had small staffs to examine claims of utility companies, and utilities undertook great efforts to maintain good relations with regulators by praising them for contributing to lower cost electricity.[38] After World War II, the cozy relationship between utilities and regulators continued—and for good reason: few contentions arose during a period when promotion of electricity use and construction of new plants brought still lower prices. As late as the 1960s, as one group of utility managers told me, a regulatory hearing convened to decide on construction of a new power plant might take half a day, with the only intervenor being an oil or coal company representative who feared further encroachment into his or her business.[39]

---

36. Bruce A. Smith, *Technological Innovation in Electric Power Generation, 1950–1970* (East Lansing: Michigan State University Press, 1977), 23. Discussions of the Averch-Johnson effect can be found in ibid., 23–25; Murphy and Soyster, *Economic Behavior of Electric Utilities* (this book evaluates several criticisms of the Averch-Johnson effect). Also see Leland L. Johnson, "The Averch-Johnson Hypothesis after Ten Years," in *Regulation in Further Perspective: The Little Engine that Might*, ed. William G. Shepherd and Thomas G. Gies (Cambridge, Mass.: Ballinger, 1974), 67–78; Sunit K. Khanna, "Economic Regulation and Technological Change: A Review of the Literature," *Public Utilities Fortnightly* 109 (January 21, 1982): 37–38; Claire Holton Hammon, "An Overview of Electric Utility Regulation," in Moorhouse, *Electric Power*, 53–54.

37. In chap. 2 of *Technology and Transformation*, I go beyond economic discussions of why managers of some of the largest utilities sought technological advances. I argue that managers generally belong to a community of engineers who see technological progress as one of their primary objectives.

38. Utility spokesmen often gave regulators exaggerated credit for reducing the cost of electricity and for providing a useful commodity to the public. See "State Regulation Has Proved Itself," *Electrical World* 93 (May 11, 1929): 915; W. J. Hagenah, "Soundness of Regulation Proved," *Electrical World* 93 (June 8, 1929): 1170.

39. Author's interview with managers of Madison Gas and Electric Company, August 21, 1984.

Regulators therefore had a fairly simple and pleasant task to perform. Because costs declined to customers, they did not need to play the role of studious antagonists. They ratified and reinforced the technological and management strategies of utility companies because everyone seemed to benefit. Looking back from the turbulent 1980s, one regulator reminisced in astonishment that "the task of state regulators was essentially one of distributing among rate payers the benefits of progressively higher efficiencies achieved by utility managers—not bad work if you can get it."[40] An academic observer of electric utility regulation noted that regulators had a "happy task of watching the industry become more efficient and, on occasion, of negotiating rate reductions."[41] This pleasant relationship between utility companies and regulators no doubt helps explain how commissions became "captured" by the industry they supposedly regulated.[42]

As beautiful as it appeared, regulation may have led to inefficiencies and wasteful behavior. For example, regulation may have encouraged utilities to promote electricity use, so that growth rates would be high and so that they would need to construct new facilities, even when other energy sources could be used more efficiently. As an example, utilities heavily promoted electric baseboard heating and electric hot water systems after World War II. Both systems convert fuel into heat with less thermal efficiency than do appliances that use oil or natural gas. Another possible inefficiency occurred when heavy promotion and construction caused a need to obtain capital. With less promotion and slower rates of growth, new equipment requirements would have been reduced, and utilities would not have been forced to enter the capital markets to obtain funding as frequently. By removing some of the competition for capital, other industries could have gained funding more easily and at lower interest rates. For these (and other) reasons, critics in recent years have argued that rate-of-return regulation has not been economically or socially efficient.[43] On the other hand, these critics did not have much of a voice (or were not heard) during the years of happy building and declining rates to consumers.

The Troubled 1970s

The world of utility managers and regulators became more complicated during the late 1960s and the 1970s as previous trends in the economy and

40. Cited is Howard Perry of the Department of Energy in Tom Alexander, "The Surge to Deregulate Electricity," *Fortune* 104 (July 13, 1981): 98.

41. Douglas D. Anderson, *Regulatory Politics and Electric Utilities: A Case Study in Political Economy* (Boston: Auburn House, 1981), 68.

42. See ibid., chap. 1 for a discussion of the capture theory.

43. McCraw notes how rate-of-return regulation has been seen as inefficient in several respects for many years (*Prophets of Regulation*, 60). Likewise, Averch and Johnson noted that this type of regulation motivates the firm to operate "inefficiently in the sense that (social) cost is not minimized . . . (Averch, "Behavior of a Firm under Regulatory Constraint," 1052). Also see Hammon, "An Overview of Electric Utility Regulation," 47.

generating technology changed radically. Some of these problems are well known and will be recounted briefly here. Of course, inflation and a slowdown in economic growth (producing stagflation) became a persistent problem. With inflation averaging 6.7 percent annually in the 1970s (compared to less than 3.0 percent per year in the 1950s and 1960s), the cost of construction and raising money through the bond markets increased dramatically. As part of the inflation, fuel prices started creeping slowly upward in the late 1960s after drifting downward (in real terms) during the 1950s and early 1960s. Meanwhile, the previously benign Organization of Petroleum Exporting Countries (OPEC) began flexing its muscle in 1970 and demanded higher royalty payments from foreign producers. The 1973 oil embargo pushed prices higher—raising oil prices almost fourfold in just a few months.[44] The 1979 Iranian revolution caused further escalations such that utilities' cost of fuel (excluding nuclear fuel) for power generation increased more than sixfold per unit of heat energy in the fifteen years after 1964.[45]

Perhaps the greatest disappointment was that these increased costs could not be mitigated by continued incremental improvements in generating technology. Unlike the previous eighty years or so, generating technology appeared to reach limits of improvement in the 1960s and 1970s such that productivity growth rates not only became smaller, but actually turned negative for several years in the 1970s. Costs and prices, therefore, increased in conjunction with the major input costs of construction and fuel. Residential consumers of power, who had become accustomed to decreasing electricity rates, watched, for example, as rates increased from about 2.2 cents per kilowatt-hour in 1967 to about 2.8 cents in 1974 and 5.1 cents (all unadjusted for inflation) in 1980.[46]

The causes for technological stagnation in power technology are many, and they constitute the major focus of my book. The loss of scale economies can be attributed to several factors: the huge size of some components of power equipment, for example, literally stretched the capability of standard metals to withstand large centrifugal forces. And new metals were excessively costly and experienced problems that had not been anticipated by manufacturers. The complexity of the big plants also caused operational problems, reducing their reliability and producing *diseconomies* of scale. But even before scale economies leveled off, thermal efficiencies hit a plateau. As early as the mid-1960s, industry journals lamented the fact that temperatures of steam (which dictated thermal efficiencies) had reached practical limits. The technology to increase efficiency to the 40 percent level existed, but the plants were expensive and unreliable to operate, thereby discounting the gains the-

44. See Hirsh, *Technology and Transformation*, chap. 9.

45. Data from Edison Electric Institute, *Edison Electric Institute Pocketbook of Electric Utility Industry Statistics*, 34th ed. (Washington, D.C.: Edison Electric Institute, 1988), 22. Also see Hirsh, *Technology and Transformation*, 111–13.

46. Edison Electric Institute, *Pocketbook*, 34th ed., 33.

oretically obtained by reaching this high point. Many of these problems resulted (at least in part) because utility managers pressured manufacturers to take greater and more frequent steps in increasing the scale of power technology. Problems existed in the equipment, but no one understood them until well after it had been deployed.[47]

Unreliable predictions of load forecasts also caused serious problems. Since World War II, load forecasting was a relatively simple task, since utilities demonstrated steadily increasing demands for power. As one utility veteran told me "if you had a straight edge, you were a load forecaster," because all one needed to do was to plot the previous decade's load growth on semi-log paper and project out to the next ten years or more.[48] But during the 1970s, when fuel costs pressed electricity costs upward rapidly, especially after the 1973 oil embargo, customers altered consumption habits. In what surprised many managers, who thought that electricity use was inelastic with respect to price (after all, everyone needed electricity, no matter what the cost, right?), consumers cut back on use dramatically. In the year after the embargo, consumption actually decreased, while over the next decade, it grew at a rate of only 2.5 percent annually. The growth, however, was not a consistent 2.5 percent each year. Some years saw growth spurts; others saw minimal gains. An industry trade journal editor lamented that planning for growth had become a "psychoanalytical crapshoot."[49]

The impact of this uncertainty affected the technology and regulation of the industry. With growth rates no longer predictable but remaining lower than the traditional rate, utilities had to rethink their technological strategy of building the biggest power units possible. Of course, due to stagnation in the technology, economies of scale no longer seemed to be automatic. But beyond this concern, managers realized that if they built, for example, a 1,000 MW unit for use in seven years and their customers only needed 500 MW, then they had overinvested in equipment that would not see economical use for several more years. In other words, the big equipment would sit idle or produce an insufficient return on investment.

Regulators, meanwhile, found themselves ill equipped to deal with the new environment and caught in the middle of disputes between utilities and consumers.[50] On the one hand, utilities sought "rate relief" for the increased costs they incurred. But rate relief to utilities meant rate hikes to customers, and regulators now learned that the happy days of satisfying all the participants in the power matrix had passed. In several cases, utilities asked regula-

47. See Hirsh, *Technology and Transformation*, chaps. 7 and 8.

48. Author's interview with Burl B. Hulsey, Jr., vice chairman of the board, Texas Utilities, April 25, 1985.

49. William C. Hayes, "Forecasting Calls for a Seer, Not an Analyst," *Electrical World* 200 (September, 1986): 7.

50. Charles F. Phillips, Jr., *The Regulation of Public Utilities: Theory and Practice* (Arlington, Va.: Public Utility Reports, 1984), 20.

tors to approve huge rate increases when new power plants were put into service. Planned for and constructed largely during the period of 7 percent annual growth rates, many of these plants came into service when large plants were no longer needed. Construction cost overruns during a period of intense inflation also put pressure on rate hikes, especially for nuclear power plants, many of which were designed during the nuclear bandwagon days of the 1960s. In a few states, regulatory commissions actually penalized utilities that built big and expensive plants, arguing that their managers had been "imprudent" in their planning in the first place. Customers should, therefore, not be held responsible for the poor business management of utility executives. Instead, the stockholders, who owned the companies and received previously increasing dividends, should bear the burden of poor management. Utilities countered by arguing that regulators were imposing a "20/20 hindsight" standard—penalizing the industry for not foreseeing what nobody else could. Moreover, regulators had already approved construction of several of these plants, so they should also bear part of the responsibility for these "dinosaurs." Rarely, however, did utilities win their points.[51]

Events such as these spurred utility managers to seek new business and new technological strategies. Because of the financial risk they incurred building large increments of power, they began, in the late 1970s and the 1980s, to avoid construction of power plants at all. As another part of this "capital minimization" strategy, some utilities encouraged conservation techniques such as providing extra insulation for electric water heaters. In addition, they often exploited "load management" techniques (such as installing equipment in cooperating businesses and homes that disconnected high-consumption equipment during peak-demand times) that reduced sharp peaks in usage. In these ways, utilities could continue to meet slowly increasing demand for power without building new plants.[52]

When demand increased above what existed (or what could be purchased from neighboring utilities), companies sought quickly installed, smaller scale generating equipment. Put into the rate base rapidly, these smaller scale plants

---

51. For a commentary on the nature of prudence reviews written by a former New York State Public Service commissioner, see Alfred E. Kahn, "Who Should Pay for Power-Plant Duds?" *Wall Street Journal*, August 15, 1985, 26. Also see Frederick Rose, "'Prudency Reviews' Are Changing the Way Utilities Set Rates," *Wall Street Journal*, October 2, 1986, 1 and 22; Bill Paul, "More States Are Tightening Rules for Electric Utilities," *Wall Street Journal*, November 13, 1986, 6; "To Win Prudence, Woo the 'Stakeholder,'" *Electrical World* 202 (June, 1988): 29–30. For details of a prudence case against the Long Island Lighting Company, see Glenn Zorpette, "The Shoreham Saga," *IEEE Spectrum* 24 (November, 1987): 33. Also see J. Ronald Fox, "The Shoreham Nuclear Power Plant (A) and (B)," Cases 0–385–249 and 0–385–251, Harvard Business School Case Studies Series (1985).

52. The risks of constructing too little new capacity is explored in Peter Navarro, "Our Stake in the Electric Utility's Dilemma," *Harvard Business Review* 60 (May-June, 1982): 87–97; Peter Navarro, *The Dimming of America: The Real Costs of Electric Utility Regulatory Failure* (Cambridge, Mass.: Ballinger, 1985).

thus lowered financial risks for their stockholders. One favorite technology has become the combustion turbine-generator. Developed in the 1940s, combustion turbines work in a way similar to jet engines, their near cousins. Essentially, these turbines burn natural gas and produce rotary power that turns a traditional electric generator. Already in use for producing power when utilities reach their peak-use times (hence, they were known as peaking units), combustion turbines had relatively low capital costs and could be constructed from mostly factory-made components within a year or two. But they did not produce large amounts of power (around 50 MW or less in the 1960s), and they cost more to operate than thermally efficient, base-load nuclear or coal units. In addition, they had an earned reputation for low reliability when used for extended periods.[53] Nevertheless, for short periods of time, the combustion turbines, which could be turned on and off more quickly than base-load units, had great advantages as peaking units.

The environment of the 1970s and 1980s, however, saw rapid development of combustion turbines for more than peaking service. Manufacturers of generating equipment, such as General Electric, Westinghouse (in concert with Japan's Mitsubishi), Germany's Siemens-Kraftwerk Union, and Switzerland's Brown Boveri, suffered from the dearth of orders for large traditional units. Westinghouse, for example, even considered leaving the turbine-generator business altogether because of the poor market.[54] Eventually realizing that the new environment would last a while, these firms began developing more appropriate (i.e., salable) technologies. Among the outcomes were refined combustion turbines that could be used as base-load units in increments of about 100 MW and with efficiencies greater than 30 percent. In a combined cycle system, where the turbine exhaust is used to create steam for a conventional steam turbine, thermal efficiencies rose above 45 percent. Some of these turbines are now entering service, with still larger combustion turbines expected in the early 1990s.[55]

The combination of load management and smaller scale technologies fit in well with utility managers' desire for more flexibility in planning for the future. Load management delayed the need for new construction, while small-scale technology allowed them to meet new demands without putting their

53. Taylor Moore, "Utility Turbopower for the 1990s," *EPRI Journal* (April-May, 1988), 6–8.

54. Richard F. Hirsh, "Westinghouse Electric Corporation—Steam Turbine Division (A) and (B)," Cases no. 687–036 and no. 687–037, Harvard Business School Case Studies Series (1986). Also see "Westinghouse Improves Profit Margins; Concern Continues to Face Longer Term Issues," *Wall Street Journal*, January 31, 1986, 6.

55. Moore, "Utility Turbopower," 8.; Office of Technology Assessment, *New Electric Power Technologies: Problems and Prospects for the 1990s* (Washington, D.C.: Office of Technology Assessment, July, 1985), 108–12. See also "Utilities Turning to Combustion Turbines to Meet Future Demand," *Electrical World* 201 (September, 1987): 40–41; "Pepco Plans GCC Capacity," *EPRI Journal* 12 (September, 1987): 38.

companies at total risk, as was the case with a few companies' nuclear power plants. (Largely because of problems with its nuclear power plant, the Public Service Company of New Hampshire filed for bankruptcy protection in 1988.)[56] Several companies have employed capital minimization approaches, and some have been rewarded with superb financial results while still being able to serve their customers reliably. As one example, Wisconsin Electric Power Company began using incentive rate structures as a form of load management in the mid-1970s. The firm found it could reduce the size of construction programs and benefit both their stockholders and customers with better financial performance and stable electric rates (or rates that went up less rapidly than the cost of living).[57]

The Public Utility Regulatory Policies Act and Partial Deregulation

Even if all electric utilities used load management techniques and smaller scale technologies, the industry would still be in flux. This is because of new public policy that, combined with the "rediscovery" of an old technology and development of new technologies, has begun a trend toward deregulation of power generation in the industry. The new policy consisted of the Public Utility Regulatory Policies Act (PURPA), one of five laws resulting from President Carter's National Energy Plan that Congress passed in 1978. PURPA had three goals: to conserve energy supplied by utility companies; to optimize the efficiency of facilities and resources used by utilities; and to provide fair rates to consumers. Much of the legislation deals with the the last concern—the development of rate structures that encourage conservation of energy and electricity. It establishes new standards for making rates and specifically prohibits the use of promotional rate structures through declining block rates—rates whose energy component is priced less as use increases—unless the utility can demonstrate that the energy component's cost actually decreases. In addition, the law requires utilities to investigate the effectiveness of time-of-day rates and other forms of load management.[58]

Another provision of the law sought to increase the nation's overall

56. Lawrence Ingrassia and Christopher J. Chipello, "PS New Hampshire Files Bankruptcy Plea," *Wall Street Journal*, January 29, 1988, 2.

57. Wisconsin Electric Power Company, *1985 Annual Report*, 2.

58. PURPA, Title I, subtitles A and B. The Electric Power Research Institute, the investor-owned utility industry's research arm, undertook several studies as part of its "Electric Utility Rate Design Study," and published extensive reports on the rate provisions, even before the enactment of PURPA. Congress began hearing testimony on the subject as early as June, 1979. See U.S. Congress, Senate, or House, Committee on Interstate and Foreign Commerce, *Implementation of the Public Utility Regulatory Policies Act of 1978*, 96th Cong., 1st sess., 1979, Serial 96–61.

energy efficiency differently, and here was a major break with past utility regulation. The law not only permitted, but encouraged, nonutility companies to take advantage of cogeneration technologies that produced steam for industrial purposes and electricity for sale to utilities. Defined as the sequential use of steam for industrial purposes and for production of electricity, cogeneration was once common in the United States. In 1922, for example, almost 29 percent of the electric power was produced by industrial plants, much of it along with steam for industrial use.[59] But as the utility industry took advantage of economies of scale and increased thermal efficiencies, it found it could offer better rates to industrial users and make it beneficial for them to leave the generation business. Successful in this pursuit, utility companies assumed an increased portion of generating activities, so that in 1960, only 10.5 percent of the power generation came from industrial plants. In 1978, nonutility plants produced only 3.5 percent of the nation's power.[60]

But PURPA sought to alter this trend by removing disincentives to cogeneration. First, PURPA eliminated the stricture that made industrial cogenerators subject to federal and state laws when they sought to sell surplus electricity. Specifically, PURPA exempted companies from portions of the Federal Power Act and the Public Utility Holding Company Act that subjected them to regulations concerning business organization and state regulation of rates and service.[61] The new law also required that relatively small producers of power (not greater than 80 MW) be able to interconnect with transmission lines owned by regulated utilities and sell them power at a rate not to exceed the utilities' cost of producing incremental power (known as the "avoided cost"). In other words, the law spurred companies to get double duty out of their energy expenditures, yielding overall energy efficiencies of greater than 50 percent (compared to less than 40 percent for large-scale power plants),[62] and to sell excess electricity to utility companies without encountering the regulatory burden that formerly discouraged them. Finally, PURPA (along with tax credit provisions of other laws passed at the same time) encouraged the use of new technologies for producing power, such as those that exploited "low-head" hydroelectric power or those that used biomass, waste, and renewable resources (i.e., wind and solar power) as primary energy sources.[63]

Despite two utility industry challenges to the law, resolved in 1982 and 1983 by the Supreme Court, PURPA spurred a tremendous amount of

59. Edison Electric Institute, *Pocketbook*, 34th ed., 6.

60. Ibid.

61. PURPA, Title II, sec. 210.

62. As implemented by the Federal Energy Regulatory Commission (FERC), PURPA imposed efficiency standards for qualifying facilities. Depending on the type of cogeneration facility used, total energy efficiency generally had to exceed 42.5 percent or 45.0 percent ("Criteria for Qualifying Cogeneration Facilities," 18 *Code of Federal Register* 292.205).

63. PURPA, Title II, sec. 210.

cogeneration and alternative technology production of electricity.[64] In parts of the country such as California, Texas, and New England, where energy and avoided costs were high, PURPA received its best reception. California, for example, witnessed independent power grow from 100 MW in January, 1982, to 1,659 MW in January, 1985. This amount is equivalent to the size of two medium-sized conventional power plants.[65] Continued interest in alternative energy—even without federal tax incentives[66]—has meant that, in 1988, independent power accounted for 6 percent of the state's 40,000 MW capacity. By 1990, the percentage was expected to rise to 10 percent.[67] As another stark example, consider Houston, Texas. In 1986, Houston Lighting and Power, a utility with a total capacity of about 11,000 MW, purchased 3,000 MW of power from cogeneration generators, with another 1,900 MW either under construction or being planned.[68] To be sure, these two examples are extreme cases. Nevertheless, in 1988, the nation as a whole depended on nonutility generation for 4–5 percent of its approximately 700,000 MW of

64. Portions of PURPA were opposed by utility companies and were subject to two reviews by the Supreme Court (Federal Energy Regulatory Commission v. Mississippi, 102 S.Ct. 2126 [1982]; American Paper Institute v. American Electric Power Service Corporation, 103 S.Ct. 1921 [1983]). The latter case established the legitimacy of PURPA and FERC rules mandating that full avoided costs were to be paid by utilities to qualified cogenerators and small power producers. It also overcame utility objections concerning the requirement to make interconnections between the producers and transmission grids. The case can be found in *Supreme Court Reporter* (St. Paul, Minn.: West Publishing Company, 1986), 1921–33. A summary and brief discussion of the the case's implications were published as "High Court Upholds Utility Rules of United States," *New York Times*, May 17, 1983, sec. D.

65. Richard Munson, "The Growing Role of Independent Electricity Producers," *Public Utilities Fortnightly* 115 (May 30, 1985): 13–14.

66. During the Reagan administration, federal tax credits for alternative energy projects were allowed to expire. Also, the 1986 tax reform eliminated investment tax credits and made depreciation schedules less beneficial to companies that invested in power equipment.

67. Stanley W. Hulett, "Promoting Independent Power: The California Experience," *Public Utilities Fortnightly* 123 (February 16, 1989): 15.

68. D. E. Simmons (Group Vice President, Power Operations, Houston Lighting and Power Co.) in U.S. Congress, Senate, Committee on Energy and Natural Resources, *Implementation of the Public Utility Regulatory Policies Act of 1978*, 99th Cong., 2d sess. 1986, 15. Speaking on behalf of the industry's trade group, the Edison Electric Institute, Mr. Simmons complained about PURPA's requirement that utilities purchase all the power provided, even when they did not need it. At the end of 1988, for example, Houston Light and Power's system capacity was 13,329 MW, with an additional 3,886 MW coming from cogeneration projects. Another 341 MW of nonutility generation was expected to be in service by the end of 1989 (Houston Industries Inc., *1988 Financial and Statistical Review*, 32–33). Overall, cogeneration seems to be the most popular of the alternative technologies. Of the almost 14,000 MW of small power production in place in 1985, 11,843 MW were from cogeneration. About 3,000 MW of this had been added since 1980. Meanwhile, by the end of 1985, more than 22,000 MW of cogeneration facilities were planned or under construction, versus only 8,400 MW for other small power production (Roger F. Naill, Frances Wood, and Patricia L. Rollin, "Cogeneration: Boom or Bust?" *Public Utilities Fortnightly* 122 [September 15, 1988]: 18–19).

current capacity.[69] Plans for more alternative electricity producers continue to grow. The North American Electric Reliability Council, a utility industry–created organization that promotes the reliability of generation and transmission systems, projects that, of the 86,200 MW of new capacity planned for the period between 1990 and 1999, 21.2 percent will come from nonutility generators.[70]

The success of PURPA in stimulating independent power has not been without problems, as has been pointed out by some utility executives. For example, managers have argued that when industrial firms produce power for themselves, utilities' expenses increase when they serve the remaining residential and commercial customers. As utilities lose their most consistent industrial customers—customers with high load factors who previously helped keep down overall costs—they must distribute increased costs to customers who cannot generate power themselves. Utility managers also argue that unregulated PURPA producers have no obligation to serve, so they can withdraw from the electricity-producing business at any time, thus leaving utilities "holding the bag" in an attempt to meet their customers' needs.[71] Another concern of utilities (such as Houston Light and Power and utilities in California) consisted of paying PURPA producers for power even when they had sufficient capacity to meet demand.[72] Likewise, some utilities found that too many PURPA producers sought to sell electricity, including those that could not guarantee the reliability or consistency of their power supplies. In these cases, customers suffer by paying more for electricity than if utilities provided it themselves.[73]

Partly to deal with these concerns, Congress and the Federal Energy

69. John H. Wile, "What Independent Producers Need to Know About the Potential Market for Power," *Public Utilities Fortnightly* 123 (February 16, 1989): 27.

70. North American Electric Reliability Council, *1990 Reliability Assessment: The Future of Bulk Electric System Reliability in North America, 1990–1999* (Princeton, N.J.: NERC, 1990), 13.

71. "Is Cogeneration in for Hard Times?" *Electrical World* 21 (May, 1987): 18; William C. Hayes, "What Level of Competition Can We Afford?" *Electrical World* 201 (August, 1987): 7. For other criticisms of PURPA, see George Melloan, "Californians Will Pay Dearly for PURPA Power," *Wall Street Journal*, March 31, 1987, 37. See Hirsh, *Technology and Transformation*, chap. 12, for other reasons for utility managers' discontent.

72. See Melloan, "Californians Will Pay Dearly," 37.

73. Spokesmen for PURPA entrepreneurs agreed that more power existed than was necessary in some regions of the country, but they countered that experience had so far shown them to be as reliable as utilities—and in some cases more reliable, depending on how one defined the term. One witness, Dr. Jan Hamrin (executive director of the Independent Energy Producers Association), argued that the reliability of PURPA producers is certainly greater than that of Pacific Gas and Electric, which came to the California Public Utilities Commission in 1977 to explain that its Diablo Canyon nuclear plant would be on line in six months. The plant did not enter service until 1985 (Senate, *Implementation of the Public Utility Regulatory Policies Act of 1978*, 1986, 286).

Regulatory Commission (FERC)—the government agency charged with implementing PURPA—have begun reevaluating portions of the law. In 1986, for example, a Senate Committee heard testimony from PURPA entrepreneurs and utility spokesmen on the benefits, unexpected costs, and unanticipated consequences of the law.[74] Soon thereafter, the FERC began procedures to clarify some of PURPA's provisions.

FERC's proposals were based on the view that, in the changing utility environment, some state regulations and PURPA provisions hindered further increases in energy efficiency and innovations in power technology. Admitting that PURPA's implementation had been uneven, the FERC nevertheless realized that the first decade of the law had provided valuable experience with cogeneration and other small power producers. For example, the commission learned that much more nonutility generation had been encouraged than anticipated and that, in some regions of the country, PURPA power provided the majority of new capacity needs.[75] But modifications were needed to fulfill PURPA's goals of energy efficiency and fair rates to customers. Among the proposed changes (not yet acted upon in 1991) included a rule that would encourage PURPA producers to compete in a bidding process for a utility's future capacity needs. Some states already had experimented with bidding systems, and FERC would ratify them or institute minor changes. In Virginia, for example, the State Corporation Commission permitted Virginia Power Company to accept bids for new capacity. In 1986, the company announced that it required approximately 1,100 MW by 1990. It received offers for more than 5,000 MW from nonutility generators. The company selected what it considered were low-cost producers that also displayed features of reliability, fuel mix, and other attributes.[76] Such bidding procedures would be consistent with the goals of PURPA but would prevent overbuilding of generating capacity.

The FERC also proposed new rules for dealing with qualifying producers and nonutility generators of power that do not meet PURPA standards (so called independent power producers). These IPPs, in some cases, are able to produce cheaper power than utilities, but since many were larger than the qualified facilities permitted by PURPA (which, on average in 1985, were only 12 MW each),[77] they were still hindered by state and federal regulation. Finally, the new rules would permit state regulators to consider factors such as reliability and existing capacity when determining avoided costs.[78]

---

74. Ibid.

75. Federal Energy Regulatory Commission, "PURPA: A Mixed Blessing," part of "FERC Notices of Proposed Rulemaking on Electricity," March 29, 1988, 3.

76. Commonwealth of Virginia, State Corporation Commission, "Staff Report," Case PUE870080, December 4, 1987, 4.

77. Munson, "The Growing Role of Independent Electricity Producers," 13.

78. Federal Energy Regulatory Commission, "Summary of Avoided Cost NOPR," March 16, 1989. A discussion of the FERC's proposed rules is included in "Balance of Power Shifts Here and Abroad," *Electrical World* 202 (April, 1988): 13–16.

Altogether, PURPA portended major structural changes for the utility industry. It did this in two steps. First, in an effort to increase the country's energy efficiency, PURPA began a modest amount of deregulation by creating a preferred group of electricity producers—the so-called qualifying facilities under PURPA protection—that had been exempted from normal regulation. These new producers enjoyed a guaranteed market of traditional utility companies who had to pay them their avoided cost for power. They also relished their freedom to enter and depart from electricity-producing enterprises whenever they wished because, unlike regulated utilities, these producers had no requirement to serve the public.

Beyond this degree of deregulation that the creators of PURPA anticipated, however, the new law and the experiences of the last decade have had another impact on the structure of the utility industry. Perhaps most important, PURPA has furthered moves for even more deregulation by stimulating discussions about the rationale for the utility industry's status as a natural monopoly. As noted earlier, natural monopolies could be characterized partially by declining incremental costs as new power plants were added to the system. But with economies of scale and thermal efficiencies of conventional plants reaching limits in the 1960s and 1970s, it appeared that traditional utilities could not further decrease marginal costs. In fact, as new plants (especially long-delayed nuclear plants) went on line, prices often rose dramatically in what became known as "rate shock."[79]

The declining cost standard was not the only one that made a utility a natural monopoly, especially if other potential producers of power also faced increasing costs. Here, however, was the snag. Could other producers of power, such as those encouraged by PURPA, produce more economically than regulated utilities? And would they be willing and able to make the heavy investment in technology that is required for electricity generation? The answer to these questions, in many cases, is yes. Experience since PURPA's passage has shown that industrial cogenerators can employ standardized equipment from manufacturers (such as GE, which promotes cogeneration as a way to make up, in part, lost utility business in conventional turbines and generators) to produce power economically.[80] They can do this because much of their investment consists of equipment for producing steam for industrial processes—an investment they would need to make anyway. The extra investment to produce electricity often turns out to benefit cogenerators, because their cost (in areas where electricity may be expensive to produce by utilities) is less than that of utilities. The electricity provided to utilities would be

79. This was usually because the costs of new plants could not be charged to customers until they became "used and useful." Hence, construction costs could not be gradually passed on to customers during the years that a plant was being built.

80. See "Cogeneration: Efficient Energy in New Applications," *Industrial Power Systems* 27, issue 4 (December, 1984).

priced the same as the electricity they would produce themselves (under the avoided cost standard); therefore consumers would pay no more than if a utility produced the power from a new plant. Moreover, these cogenerating companies find they can finance and construct the plants without the assurances of returns provided by utility regulation. In this sense, nonutility generators often can provide power for customers as cheaply as utilities while, at the same time, reducing the financial risk incurred by utilities, their stockholders, and customers.

PURPA has also challenged the notion of traditional utilities as natural monopolies on the grounds that utilities may not make the most efficient use of resources. In fact, since one of the goals of PURPA was to increase energy efficiency of power production, the law implicitly acknowledged that utilities have been less efficient than possible in producing electricity. Passed during a period of heightened awareness of energy use, PURPA specifically sought increased overall efficiency for the most important of reasons: for the "protection of the public health, safety, and welfare, the preservation of national security, and the proper exercise of congressional authority under the Constitution . . . ."[81] The existence of producers of power that make better use of resources than utilities further undermines utilities' claim for natural monopoly status.

As a concrete example of how the principles of natural monopoly may no longer apply to power generation, consider Cogentrix, Inc., of Charlotte, North Carolina, a company that builds and operates cogeneration plants for industrial firms.[82] In one venture, the firm entered into agreements with Pfizer, Inc., and Carolina Power and Light Company (CP&L). Pfizer needed steam for production of citric acid at its Southport, North Carolina, plant, and CP&L needed extra power. Cogentrix offered to build, at its own expense and risk, a 110 MW coal-fueled power plant adjacent to the acid plant that would supply steam to Pfizer and about 105 MW of electricity to CP&L. Using standardized equipment, designed in conjunction with Duke Power Company (an acknowledged leader in using power generation technology), Cogentrix erected the plant in just fourteen months (completed in 1987) at a cost of about $800 per kilowatt of electric capacity.[83] For comparison, construction of larger, conventional fossil-fuel plants cost about $1,500 per kilowatt, while delay-ridden nuclear plants sometimes exceeded $4,000 per kilowatt.

81. PURPA, Preamble to findings, sec. 2.

82. Cogentrix plants would be considered "independent power producers" rather than "qualified facilities" due to their large capacity.

83. "A 110-Megawatt Cogeneration Plant to Supply Steam to Pfizer's Citric Acid Plant While Generating Electricity for the Carolina Power and Light Company," *PR Newswire*, August 21, 1986, 82 (*PR Newswire* is accessible through the Dow Jones News Retrieval computer service; this story had an accession number of 04348999). More information about Cogentrix and the Southport plant came from Cogentrix's 1987 *Annual Report* and promotional literature provided by the company. For other examples of cogeneration successes, see Bill Paul, "Cogeneration is Rapidly Coming of Age," *Wall Street Journal*, March 2, 1987, 6.

This example questions the notion of natural monopoly and traditional regulation in the utility industry on several fronts. The first deals with large-scale technology. Because of limitations in traditional technologies for producing electric power, economies of scale may no longer exist. As Cogentrix has demonstrated, moderately sized plants, especially those that produce both electricity and steam for sale, can be financially successful and beneficial to a number of stakeholders in the power matrix. The implication of this realization, of course, is profound. If the traditional utility industry can no longer demonstrate increasing economies of scale (or even lower costs than potential competitors), then one rationale for its natural monopoly status no longer remains valid. The example also invalidates other arguments for natural monopoly. If entrepreneurial companies such as Cogentrix, which was formed only in 1983 and by 1987 had constructed plants with total capacity of about 500 MW, could manage engineering and financial risks successfully without relying on a guaranteed profit, then high capital expenditures do not necessarily create barriers to entry. Finally, the company has shown that it could provide increments of power quickly and with higher resource efficiency than could traditional utilities.

The New Environment for Technological Development

The example of Cogentrix also demonstrates that partial deregulation has provided incentives for development of new technologies or novel arrangements of traditional technologies. But these incentives are not equally offered to utilities and nonutility generators. PURPA producers and independent power producers can profit without limit if new technologies are successful in reducing production costs. Since nonutility producers do not receive payments based on their cost of investments (as do utilities), they have incentives to develop techniques that produce electricity as cheaply as possible so they can maximize profits. They would act like other businesses operating in an open, unregulated environment.[84]

Restrained by more traditional regulation, however, utilities must still act in a risk-averse manner that may hinder technological advances. Because of possible prudence hearings, regulated utilities must impose stringent economic performance analyses on investments in new technologies.[85] In many cases, they refuse to build new technologies because of regulatory risk.[86] Utility managers realize that under traditional regulation, if a risk ends in

84. Federal Energy Regulatory Commission, Office of Economic Policy, "Regulating Independent Power Producers: A Policy Analysis," FERC staff paper (October 13, 1987), 33.

85. A discussion of the nature of risk in utility construction is in John Stutz, "Risk Sharing in a Regulated Industry," *Public Utilities Fortnightly* 117 (April 3, 1986): 29–34.

86. A good discussion of institutional deterrents to technological progress is included in Abraham Gerber, "Reliability, Research, and Efficiency," *Public Utilities Fortnightly* 116 (August 22, 1985): 30–33. Also see Office of Technology Assessment, *New Electric Power Technologies*, 69.

failure, they suffer because of possible disallowance of their investment. If successful in the risky venture, however, the cost savings usually accrue to ratepayers rather than to shareholders. In other words, regulation creates a risk-reward equation that is asymmetrical and discourages technological innovation on the part of utilities and their suppliers.[87]

Of course, R&D in technology continues to be performed in the electric utility industry, but it is cautious research aimed at solving specific problems. Moreover, the research is largely coordinated by an industry-created organization—the Electric Power Research Institute—that receives funds from individual utility companies and must be responsive to the needs of its "clients." As a result, the EPRI has sponsored much research on pollution abatement technologies, such as fluidized-bed combustion, which suspends crushed coal on an air bed and burns it with limestone (or other chemically active "sorbents") to minimize emissions. Another recent EPRI-sponsored venture is the integrated gasification, combined-cycle (IGCC) power plant. The technology converts coal cleanly into a synthetic gas that powers a combustion turbine and generator. Hot exhaust from the turbine produces steam that turns a conventional turbine to produce still more electricity. While utilities support work on these technologies, they are still careful about implementing them because of regulatory disincentives to risk taking. Demonstration plants using fluidized-bed combustion and IGCC technologies are now beginning to be used by utilities, but their costs are often shared by the EPRI and government agencies.[88] Without such cooperative funding and risk sharing, utilities might be less inclined to experiment with the new technologies.

In contrast, technological innovation on the deregulated side of power production has been daring. R&D efforts in cogeneration technologies, for example, have thrived as numerous small power equipment companies join the large firms to cater to a growing market. Other technologies have also been advanced rapidly in the deregulated environment. The FERC noted, for instance, that fluidized-bed combustion for small-scale furnaces that burn waste or fuels with low energy density was inspired by PURPA. Likewise, geothermal power production from wet steam sources and combined-cycle gas combustion generation were largely undeveloped before PURPA. But with the manufacturing industry's push of the last source, for example, they

87. Federal Energy Regulatory Commission, "Regulating Independent Power Producers," 33.

88. For example, a 160-MW atmospheric fluidized-bed combustion demonstration plant has been built for the Tennessee Valley Authority, with participation from several other utilities, coal companies, manufacturing firms, the state of Kentucky, and the Department of Energy ("AFBC 160-MW Demonstration Plant," brochure published by the Atmospheric Fluidized Bed Development Corporation). Also see Arnold M. Manaker and Patricia B. West, "TVA Orders 160 MWe Demonstration AFBC Power Station," *Modern Power Systems* (December-January, 1984): 59; "AFBC Will Soon Be an Option, says EPRI Manager," *Electric Light and Power* 64 (May, 1986): 24; "How Fluidized Bed Technology Works," *Electrical World* 199 (June, 1985): 106–7.

are now firmly established.[89] As another example, consider the "Kalina cycle" system, one that uses a mixture of ammonia and water instead of only water in a steam turbine. Because ammonia vaporizes at a lower temperature than water, the cycle uses less energy to produce the steam that turns a turbine and generator like conventional systems. Waste heat from the turbine is used to dilute the ammonia mixture with water, which allows the ammonia to condense at a higher-than-normal temperature. Overall, the system promises about 50 percent efficiency and has been installed in a cogeneration plant to produce steam for a greenhouse.[90] The congressional Office of Technology Assessment (OTA) further noted that several nonutility organizations (along with utilities in a few cases) have pushed ahead with other forms of technology, such as wind turbines, solar-thermal electric systems (those that use the sun to convert water into steam that then passes through a turbine), photovoltaics, geothermal stations, and fuel cells.[91] Because of the forced caution exercised by regulated utilities, the OTA noted that "projects initiated under the Public Utility Regulatory Policies Act . . . have served as the principal test bed for first generation commercial applications of many new generating technologies."[92]

Future technological development may also be affected by the basic asymmetry of incentives provided to the partially deregulated utility industry. While coordinated utility research will continue with the EPRI, less emphasis will be placed on low-cost generation and transmission technologies. Instead, as one utility executive has argued, the traditional utility industry will work on providing expanded services to customers (such as ways to improve productivity and product quality) and appropriate new products (such as electric vehicles). The new research would be aimed at increasing sales of power to customers (mostly residential) who do not have the option of producing electricity for themselves, in order to make up for revenue losses that result when industrial companies generate their own power.[93]

The new driving force for development of generation technologies may, therefore, come from the unregulated, small-power generation industry.

---

89. Federal Energy Regulatory Commission, "Regulating Independent Power Producers," 33.

90. "A Quantum Leap for Power Generation?" *Chemical Week* 135 (October 3, 1984): 20–21; Calvin Sims, "Steam System May Improve Power Plants," *New York Times*, February 4, 1986, sec. C; and Alexander I. Kalina and Herman M. Leibowitz, "Kalina Cycle Promises Improved Efficiency," *Modern Power Systems* 7 (January, 1987): 19–23. Despite its initial promise, the Kalina cycle did not win initial FERC approval as a PURPA producer because the commission doubted the system produced enough energy to qualify as a cogeneration system. But the manufacturer of the system planned to reapply for certification (John Maggs, "FERC Nixes PURPA Status for First Kalina Cycle System," *Energy User News* 11 [July 7, 1986]: 1 and 9).

91. Office of Technology Assessment, *New Electric Power Technologies*, 27.

92. Ibid., 8.

93. Lawrence D. Hamlin, "Electric Utility Research and Development in a New Competitive Environment," *Public Utilities Fortnightly* 123 (June 8, 1989): 21–26.

Though fragmented into cogeneration, solar, wind, and other sectors, the industry remains unhindered by regulators and motivated only by its desire to develop technologies that can produce electricity with greater efficiency than traditional utilities. One already sees much innovation occurring. Aside from the traditional manufacturers of heavy equipment for utilities, start-up firms have been active in developing small-scale and efficient technologies for the new market (e.g., Exergy Inc., which developed the Kalina cycle, and the Fayette Company, which built a demonstration Kalina plant as an adjunct to its normal wind-powered electricity-generating system business). Many of these firms, it has to be admitted, made use of tax advantages that were available before 1986 (such as alternative energy and investment tax credits), but many remain active because of remaining incentives. While one might argue that the asymmetry of incentives is not fair and that competition between unregulated and regulated electricity producers is not being conducted on a level playing field,[94] one nevertheless must acknowledge its impact on the development of technologies that previously had few champions.

Conclusions

Technology and regulation in the electric utility industry have played both supportive and antagonistic roles during the twentieth century. From the beginning of regulation in the early 1900s and until the 1960s and 1970s, incremental technological advances in standard turbine, generator, and transmission technologies provided economies of scale and decreasing unit costs. Regulation supported continued advances in this technology by remaining relatively benign and unobtrusive, providing the appearance of governmental oversight and the legitimization of a natural monopoly. Little criticism of the system emerged because its costs and prices fell continually. Likewise, regulators themselves benefited as they took credit for monitoring an industry that, for much of the century, prided itself on helping enrich the lives of the country's masses.

The beautiful technological and regulatory superstructure of the industry encountered hard times in the 1960s and 1970s, as thermal efficiencies of the standard technology failed to improve and scale economies in large equipment seemed to vanish. Coming at a time when inflation raged, fuel prices soared, and consumers took a more activist stance, technological stagnation meant that productivity could not improve as it had in the past and that higher unit costs would be passed on to electricity users. Understaffed regulatory commissions found that their work had become more difficult, since the system that brought benefits to everyone no longer existed. Utilities sought rate relief, while consumers pressed for cheap electricity. The conflict put

94. See Bruce W. Radford, "Competitive Bidding and the Level Playing Field," *Public Utilities Fortnightly* 122 (September 15, 1988): 6–8.

regulators in the middle of contentious hearings. During the 1970s, they began (in some states) questioning the behavior of utilities, which planned huge power plants that no longer were needed due to conservation efforts spurred by higher prices. Backward-looking prudence reviews by regulatory bodies motivated utilities to seek new technological strategies that would contend with slowly rising demand for power by providing small increments of capacity. Small-scale technologies such as gas combustion turbines re-emerged from the manufacturers of power equipment in modified form, and they became popular among utilities as a means to reduce regulatory risks and to minimize capital spending. In short, regulation in a different environment engendered the abandonment of one technological strategy and the adoption of another.

Further complicating the flux in the industry was the implementation of a public policy designed to help mitigate the energy crisis. Complications arose, however, because of the policy's unintended structural and technological consequences. The Public Utility Regulatory Policies Act of 1978 counted partly on the resurgence of an old technology—cogeneration—and the introduction of alternative energy systems that would make better use of the country's energy resources. While the goals of the policy were laudable, the law began a process of deregulation in the industry by creating a class of electricity producers exempt from traditional regulation. Meanwhile, the act offered incentives for entrepreneurs who could develop or exploit technologies for producing power. As a result, R & D on novel, small-scale power technologies flourished, providing further opportunities for the nation to produce electricity more efficiently in the future.

While offering new technological avenues to pursue, PURPA motivated people to begin questioning whether the rationale for utilities as a natural monopoly still existed. After all, the PURPA experience has shown that previous impediments to entering the market of producing electricity did not exist. Moreover, nonutility generators demonstrated that they could provide increments of capacity quickly and at costs below those provided by utilities. Since large-scale technology used by utilities no longer offered traditional economies, and since utility investors (and managers of utilities) found it better to avoid construction of large plants, there appeared to be less justification for maintaining the natural monopoly status of utilities.

This history of technology and regulation suggests several lessons. First, it teaches that even the well-intended government regulation of industries must be reevaluated frequently to determine whether the original rationale for regulation makes sense. In the utility industry, regulation appeared to bring universal benefits until previous trends in both the business environment and technological progress changed markedly in the 1970s. Reevaluation of the regulatory rationale has led to the industry's restructuring, a move that was aided by the implementation of PURPA. This lesson has already been learned in other industries in the United States. Technological change also played an important role in the restructuring of the long-distance telephone industry, for example.

For individuals and corporations involved in the development of technology, the recent experience of the utility industry offers another lesson. Namely, one must constantly monitor and attempt to anticipate the effects of regulatory change on technological strategies. Within the regulatory framework that existed before 1970, manufacturers of power generating equipment pursued R&D on large-scale technologies because their customers—utility companies—benefited from them. But when regulation spurred greater risk aversion and a desire for more modular, incremental capacity additions, manufacturers needed to shift R&D strategies to the production of reliable and efficient gas combustion turbines, cogeneration equipment, and other small-scale technologies. While regulation supported one technological strategy for a long time, there could be no guarantee that the regulatory environment would always support it. Therefore, R&D managers must remain alert to changes in the regulatory climate.

Finally, policymakers should learn from this history that they must frequently reevaluate policy to assure that the original goals of the policy are being achieved. They should also analyze whether the policy has spawned unintended and counterproductive consequences. For example, the overwhelming success of PURPA in spurring cogeneration also provided incentives for companies to use oil and natural gas—fuels whose use was discouraged by regulated utilities because of their value as a versatile resource that should have been conserved.[95] More significantly, PURPA did not necessarily intend to restructure the utility industry. Designed to conserve energy, the law began a series of events that may cause further restructuring. At the same time, the law created asymmetrical incentives to the regulated and unregulated parts of the industry. Was it the goal to provide new opportunities for small-scale production while eliminating incentives (and providing disincentives) for R&D on large-scale technologies—technologies that may someday be desirable again? These must be areas of concern for policymakers.

---

95. The Powerplant and Industrial Fuel Use Act of 1978 (PL 95–620) restricted the use of oil and natural gas by utilities as a way to conserve the fuels for better uses. Because cogenerators could readily obtain exemption from the law, utility managers often argued that society as a whole did not benefit from the arrangement (Walter J. McCarthy, Jr., "The Public Interest in Cogeneration," *Public Utilities Fortnightly* 133 [September 15, 1988]: 14). Cogenerator entrepreneurs countered that these arguments served coal interests and that overall energy efficiency increased when their facilities used the fuels (Cogeneration Coalition of America, "Implementation of PURPA and Development of Cogeneration and Small Power Production Facilities," in Senate, *Implementation of the Public Utility Regulatory Policies Act of 1978*, 255). The law was repealed in 1987. See George H. Lawrence, "Repeal of Fuel Use Act Has Set Stage for a Significant Expansion into New Markets," *Oil Daily*, December 21, 1987, 6. In 1989, natural gas provided 11 percent of the energy used by utilities, but nearly 50 percent of new power plants under construction were planning to use the fuel (Mark Ivey, "Why Natural Gas is Burning Brighter," *Business Week* [August 28, 1989]: 68).

Overall, the theory of regulation of a natural monopoly in the electric utility industry appeared to apply well for several decades. But regulation depended, in part, on the continued integrity of a technological superstructure that crumbled in the 1970s. As a new public policy began having its effects, the superstructure deteriorated more, and critics called into question the rationale for regulation of the industry in general. They argued (among other things) that the interdependence between regulation and technology no longer existed, and that a competitive environment for electricity production could now be engineered. Not yet completed, the story of deregulation in the utility industry will revolve around interest-group politics (as usual) and trends in technological developments that further erode the claims of natural monopoly status for utilities.

Contributors

Clayton A. Coppin is senior research fellow, Center for the Study of Market Processes, George Mason University, Fairfax, Virginia.

Robert W. Crandall is senior fellow, The Brookings Institution, Washington, D.C.

Jerome Ellig is assistant professor of economics, George Mason University, Fairfax, Virginia.

Jack High is Newcomen fellow, Graduate School of Business Administration, Harvard University, Boston, Massachusetts.

Richard F. Hirsh is professor of history, Virginia Polytechnic Institute and State University, Blacksburg, Virginia.

Robert D. Tollison is Duncan Black professor of economics and director, Center for Study of Public Choice, George Mason University, Fairfax, Virginia.

Richard H. K. Vietor is professor of business administration, Graduate School of Business Administration, Harvard University, Boston, Massachusetts.

Index